For my family . . . past, present, and future.

FOREWORD

READING THIS BEAUTIFUL book of devotions reminds me of what philosopher Mortimer Adler observed in his classic, *How to Read a Book*:

> There is only one situation I can think of in which men and women make an effort to read better than they usually do. When they are in love and reading a love letter, they read for all they are worth. They read every word three ways; they read between the lines and in the margins. They may even take the punctuation into account. Then, if never before or after, they read.

It is clear from Chapin Garner's devotions that he reads the Bible as if it is a love letter. He reads scripture for all he's worth, with focused attention on each line and between the lines, as one would read a love letter. And that is fitting, because Chapin understands scripture as an expression of God's fierce and abiding love for God's people.

It is also fitting that these little gems of spiritual writing are called daily "devotions," because they are love letters, as well, expressing devotion to the God revealed in scripture. These days there is no lack of writing about God or about Jesus Christ. Nevertheless, this writing *about* is quite different from expressing devotion. It is the difference between writing about a loved one and writing a love letter. Chapin's reflections here are so aptly called "devotions" because they do indeed express devotion, a deep love for God.

Anyone who takes the time to read and reflect on these devotions will find their own relationship with God deepened. Or, to put it another way, these devotions have the power to deepen the reader's devotion to God. So "make an effort to read better than [you] usually do." Read for all you are worth. But only if you are willing to have your life forever changed.

Martin B. Copenhaver

INTRODUCTION

THE COVER ART for this devotional book is taken from a photograph that my wife, Tammie, captured when we were on a family pilgrimage to Israel. She and my daughter were on the women's side of the Western Wall offering their prayers, while my son and I were in the larger and more prominently placed men's section. As she took pictures, she caught this dove in flight in front of an open door in the upper reaches of the Wall. For me, it is one of the most moving images of the Holy Spirit I have ever seen. I also love the fact that this movement of the Spirit was captured, not in the men's section of the Western Wall but in the less prominent and far smaller women's area. It is a wonderful testament to the truth as described by Jesus in the Gospel of John, that the Spirit really does move as it chooses, and you can sense its presence, but you don't know where it comes from or where it goes . . . and it often shows up in the most unexpected moments and places.

This devotional book has been a similar movement of the Spirit. I began writing short devotional passages after my father died in 2006, as a way to honor his memory and manage my own grief. There was little rhyme or reason for my selection of certain passages of scripture, and some texts were utilized more than once. As the Spirit moved during my own daily devotions, I wrote down my reflections on particular passages. Therefore, this volume is not a systematic treatment of a certain biblical book or testament. Rather, it is a collection of scriptural meditations that move through the entire biblical canon as the Spirit has led. For me, they are like a picture of a dove framed in an open doorway —the Spirit moved, and I tried to capture in words what I experienced.

For people who are seasoned in the practice of devotional reading, I have very little to say in regard to the use of this book. I hope and pray that the biblical grounding and Christ-centeredness of this volume will help guide you into an even more expansive relationship with God. For those new to devotional reading, I suggest that you take a few moments at the beginning of your day to reflect on the message for that day. (Be sure to read the extended passage of scripture as indicated, so you can get the full context of the message.) When you begin your day with scripture, meditation, and prayer, it has a way of moving with you and informing all the interactions of your waking hours. For those of you who are more inclined to do your devotional reading at night, while that has not been my practice, I trust that the Holy Spirit can work in your sleeping hours with an equal measure of transformational power.

For years now, the members of my own faith community have used these devotional reflections as a passageway—or open door, if you will—for the movement of the Spirit in their lives. I now offer these reflections to you, in the hope that you will enjoy them and share them with others. For as the apostle Paul wrote to the Christians in Corinth, *"Where the Spirit of the Lord is, there is freedom."* Like a dove flying into an open doorway, God's Spirit can enter your life in ways that allow you to love and live more freely and faithfully.

Stephen Chapin Garner

January 1

CREATION

Read: Genesis 1:1—2:4

In the beginning when God created the heavens and the earth,
. . . God said, "Let there be light;" and there was light.
GENESIS 1:1 & 3

IN THE BEGINNING, as it is to this day, words bring forth life. The ancient and holy story of the first chapter of Genesis tells of the origins of creation. All things began with the spoken word. Light and darkness, sky and sea, earth and vegetation, animals and humankind were spoken into existence. God speaks, and life forms.

Words are powerful things. They can build up, or they can tear down. They can be used to heal or to hurt. They can bring peace or incite war. In the beginning, God spoke and goodness came into being. The same can happen with our words. A carefully timed compliment can lift spirits. A word of encouragement can give shape to a life. A loving word can lead to intimacy that literally gives birth to life.

How can your words bring life to others?

Lord, you have spoken all things into being. I owe my own existence to your word. Your words are life-giving. Help me to choose my words carefully, so that when I speak, life abounds. In Jesus' name, I pray. AMEN.

ADAM AND EVE

Read: Genesis 2:4b—3:24

> *Then the Lord God said, "It is not good that the man should*
> *be alone; I will make him a helper as his partner."*
> *GENESIS 2:18*

IN THE STORY of Adam and Eve, relationship is primary. We may not know the *how* of creation, but this ancient story attempts to explain the *why* that gave birth to the world and humankind. Man was created to be with God, and woman was created to be with man. God wanted company, and God wanted us to enjoy relationships as well. We were built, birthed, and created to be in union with others and with God. That is why Adam and Eve hiding from God is such a heartbreaking scene in this story. The God who wanted nothing more than companionship is abandoned by creation itself. After eating from the Tree of the Knowledge of Good and Evil, Adam and Eve hid in the bushes in an attempt to avoid God. Whatever the historicity of this ancient story is, the message is undeniably true. God created us for relationship, and yet, we so often hide ourselves from God and others. It was so from the very beginning, and God has been trying to find us ever since.

Do you hide from God?

Lord, find my hiding place. Call me from out of the bushes. Deliver me from my shame, and forgive me so that I can once again delight in our relationship. Help me also to receive the relationships I have with others as gifts, worthy of my time, attention, and thanksgiving. In Jesus' name, I pray. AMEN.

PROVISION FOR THE SINFUL

Read: Genesis 2:1—4:16

And the Lord God made garments of skins for the man and for
his wife, and clothed them. . . . And the Lord put a mark on Cain,
so that no one who came upon him would kill him.
GENESIS 3:21, 4:15B

ADAM AND EVE were kicked out of the Garden of Eden for eating the forbidden fruit, and Cain was forced to restlessly wander the earth because he killed his brother Abel. All three did something terribly displeasing to God, and yet, even in punishment, God made provision for each of them. God made clothes for Adam and Eve, and God put a mark on Cain to ensure his safety. This is testimony that God will not abandon even the most egregious of sinners. Even when God punishes, God continues to provide.

Why does God continue to provide for us when we turn against God's wishes?

Lord, you are so good to us . . . You are even good to us when we are bad to you. Grace upon grace, you offer us. Thank you. In your name, I pray. AMEN.

January 4

BROTHER'S KEEPER

Read: Genesis 4:1–16

> *Then the Lord said to Cain, "Where is your brother Abel?" He*
> *said, "I do not know; am I my brother's keeper?"*
> GENESIS 4:9

THE STORY OF Cain murdering his brother Abel is punctuated by this memorable exchange between God and Cain. Knowing of Abel's murder, God asked the offending brother for the whereabouts of Abel. Cain's dismissive response indicated that he believed he was not responsible for keeping track of his brother. The comment is nearly as callous and unfeeling as the murder itself—and it is a sentiment many of us share. We do not feel responsible for keeping tabs on other people. We say, *"I'll do my thing, you do your thing, and let's just keep out of each other's way."*

This story indicates, however, that we should not only refrain from harming others but we should also take a deep interest in them. Even people with which we are at odds, warrant our care and attention. God sees all of us as a single family unit; therefore, we are beholden to take care of and keep an eye out for one another. A touching reminder of this kind of familial care is the protection that God promised to afford Cain even after Cain's egregious act. God marked Cain as a means of taking care of him. Should we be our brothers' and sisters' caretakers? Yes!

Who should you be keeping track of?

Lord, I would really like to limit my involvement with certain people. If I am to be honest, the people I would like the most distance from are often those with whom I live at rather close range—my family. But you remind me of my responsibility to care for and keep track of the people around me. If you are my keeper, then I should be responding to that grace by taking care of others. In your name, I pray. AMEN.

January 5

Noah and the Ark

Read: Genesis 6:1—9:17

So the Lord said,"I will blot out from the earth the human beings I have created . . .
for I am sorry that I have made them."
GENESIS 6:7

GOD GETS ANGRY. The Gospels attest that Jesus got angry. And that anger, according to the Bible, is often directed at us. As in the time of Noah, there must be moments when God laments ever birthing us into existence. There must be times when we frustrate God, and God's temper is loosed on us. Now, the wrath and vengeance of God has been out of vogue for quite some time. We prefer to think of God as loving, nurturing, and unfailingly gracious. That may all be true, but even the most loving of parents get furiously angry with their children from time to time. Just because parental love is enduring doesn't mean the anger isn't real.

We want God to conform to our desires, just as we wanted our parents to bend to our wishes when we were growing up. We want the God we have come to know through Jesus Christ to be around for our wish fulfillment, but not for our rebuke. If we want a real relationship with God, however, we must embrace all of God—God's love, God's mercy, and even God's anger. Perhaps it is time for us to stop being offended by divine anger and allow ourselves to be corrected by it. Through the story of Noah, we learn that God has promised never to blot human-kind from the earth again—mercy and forgiveness are God's rainbow covenant with us—however, God still has every right to get angry with us.

Why might God get angry with you?

Lord, I don't like thinking about your wrath, probably because I know I deserve it. I do trust that in the end your love for me wins out, but there must be times when you become deeply frustrated with me. Forgive me when I choose a caricature of you, rather than the real you. What I want more than anything else is all of you in my life—your holy love, your holy anger, and your Holy Spirit. Forgive me and fill me . . . In Jesus' name, I pray. AMEN.

— 5 —

Tower of Babel

Read: Genesis 11:1–9

> *And the Lord said, "Look, they are one people, and they have all one language;*
> *. . . nothing that they propose to do will now be impossible for them."*
> *Genesis 11:6*

MANY BIBLE STORIES are perplexing and disturbing. We know these are stories told by ancient people who were doing their best to express their understanding of God and the world they saw around them. The story of the Tower of Babel, which many of us remember from our childhood, strains our religious sensibilities. Why, according to this story, did God need to confuse and scatter the people? What were they doing wrong? They were working together in harmony. They had a strong vision for their future. They were making impressive progress as a society. How could God be against that?

Unless, in the desire to make a name for themselves, they forgot the very purpose of their own creation. They had been created to be in relationship with God. They were not supposed to secure a place for themselves in the cosmos—they were supposed to adhere their lives to the presence of God. Independence and innovation were not to be their goals—dependence and cooperation with God were supposed to be their primary pursuit. All the progress in the world wasn't nearly as important as partnership with God. Towers fall, societies crumble, names are forgotten, but our relationship with God endures forever.

Are you working for yourself, or are you in partnership with God?

Lord, too often I try to make a name for myself. I suspect I do this because I do not really trust in your presence. I feel alone much of the time. I feel like a grain of sand amidst the great expanse of the cosmos. I desperately try to compensate for my smallness by doing more sizable works. However, I have this sneaking suspicion that my life and memory are ultimately bound to you . . . therefore, our partnership should be my first priority. Help me to get this straight. In Jesus' name, I pray. AMEN.

Unsettled

Read: Genesis 11:27—12:5

Now the Lord said to Abram, "Go from your country and your kin-
dred and your father's house to the land that I will show you."
GENESIS *12:1*

MANY YEARS EARLIER, Terah, Abraham's father, had felt drawn to uproot his family from their home in Ur to travel to the promising land of Canaan. However, and for reasons unknown to us, Terah aborted the journey when he arrived in town Haran. Perhaps the journey had already taken too much of a toll on his family. Perhaps the kids complaining in the back of the caravan became too much for him. Or, it is entirely possible that Haran looked promising enough. Why risk going all the way to Canaan when it might not live up to Terah's expectations? So Terah settled in Haran with his family, and his journey ended.

However, for Abraham, the journey was just about to begin. In the deep of the night, or from the depths of his heart—or from wherever it is that God is able to catch our attention—God began to call to Abram. *"Go. Leave Haran behind. Follow me to Canaan . . . You will be the father of many children. You will be blessed. And your life and legacy will be a blessing for the entire world."* Terah settled for less than what God called him to do and be, and he became no more than a footnote to history. Abraham traveled to Canaan and became the father of three great faith traditions: Judaism, Christianity, and Islam.

Like Terah, we will always be tempted to settle for less than God hopes for us. But thankfully, God has a way of shaking things up and presenting us with opportunities that can provide us with more than we ever dreamed. God has a way of drawing us into an adventure of faith where settlers become travelers who are blessed in the journey. All we need is a willingness to risk our present situation in order to embrace the promise of a future that God envisions for us.

Have you settled for less than God desires for you?

Lord, I have settling tendencies. Fill me with the vision and courage of a traveler. Help me to break from my present situation to take hold of the future you call me into. In your name, I pray. AMEN.

EXPOSURE

Read: Genesis 12:1–3

> *Now the Lord said to Abraham, "Go from your country and your kin-*
> *dred and your father's house to the land that I will show you."*
> *GENESIS 12:1*

SOMETIMES WE FIND ourselves in a rut. Stuck. Stagnant. We get into a certain rhythm, or a certain routine, or a certain mindset and we cease to grow. We go to the same job, we go to the same restaurants, and we hang out with the same friends . . . and in time we become bored and boring people. We become narrow-minded. We live life with blinders on, unable to see other ways of living.

God calls us forth into new experiences, new adventures, and new journeys with the intent of unfolding a world of opportunity to us. God wants to broaden, deepen, and enrich our living, so God encourages our exposure to new ideas, new places, and new people. Exposure to that which is new and unfamiliar to us is a pathway to a land and life of promise.

Where can you go this week that will expose you to new experiences and opportunities?

Lord, expose me. Push me out of the rut I am in, break me out of the unhealthy relation-ships I am in, drag me out of the unproductive patterns of living I am in. Take me to new places, help me to meet new people, give me a new perspective on life. Move me. Don't allow me to limit myself. I need to know my options if I am ever going to live fully for you. In your name, I pray. AMEN.

CALL OF ABRAM

Read: Genesis 12:1–9

Abram was seventy-five years old when he departed from Haran.
GENESIS 12:4C

THE BIBLE DOES not support the traditional American ideal of retirement. The vision of a leisurely, carefree retirement at age sixty-five or younger, when you no longer work but spend your time playing golf or bridge or shopping could not be less biblical. One cannot retire from the work of ministry. God's call on our lives is a lifetime call. Even as we draw toward what we believe to be the end of our days, God might call us to make some great, life-changing journey of faith.

This reality is actually a great blessing. At the very age when too many people begin to feel useless and forgotten, just when the joy of retirement has evolved into aged loneliness, the Spirit of God speaks to us saying, *"I am not done with you yet, get up, go—we have work to do!"* How joyous it is to realize that God does not discriminate based on age—we are never too old to do important, world-transforming work.

What are your retirement plans?

Lord, there are days when I long to retire from the demands that life places on me. I want a steady enough stream of income to allow me to relax and do what I want with the rest of my life. However, I quickly realize that playing by my own rules and governed by my own timetable, I lack a sense of personal fulfillment, as if I am doing nothing of particular importance. Lord, call me out of retirement, or away from my dreams of retirement, and engage me in your kingdom work. In Jesus' name, I pray. AMEN.

January 10

SARAH AND HAGAR

Read: Genesis 16:1–15; 21:1–21

Sarah saw the son of Hagar the Egyptian, whom she had borne to Abraham, play-
ing with her son Isaac. So she said to Abraham, "Cast out this slave woman with her
son; for the son of this slave woman shall not inherit along with my son Isaac."
GENESIS 21:9–10

SARAH AND HAGAR had behaved badly toward one another—they had history—and Sarah had held a grudge. That grudge ended in Abraham banishing his son Ishmael, and his mother Hagar, into the wilderness with nothing more than enough bread and water for a single day. The women's animosity toward each other—while not entirely rational—was completely understandable. Before Sarah had given birth to Isaac, she had been jealous of Hagar's fertility. When Hagar gave birth to Ishmael, she felt proud that she could accomplish something her mistress could not do for Abraham. A corrosive combination of insecurity and jealousy devolved into a careless and heartless outcome.

Of all the bad actors in this story, Abraham must be held most accountable. As the women lost their cool and their better judgment, Abraham stood by and did nothing. He watched two women mistreat one another on his account, and he failed to intervene. He was a bystander who was willing to watch, but unwilling get involved. When people lose their better judgment—which happens to us all—those standing by must intervene for the good of all involved. Blessed are the peacemakers, not the bystanders.

What situation do you need to address so that relationships are not permanently damaged?

Lord, I don't like conflict and I don't like getting involved in other people's business. I have
heard myself and others say that more times than I can remember. Perhaps it is a cop-out, a way to
avoid the guilt of standing idly by while people injure themselves and others. Give me the courage to
step up and into conflict when I can be a voice and presence for peace. In Jesus' name, I pray. AMEN.

Faith That Shows

Read: Genesis 17:1–27

> *"You shall circumcise the flesh of your foreskins, and it shall*
> *be a sign of the covenant between me and you."*
> Genesis 17:11

What a strange and painful ritual to observe as a sign of a promise from God! Abraham and all the men in his family, and all the men in his company, had to be circumcised as a sign that they were in a relationship with the Lord. After circumcision, there was no mistaking—one was a Jew, a follower of Yahweh, a member of God's chosen people. Once circumcised, it was a form of identification that could not be undone. One was marked for life.

The truth of circumcision is that somehow our faith and our relationship with God should show. As people of faith, our faith should be evidenced in our lives, in our relationships, in our business dealings, and perhaps even in our bodies somehow. Jesus said to his followers, *"By this everyone will know that you are my disciples, if you have love for one another."* Simply put, our faith should show.

How can people recognize your faith in your daily living?

Lord, when people look at me, they should be able to tell that I follow you, that I love you, and that my life is offered to you. Help me to circumcise the whole of my life so that when people see me, they somehow catch a glimpse of you. In your name, I pray. AMEN.

January 12

SODOM AND GOMORRAH

Read: Genesis 18:1—19:29

> *Then Abraham said, "Oh do not let the Lord be angry if I speak just once*
> *more. Suppose ten [righteous people] are found there."The Lord answered,*
> *"For the sake of ten I will not destroy Sodom."...Abraham went early in*
> *the morning to the place where he had stood before the Lord; and he looked*
> *down toward Sodom and Gomorrah and toward all the land of the Plain*
> *and saw the smoke of the land going up like the smoke of a furnace.*
> GENESIS *18:32 &19:27–28*

ABRAHAM DID HIS best negotiating in an attempt to save his nephew, Lot, from destruction. God, in the form of three men, came to Abraham's tent and let the
old man know of the divine intention to obliterate the sinful cities of Sodom and
Gomorrah. Fearing for his nephew's life, Abraham bargained with the Lord to
spare the city of Sodom if only ten righteous people could be found in the city. God
agreed. God was moved by Abraham's plea. However, the next day, as Abraham saw
the smoky mushroom clouds of God's wrath in the valley below, he learned that
while it is possible to move God, God resists being controlled.

We all try to strike bargains with God from time to time, and the Bible attests
to the fact that God not only hears our pleas but also responds to them. But the willingness of God to be deeply moved and involved in our lives does not mean God is
controlled by our desires. In the end, God is God, and we are not. God will do what
God will do, whether we like it or not. Perhaps we should spend less time trying to
manipulate God and more time worshiping the One in whose charge are all things.

Do you try to control God or worship God?

Lord, I want to manage you like I try to manage all other aspects of my life. But thank-
fully you resist and refuse my control. Thank you for the many times you remind me of my
place —on my knees, head bowed, waiting on you. In Jesus' name, I pray. AMEN.

January 13

SACRIFICE OF ISAAC

Read: Genesis 22:1–19

> *After these things God tested Abraham. . . . God said, "Take your*
> *son, your only son Isaac, whom you love, and go to the land*
> *of Moriah, and offer him there as a burnt offering."*
> GENESIS 22:1A & 2

ABRAHAM HAD TWO sons. His first son, Ishmael, birthed by Sarah's servant Hagar, was sent away into the wilderness with Hagar because of jealousy within Abraham's household. Therefore, the sacrifice of Isaac represented the second time Abraham would lose a son. Whatever we make of God testing Abraham's faithfulness, the prospect of losing a child makes a parent's blood run cold. Our children are our most precious possessions, and we treat them as such. We don't ever want to lose them . . . even when they frustrate us.

However, our children are not *our* possessions, they are *God's*, and inevitably we have to turn our children over to that divine relationship. Like all things in life, we need to let go of that which is dear to us . . . because it is not ours. We are finite beings who are merely stewards in this life, managing the resources and relationships entrusted to our care. Whether it is handing over a set of car keys to our sixteen-year-old, dropping a newly minted college freshman off at their dorm room, or watching as a son or daughter takes the hand of another in marriage . . . we need to let go. We need to let go and trust that the God who has been a faithful provider for us will be so for those we love and desire to hold on to. As the religious cliché goes: Let go, let God.

What child, or significant relationship, are you having difficulty letting go of?

Lord, I cannot imagine sacrificing my children, and yet, in a way that is exactly what we do. We tend to their needs for only a while, then offer them back to you, trusting that you will take care of them more completely than we ever could. Please strengthen that trust when it is not as durable as it could be. I pray this in the name of a Son, offered to the world by a Father, Jesus Christ, our Lord. AMEN.

January 14

GIVING TO GET

Read: Genesis 22:15–19

> *Abraham, because you have done this, and have not withheld Isaac, your*
> *only son, I will indeed bless you, and I will make your offspring as numer-*
> *ous as the stars of heaven and as the sand that is on the seashore.*
> GENESIS 22:16–17

GOD INTENDS FOR us to have everything we need. Food, clothing, shelter, friendship, love, and fulfilling vocations and avocations are all part of God's plan for us. But often there is a barrier that prevents us from receiving all that God is prepared to give us. In the Bible, blessing is only fully released into someone's life when they are finally willing to give up the thing they love most in the world. God is supposed to be our first priority and our first love, but other loves and priorities have a way of crowding God out of our lives. Therefore, we may have to be willing to sacrifice something that has become dear to us if we want to enter into God's abundant favor.

When you finally give up that thing that has become too dear to you—when you finally make God your first priority and love—abundant blessings follow, and what you give is forever outweighed by what you get in return.

What passion, love, or lust might you need to give up for God to take a more central role in your life?

Lord, I love so many things. Work, play, family, food . . . there is so much of life I enjoy. I admit that I place many things before you in my life. My priorities are out of line. Help me to reorder my life so that all that I am and all that I do centers in you. Help me to stop clinging so tightly to the things I have, so that my hands and my heart can be open to you. In Jesus' name, I pray. AMEN.

January 15

JACOB AND ESAU

Read: Genesis 25:19–34; 27:1—28:9; 32:3—33:17

Esau ran to meet Jacob, and embraced him, and fell on his neck and kissed him, and they wept. . . . Then Esau said, "Let us journey on our way, and I will go alongside you."
GENESIS *33:4 &12*

As ESAU MARCHED toward Jacob with four hundred armed men, Jacob must have feared for his life and the safety of his family. After having dealt so treacherously with his brother Esau, by cunningly obtaining his birthright and stealing his blessing, Jacob knew he deserved nothing more than his brother's wrath. After years of estrangement, Jacob met Esau on the fields of the Jordan Valley—to be embraced and kissed by his brother must have seemed nothing short of miraculous.

There is something about the passage of time and the richness of God's blessing that can heal even the deepest of wounds. Esau had been injured by his younger brother, but during the years that followed God had generously blessed Esau. With enough time and with adequate recognition of God's goodness to us, how can we hang on to old grudges? If God blesses and forgives sinners like us, how can we withhold our blessing and forgiveness of others? Because of all the grace and mercy Esau received from God, he could not help but offer the same grace and mercy to his brother Jacob. Forgiveness is a gift we can give, because it is a gift we have received.

What old injury or lingering grudge do you need to forgive and forget?

Lord, you have blessed me so abundantly and for such a long time—and I know I deserve none of it. If I, as undeserving as I am, have been blessed and forgiven by you, how can I withhold those gifts from others? I should not, but I do. Grant me the courage and the resolve to rise above past injuries and current estrangements, to offer the love, mercy, and forgiveness you have so willingly offered me. In Jesus' name, I pray. AMEN.

January 16

THE FACE OF GOD

Read: Genesis 32:22—33:20

*So Jacob called the place Peniel, saying, "For I have seen
God face to face, and yet my life is preserved."*
GENESIS 32:30

*Jacob said to Esau ". . . for truly to see your face is like seeing the
face of God—since you have received me with such favor."*
GENESIS 33:10

THERE ARE MANY disturbing images and actions attributed to God that are written down in the book of Genesis. From a casual reading, it would seem that *"In
the beginning,"* God was quite an angry character who was ready to dole out swift
and harsh punishment when directives were ignored. However, tucked away in the
story of Jacob and his older brother Esau is a sighting of the God many of us have
come to know through Jesus Christ.

After Jacob came face to face with God during a night of wrestling, he
encountered the older brother whom he had dealt treacherously with in the
past. Esau had every right to be furious with Jacob. The last time they had been
under the same roof, Esau had vowed to kill his younger sibling. However, when
they finally reunited, Esau embraced Jacob and offered him complete forgiveness and love. Receiving such a gift of grace and mercy, Jacob responded to
Esau, saying that to see Esau was like seeing God face to face. Jacob would have
known, because he had spent the previous night wrestling with God. Perhaps,
when we encounter love and forgiveness and mercy, we are, in fact, standing in
the presence of God. For those who think that the God represented in the Old
Testament is all about vengeance, they should read the story of Jacob and Esau,
and think again.

What does God look like to you?

Dear Lord, perhaps it is true that whenever we receive love, grace, mercy, and forgiveness . . . you are inviting us to receive you . . . because that is who you are. Thank you. I accept. In your name, I pray. AMEN.

January 17

Joseph and His Brothers

Read: Genesis 37

Joseph's brothers said to one another, "Here comes this dreamer. Come now, let us kill him and throw him into one of the pits; then we shall say that a wild animal has devoured him, and we shall see what will become of his dreams."
Genesis 37:19–20

There are so many disturbing elements to this story of Joseph and his brothers. There is a father loving one son more than the others, and a son who seemingly takes pleasure in boasting of dreams of dominion over his brothers, and brothers who plot and carry out harmful actions against their younger sibling. What is most shocking is that this is the very family the Bible tells us serves as the source of God's revelation in the world. Somehow, Jacob's dysfunctional family serves as God's ambassadors to the world. This might cause even the most faithful person to question God's better judgment.

And yet, this dark and troubling story is punctuated by a few pinpricks of light. There was Reuben, who convinced the others not to kill Joseph in the hope of rescuing him later. There was Judah, who lobbied his brothers to sell Joseph into slavery instead of letting him die in a pit. And there was Joseph himself, who fostered a belief that somehow God was still in control of the whole mess. Perhaps those little pinpricks of light in the darkness are all God needs to work powerfully in our world and in our lives.

Can you identify little slivers of light that have broken into your life and allowed God to work with you in truly important ways?

Lord, the story of your family—a story of which we are very much a part—is a story littered with malfeasance, treachery, and sin. It is amazing you choose to work with us. There are moments when we show glimmers of what we might be, but those hopeful moments seem as fleeting as a candle in the wind. And yet, you continue to walk with us, work with us, and love us in the hope that your light might be more fully and more consistently reflected in our own living. Let just such a light shine through me today. In Jesus' name, I pray. AMEN.

January 18

JOSEPH'S FAMILY REUNION

Read: Genesis 42–45

God sent me here before you to preserve for you a remnant on earth, and to keep
alive for you many survivors. So it was not you who sent me here, but God.
GENESIS 45:7–8A

GOD HAS A plan. That is what Joseph said to his brothers. Selling Joseph into slavery was not a result of his brothers' hateful intentions, rather it was God's way of insuring that God's people found preservation in the land of Egypt. Because Joseph was taken to Egypt and rose to power there, when famine engulfed the land, Joseph could provide safe haven for his entire family. Bad intentions led to a good outcome—that may be the real truth of this story.

The idea that the unfortunate things that happen to us in life are all a part of God's plan might be a naïve way of looking at life. It is a way of holding out hope that our misfortune is just a prelude to greater blessing. It is well worth questioning whether the bad things that happen to us in life are part of God's design, but the Bible and our life experiences teach us that God certainly has the ability to bring wonderful outcomes out of the worst circumstances.

Think of a time when an unfortunate circumstance led to a great blessing.

Lord, I struggle to think that you intend bad things to happen to your people. Through the life of Jesus, and the many Christian witnesses that have followed, we are told of your infinite love and care. Your plan for our lives does not include harm, but even when we are injured you are able to preserve us and restore us in the most remarkable of ways. Thank you for bringing good outcomes out of bad situations. In Jesus' name, I pray. AMEN.

January 19

Water and Salvation

Read: Exodus 2:1–10

The daughter of Pharaoh came down to bathe at the river, while her atten-
dants walked beside the river. She saw the basket among the reeds and
sent her maid to bring it. When she opened it, she saw the child.
Exodus 2:5–6a

In the Bible there is a connection between water and the salvation of God. God cleansed the world of sin through the story of Noah and the flood. Pharaoh's daughter drew the infant Moses out of the Nile. Moses, in turn, led the Hebrew people through the Red Sea and away from slavery in Egypt. After forty years in the wilderness, the Israelites had to cross the Jordan River to inherit the promised land. John baptized people in the Jordan River to symbolize God's ability to wash away sins. And we engage in baptism today as a continuation of that symbolic ritual—water and salvation tend to go hand in hand in the Bible. We also know that life itself is fed by water—where there is no water there is no life, and where water exists life abounds. Is it any wonder that human beings are drawn to water as if we have some deep spiritual connection to it? Can it be a surprise that the seaside and the lakeside and the riverbed can feel like very thin places where the Spirit of God and our own spirit mingle? Water has properties that go far beyond its molecular makeup—water is spiritual, sacred, and salvific.

What is your favorite body of water, and why do you think it calls to you?

Lord, we are made of water. The salt content of our bodies is in equal measure to the salt
of the seas from which we emerged. Life and water are intrinsically linked. It is no surprise
that you use water as a symbol of cleansing, salvation, and new birth. No wonder I sense you
in the lapping of waves and the drumming of a rainstorm and the gurgling of a forest brook.
Like Moses, continue to draw me up out of the waters of your creation to new and even more
vibrant life. In Jesus' name, I pray. AMEN

January 20

MOSES AND THE BURNING BUSH

Read: Exodus 3:1–15

God said to Moses, "I AM WHO I AM." He said further, "Thus you
shall say to the Israelites, I AM has sent me to you."
EXODUS 3:14

GOD REFUSED TO be controlled. The mysteries of God would not be explored and exposed by Moses' turning aside to thoroughly inspect a burning bush in an attempt to explain it. Pharaoh would not keep God's people bound when God chose to set them free. God's name would not be made known just for the mere asking of it. God simply *is*, and the only appropriate response to God's awesome presence and power is worship.

This is not a comforting reality for those of us who like to be in control. We are proud people who don't like to be told what to do. But for Moses, an alien in a foreign land, a murderer in hiding, and an unlikely leader in the making, the proclamation that God was in control must have been somewhat liberating. God *is*, Pharaoh *is not*. The promised land was Israel's future, Egypt was not. God was in control, Moses was not.

How do you respond to a God who refuses your control?

Lord, I desire to domesticate you. I want to control you. I want to craft you in an image that is pleasing to me. I want to call you by your first name. But you rightly refuse my will by refusing my arrogant requests. Thank you for putting me in my place. In Jesus' name, I pray.
AMEN

CELEBRATING FREEDOM

Read: Exodus 12:1–32 & Matthew 26:17–25

This day shall be a day of remembrance for you. You shall celebrate it as a festival to the Lord; throughout your generations you shall observe it as a perpetual ordinance.
EXODUS 12:14

On the first day of Unleavened Bread the disciples came to Jesus, saying, "Where do you want us to make the preparations for you to eat the Passover?"
MATTHEW 26:17

THE TWO MOST significant events in the Bible are the exodus in the Old Testament, and the resurrection in the New Testament. Both events have to do with freedom—freedom from slavery and freedom from death. The exodus has been celebrated in the remembrance of Passover for as many as 3,500 years—Jesus celebrated Passover with his disciples just before his crucifixion in Jerusalem. We have been celebrating Jesus' resurrection in Easter remembrance for nearly 2,000 years. These are both extraordinary rituals that have guided the lives of countless people throughout human history. They both testify to the fact that while bondage and death are real, slavery and death will not endure, because slavery and death have no power over God. Our Easter and Passover remembrances have a way of reminding us that what seems so frightful and unalterable to us is simply another opportunity for God to work in liberating ways in our lives and our world. Our job is to celebrate that freedom, and our God who inspires it!

Where do you need to feel free in your life?

Lord, I do feel in bondage in so many ways in my life. I long for a sense of release from the burdens I bare. I want to be able to breathe easily—trusting that somehow all will be well. I so long to feel exodus and Easter joy, where new life not only seems possible —it also is downright visible and tangible! For this I long and I pray, in your name. AMEN.

January 22

SHOWDOWN

Read: Exodus 14

The Lord will fight for you, and you have only to keep still. . . . And
the Egyptians shall know that I am the Lord, when I have gained glory
for myself over Pharaoh, his chariots, and his chariot drivers.
EXODUS 14:14 & 18

IF WE ARE to accept this story as it is related to us, then we are invited to believe that parting the Red Sea was God's way of proving himself to all parties in this conflict. To the Hebrews, God would prove able to provide for all their needs. To Moses, God would prove to be a faithful companion on the journey. To the Egyptian army, God would prove to be Lord over all—able to move heaven and earth and part seas for those who follow him. To Pharaoh, God would prove that earthly power has no dominion over heavenly power. In the showdown between God and the great king of Egypt, God won.

We may not feel the need for God to prove God's self to us—and God may feel even less need to do so. However, it is important to remember who claimed ultimate victory in this showdown. Pharaoh commanded soldiers and chariots and the great warhorses that drove them. Pharaoh had power over slaves and the ability cast fear into the hearts of all his subjects. But God commanded the winds and the waves and the heart of a man named Moses. In this showdown by the Red Sea, God planned to capture the hearts of the entire Hebrew people—hearts that had formerly been enslaved to Pharaoh. God won. A nation of wandering Israelites was formed. And this story has been told and retold ever since. Pharaoh may have been king of Egypt, but God is Lord of all.

What pharaoh do you fear?

Lord, I don't think of myself as a slave, but I do feel like there are powers that exercise
influence over me. Which is to say, I feel weak at times . . . or, at least, not strong enough to

effect much change in my life or the world. I can feel like a pawn sometimes in a game that is being played over which I have little or no control. Help me to remember that you are Lord over all, and there is no earthly power that will claim victory over you. And if I follow you, I dare to believe that I will be able to share in your victory. You are my Lord, I will not fear the rule of any other. In Jesus' name, I pray. AMEN.

January 23

DESERT PROVISION

Read: Exodus 16

In the evening quails came up and covered the camp; and in the morning there was a layer of dew around the camp. When the layer of dew lifted, there on the surface of the wilderness was a fine flaky substance, as fine as frost on the ground.
Exodus 16:13–14

THE ISRAELITES WERE complaining that they had no food to eat in the desert. They asked Moses why he had to lead them out of Egypt so that they could die in a wasteland. Moses countered saying that their quarrel was not with him but with God. In truth, Moses might have had the same questions lurking in his own heart. How was he going to feed so great a multitude of people in the desert? The answer, of course, was that *he* was not. It was not Moses' job to feed the people—that was God's responsibility. What Moses and the Israelites needed to do was to trust that the God who had brought them out of Egypt and into freedom could provide meals for them in the desert. The wandering band of Hebrews needed to learn to trust in God's provision.

Lo and behold, the Israelites discovered that there was just enough quail and manna in the desert to meet their needs. That didn't mean they had all they wanted. Unfortunately, the complaints of the wandering Hebrews would continue, but they would not starve in the desert. Even in a place of desolation, God provides.

Do you grumble about unfulfilled wants?

Lord, I know there are too many times when I doubt your provision. Even though you have faithfully provided for all my needs, when the next challenge I must face presents itself, I begin to worry and grumble about not being able to make it through. If I can't figure a situation out, if the resources I need are not readily at hand, if the obstacles before me appear greater than my ability to overcome them, I assume I am lost. Why don't I assume that in such situations you will provide? You always have. It's true that I have plenty of limitations—left on my own I would die in the desert. But I am not alone. You are with me. And you promise to provide. Help me to trust in that provision. In Jesus' name, I pray. AMEN.

January 24

DELEGATING AUTHORITY

Read: Exodus 18:13–27

> *Moses' father-in-law said to him, "What you are doing is not good.*
> *You will surely wear yourself out, both you and these people with*
> *you. For the task is too heavy for you; you cannot do it alone."*
> *EXODUS 18:17–18*

YOU CAN'T DO it all yourself. If you think you can—you're wrong—and you will wear yourself out, and you won't do your best work. That was the assessment of Moses' father-in-law, Jethro. Jethro went on to say that Moses had to learn to delegate tasks and share his authority with others whom he trusted. Moses needed to be careful in his selection of people he would put in charge, but he needed to have others share the burdens and blessings of leadership with him.

This is a reality of leadership that is as true today as it was in Moses' time. Great leaders don't do everything—in fact, the mark of a truly fine leader is often their ability to cultivate the leadership abilities of others. Some people like to be big shots, believing that they are the only ones who can do a particular job. There are other folks who don't delegate because they don't believe things will be done well if they are not involved themselves. And still others do not share tasks because they don't want to impose upon others by asking people to join them in their work. All these are pathways to leadership peril. Leadership requires delegating authority, and when that happens, organizations, communities, and relationships begin to grow stronger. Moses took his father-in-law's advice and the Hebrew people were strengthened by Moses' actions.

What tasks or authority do you need to share with someone else?

Lord, I feel best when I do something myself, because I feel I know how things should best be done. However, my compulsion to do everything may squelch the leadership potential of others. It also limits what can be done, because there are natural limits on my time. Lord, help me to delegate, help me to share tasks with others, help me to empower others to positions of authority . . . so that we both grow and our work is done even better. In Jesus' name, I pray. AMEN.

January 25

THE TEN COMMANDMENTS
AND THE GOLDEN CALF

Read: Exodus 20:1–21; 32:1–20

> *"You shall not make for yourself an idol, whether it is in the form of any-*
> *thing that is in heaven above, or that is on the earth beneath, or that is*
> *in the water under the earth.". . . Aaron took the gold from them, formed*
> *it in a mold, and cast an image of a calf; and they said, "These are your*
> *gods, O Israel, who brought you up out of the land of Egypt!"*
> EXODUS 20:4; 32:4

THE ISRAELITES MUST have gotten off on a technicality. Moses was up on Mount Sinai conversing with God while the Israelites were lamenting being left alone. God was giving Moses laws to live by, while Aaron was left to manage people who feared they would die in the desert. God said, *"I am the jealous type. So, don't make idols,"* while Aaron was fashioning a golden calf for the people to worship. Only through Moses' intercession were the Israelites saved from God's wrath.

It is a painful story: as God was giving the law, the people were already breaking it. Their only defense was that they didn't know any better—a technicality. Once they read the stone tablets they understood their offense. Which is not to say they behaved much better . . . nor do we. We still make and worship idols, and God still does not appreciate it. We worship wealth, success, beauty, and so much more! When will we learn?

What idol do you need to grind into dust and be rid of?

Lord, when it comes to the many things we worship, we cannot claim that we don't "know"
any better. The plain truth is that we just don't "do" any better. We know your laws, we know
your requests of us, we even know when we break your heart . . . but that doesn't change our
behavior all that much. Forgive us, remain with us, and keep pointing us in a better direction.
In Jesus' name, I pray. AMEN.

Driver's Seat

Read: Exodus 25:10–22

> *Then you shall make a mercy seat of pure gold; two cubits and a half shall*
> *be its length, and a cubit and a half its width. . . . You shall put the mercy*
> *seat on the top of the ark; . . . There I will meet with you, and from above*
> *the mercy seat, from between the two cherubim that are on the ark of the*
> *covenant, I will deliver to you all my commands for the Israelites.*
> *Exodus 25:17, 21a, 22*

WHEN GOD INSTRUCTED Moses to have the Israelites build the Ark of the Covenant, God commanded that a seat be placed on top of the Ark. The "mercy seat" was the location where God would meet with the Hebrew people to give them direction. For generations, the Israelites would bring the Ark of the Covenant with them wherever they went. When they went into battle, the Ark of the Covenant—a box with a seat on top—would travel with them. While this must have looked like foolishness to Israel's adversaries, it was profound and powerful symbolism to the Hebrew people. God traveled with them. God moved with and among the Israelites. From the Ark of the Covenant, God gave direction and instruction to the Hebrews. In a very real way, God was in the driver's seat!

Is God a passenger in your life or the driver?

Lord, I charge off in any direction I choose. This allows me to feel in control. But deep down, control is not what I crave. I long for you. I desire your direction. I want you in the driver seat of my life. Please, Lord, take the wheel . . . I offer it to you. In Jesus' name, I pray. AMEN.

January 27

SHINING

Read: Exodus 34:29–35

> *When Aaron and all the Israelites saw Moses, the skin of his face*
> *was shining, and they were afraid to come near him.*
> *EXODUS 34:30*

AFTER SPEAKING AND interacting with God, Moses looked different to those who saw him. He was radiant. He shined. Something of the light and life of God shown through him.

There really is a glow that accompanies the lives of people who attempt to make time for God. Time spent in prayer, time spent in spiritual reading, time spend in worship has a way of transforming and enlightening people. There are times when you can just look at someone who seems aglow with the presence, or perhaps peace, of God. When we attempt to spend time in the presence of God, it stands to reason that something of God's presence should rub off on us. It did for Moses.

Have you seen someone who appears to shine with the Spirit of God?

Lord, light up my life. Allow your presence to fill my person. Help me to look different as a result of being made different through your grace and love. I will try to find a way into your presence so that part of you can rub off and travel with me. In Jesus' name, I pray. AMEN.

January 28

RULES

Read: Leviticus 1:1–9

The Lord summoned Moses and spoke to him from the tent of meeting, saying: Speak to the people of Israel and say to them:When any of you bring an offering of livestock to the Lord, you shall bring your offering from the herd or from the flock.
LEVITICUS 1:1–2

COUNTLESS PEOPLE OVER the generations have decided at one time or another to read through the entire Bible from beginning to end. It is a well-intentioned desire, and it is rewarded with some truly captivating stories from Genesis and Exodus. But then the reader encounters the book of Leviticus, and after a chapter or two their resolve erodes, and the Bible is closed. Leviticus is a recounting of the laws God gave to Moses—laws that extended well beyond the Ten Commandments—that would serve to govern all aspects of communal life for the Hebrew people. There are laws for worship and sacrifice, for washing dishes and bathing one's body, for settling grievances and leveling judgments, and for just about every other activity or interaction within the community. To a contemporary reader, these laws can seem both dry and severe, and we quickly become grateful we do not have to live under their authority. In fact, with an air of superiority, we tend to dismiss these laws as something the poor Jews have to deal with, while more enlightened and liberated Christians can faithfully ignore them.

What we often miss is the power of rules and regulations. We often take the rule of law that protects our own society for granted. And we forget what a preserving force Judaic law was in antiquity. There are reasons why the Hivites, Jebusites, Canaanites, and Philistines don't exist anymore while the Jews continue to endure, even having faced the most unspeakable attempts to sweep them from the face of the earth. One of those reasons is their devotion to the law. Laws protect life. Rules safeguard relationships. And strict regulations can save entire societies. The book of Leviticus might weary the contemporary reader, but that book of laws has sustained the Jewish people for nearly 3,500 years. Therefore, it might be worth our reading.

What rule or law has been particularly beneficial to your life?

Lord, we chafe under certain rules and regulations. We don't like thinking about having our freedoms limited in any way. And yet the rule of law ensures our liberty. Without laws, we have chaos, which harkens back to the dawn of creation when the world was nothing more than a formless void. You give the world shape, Lord. And your laws set appropriate limits for our lives. Help us to appreciate your call to regulation for the gift it is. In your name, I pray. AMEN.

First Fruits

Read: Leviticus 23:9–14

Speak to the people of Israel and say to them:When you enter the
land that I am giving you and you reap its harvest, you shall bring
the sheaf of the first fruits of your harvest to the priest.
Leviticus 23:10

As the Hebrews wandered in circles in the Sinai desert for forty years, they became acutely aware of all that they did not posses. As nomads they had no land to call their own, they did not have established dwellings, and they did not have fields and crops to sustain themselves. They were forced to rely solely on the provision of God. And God provided. So, as they began to contemplate what life could be like in a land that was said to flow with milk and honey, they probably didn't have an issue with offering the first fruits of their labor and the very best of their produce to God as a way of expressing gratitude. How hard is it to think of being generous with that which you do not possess? But once you have received the gift and lived in the land for some time, once you begin to reap what you believe to be the rewards of your own labor, once you feel like the owner of all that you have—how much more difficult it is to part with what you believe is rightfully yours!

But all that we have is a gift from God—whether we recognize that fact or not. God gives us life, God has created the world we live in, and God promises to provide for us whether we find ourselves in the breadbasket of the world or in a barren desert. God rightfully deserves the best of what we have. Offering God the first fruits of our harvest—whatever that harvest might be—is a wholly appropriate gesture of thanksgiving. How easy it should be to offer that which we have to God, who promises to always supply us with more! Why, then, is it so difficult for us?

Do you offer the best of what you have to God?

Lord, I give you my leftovers if I remember to give you anything at all. I feel entitled to what I have. I believe I have earned it. But if I take a moment to step back and survey the abundance of this world, and how little I actually produce in it, I find I am reminded that everything belongs to you. My claim on this world and all that I have is tenuous and temporary at best. In truth, I own nothing —I am squatter in your world —all things are yours. Help that realization to fuel my generosity. In Jesus' name, I pray. AMEN.

January 30

ANCIENT BENEDICTION

Read: Numbers 6:22–27

The Lord bless you and keep you; the Lord make his face to shine upon you, and be
gracious to you; the Lord lift up his countenance upon you, and give you peace.
NUMBERS 6:24–26

GOD INSTRUCTED MOSES to have Aaron pronounce this blessing over all the people
of Israel. It is an ancient blessing that demonstrates God's desire to shower people
with goodness. Safekeeping, a lighted way, and the hope for both gracious and
peaceful living are all a part of God's most basic desires for us. The priests were
to offer this benediction as a way of sending people out into the world, mindful of
God's desire to bless them wherever they might go. And to this day, every time we
hear this blessing pronounced in our churches, it is a reminder of our connection
with people of faith throughout the generations. This benediction may be ancient,
but God's ability to bless us is renewed each day and in every age.

When was the last time this blessing was pronounced over you?

Lord, thank you for sending me out into the world with words of encouragement that
remind me of your presence in my life and your interest in all I do. Thank you, also, for the
unbroken line of faith that connects those words from Aaron's mouth to my ears. Your faithful-
ness has been experienced through every generation leading up to my own. What a blessing to
be reminded that your love and interest in us is never diminished. In your name, I pray. AMEN.

January 31

LITERALLY?

Read: Numbers 15:32–36

> *Then the Lord said to Moses, "The man shall be put to death;*
> *all the congregation shall stone him outside the camp."*
> *NUMBERS 15:35*

FROM TIME TO time there are people who claim to take the Bible literally. It is unclear what *taking* means. Does it mean believing that every word of scripture was personally uttered by God? Does it mean that they live according to the letter of the law themselves? Does it mean the Bible is the operation manual for life on earth—just follow the instructions and all will be well? More often than not, "taking the Bible literally" means picking and choosing passages of scripture that confirm a bias or further an argument. In truth, no one lives his or her life strictly adhering to each command of the Bible. If we did, the vast majority of Christians—and Jews for that matter—would either be dead or incarcerated for murder.

In this passage of scripture, a man was put to death for doing work on the Sabbath. A man was caught picking up sticks, and his life came to an end when his community started throwing stones in his direction. Imagine being condemned to death for missing church or for taking children to soccer practice or for doing bills on a Sunday afternoon? If a person does any work on Sunday, they are breaking the commandment to rest and keep the Sabbath holy. Scripture cannot be lived literally, but it can be taken seriously. While the Bible may not be a step-by-step manual for living, it can be a centrally important guide for our lives. The Bible is a living document, which is meant to be continually reinterpreted through the leading of the Spirit and our own life experience. For instance, breaking the Sabbath may no longer be an offense punishable by death, but forgetting our call to Sabbath can still rob us of life.

How do you decide what commands you will obey?

Lord, Holy Scripture is both disturbing and enlivening. It is amazing how the same words that Moses spoke thousands of years ago can speak to me today—even, or perhaps especially, if those words trouble my spirit. The application of scripture may be different in our culture, Lord, but the truth of your word remains constant. Help me to know how to faithfully interpret all that you have said and continue to say. In Jesus' holy name, I pray. AMEN.

February 1

LEADERSHIP TRANSITION

Read: Numbers 27:12–23

So the Lord said to Moses, "Take Joshua son of Nun, a man in whom is the
spirit, and lay your hand upon him; have him stand before Eleazar the
priest and all the congregation, and commission him in their sight."
NUMBERS 27:18–19

HOW DO YOU replace Moses? How do you transition from an iconic leadership figure to another person who must follow in their footsteps? How does leadership succession work so that a newly minted leader feels empowered to do the job assigned to them? It is a daunting challenge that so many communities, organizations, corporations, and institutions are forced to wrestle with. A charismatic and galvanizing leader dies, retires, or leaves for another job, and questions of succession fill people with tremendous anxiety. What is to be done?

The leadership transition between Moses and Joshua had several important steps. First, Joshua was selected based on the belief that he had the right gifts for the job. Second, Moses placed his hands on Joshua, physically demonstrating his own affirmation of this young man. And, finally, other leaders, such as the priest Eleazar, stood in support of Joshua. All these proceedings were done in plain sight of the people who would wind up following Joshua. How do you transition leadership successfully? Pick a gifted person. Secure the blessing of prior and current leadership. And make sure the people in the organization are witnesses to the entire process. There should be no secrets in succession.

Have you witnessed a leadership transition that worked particularly well?

Lord, you not only care about us as individual people, you also care for the institutions
and organizations and communities that we inhabit. You care about faithful leadership, and
about healthy transitions in leadership. You also know that secrecy often undermines succes-
sion. Please safeguard our leaders, and when it is time for transition, help us to engage in a
thoughtful and faithful process of succession. In Jesus' name, I pray. AMEN.

February 2

DEBT FREE

Read: Deuteronomy 15:1–8

You will lend to many nations, but you will not borrow; you will
rule over many nations, but they will not rule over you.
DEUTERONOMY 15:6

PARALYZING PERSONAL AND national debt is an epidemic in our country. As Americans we have a combined consumer debt in the trillions of dollars. This is dwarfed, of course, by our national debt, which is dozens of times greater. Forty percent of U.S. families spend more than they earn. An average of 1.5 million U.S. households file for bankruptcy each year. The average personal credit card debt is equal the cost of a year of college.

When we are financially bound, we can't be spiritually free. The Bible is clear—you don't want to be in debt. The apostle Paul wrote to the Romans, "*Owe no one anything, except to love one another.*" In Proverbs it says, *The borrower is the slave of the lender.* And that is, in part, what this passage in Deuteronomy says. Moses gave the Israelites some banking advice: *You will lend to many nations, but you will not borrow; you will rule over many nations, but they will not rule over you.* Lenders rule, borrowers pay. When you go into debt, you lose your power. You become a slave. Your creditors rule your life. God did not create you to be ruled by Visa, American Express, or Mastercard —there is nothing priceless about those relationships! You were not created to be a slave; you were created to be free. You we not created to be a debtor, you were created to be a disciple.

Are you a debtor?

Lord, my desire to purchase things is insatiable. I see something I want, and I go out and get it. I often buy things I don't really want and don't really need, because there is an emptiness inside me and I don't know how else to fill it. Help me, Lord. I am financially bound, help me to be spiritually free. In Jesus' name, I pray. AMEN.

February 3

CAN'T GO BACK

Read: Deuteronomy 17:14–20

You must never return that way again.
DEUTERONOMY 17:16

AFTER ESCAPING SLAVERY, the Israelites were never again to return to Egypt. When they first fled into the desert, they longed for the savory food, the good drink, and the adequate shelter they'd had in that foreign country. They cried out against God saying, *"Why have you brought us out of the land of Egypt to kill us in the desert?"* Even after the Hebrew people established themselves as a stable nation, when threatened, they would always consider returning to Egypt for warhorses, chariots, and national alliances, which they believed would keep them safe. When times were difficult, the Israelites longed for the safety of their old, enslaved lives. But God told them never to return. Once the bonds of the past have been broken, one never returns to the prison again. One never goes back, one just moves forward.

Are there any old and unhealthy relationships, situations, or habits in your life that beckon you back into bondage?

Lord, when you free us from the chains of the past, you command us never to go back. There are moments, however, when I am tempted to return. An old flame, a trusty addiction, an unhealthy but familiar working relationship can seem preferable to my present troubles. But the difficulties of the present are never worth returning to the slavery of the past. Help me to move forward with you without looking back. In Jesus' name, I pray. AMEN.

February 4

RULES OF DISENGAGEMENT

Read: Deuteronomy 20:1–9

Has anyone planted a vineyard and not yet enjoyed its fruit? He should go back
to his house, or he might die in the battle and another be first to enjoy its fruit.
DEUTERONOMY 20:6

IN THE BIBLE there are reasons to go to war, and there are reasons to avoid the battlefield. If you had just built a house but had not dedicated it, if you had planted
a vineyard and not enjoyed its fruit, if you were engaged but had not yet married
. . . you should disengage from the battle to first enjoy the blessings of life. Even
when the land of the Israelites was threatened, God did not want a single person
to lose out on the opportunity to enjoy life.

Home, food, drink, intimacy with a life partner—the extravagantly simple
pleasures of life—are experiences not to be missed. Miss the battle before you
miss the joys of life. But for those of us who have tasted some of the goodness of
life . . . the battle, the hardships, the front line fight for God's will to be done in
our world and in our lives . . . that battle is ours. For God, no one should go to the
grave without savoring a bit of the beauty of life first.

What activities fill you with pleasure?

Lord God, before duty is your command to take pleasure—not to live a life of indulgence,
but to taste some of the fruits of this world before we come to our earthly end. You desire us to
be happy, even for this brief moment of life. How amazing that you even care for our pleasure,
insisting that we make time for it! In Jesus' name, I pray. AMEN.

February 5

No Cheating!

Read: Deuteronomy 25:13–16

All who act dishonestly are abhorrent to the Lord your God.
DEUTERONOMY 25:16

WE LIVE IN an age where corporations and corporate leaders appear willing to do whatever it takes to increase their profit margins. As a result, customers, employees, and the entire economy can be injured. This was true in biblical times as well—cheating in business is nothing new. In Deuteronomy, God warned merchants against carrying two weights in their bags—one large and one small. God instructed merchants that when weighing out a transaction, they were to use "*only a full and honest weight; you shall have only a full and honest measure, so that your days may be long in the land.*"

God cares about the way we do business, because the way we do business has an impact on people God loves and cares for. As people of faith, even in an often cutthroat business environment, we are charged to conduct ourselves with integrity and honesty.

Are you honest in all your business and relational dealings?

Lord, you promise that if I conduct my business with integrity, you will bless me. However, I see so many people around me cutting corners and making huge financial gains. It is tempting to follow their example. Help me to trust that if I strive to do what is right, you will allow me to do very well. In Jesus' name, I pray. AMEN.

February 6

CHOICE

Read: Deuteronomy 30:11–20

> *I have set before you life and death, blessings and curses. Choose life . . .*
> *DEUTERONOMY 30:19*

GOD SETS CLEAR boundaries for us. God outlines behavioral territory that is safe for us, and God also defines for us places of danger. There are blessings and curses to be had in life, and we have been given the freedom to choose a path that can lead in either direction. God has given us rules to live by, intended for our benefit and blessing. When we choose to disobey, we often find our lives accursed . . . that is the cost of freedom. God has set life and death, blessings and curses before us. God is not dispassionate, however; God desires that we choose the way toward life and blessing.

Do you exercise the freedom that God has given you in life-giving ways, or do your choices bring curses to bear on your life?

Lord, you have mapped out life for us, and like a loving parent you have made strong recommendations about how we should live in order to live well. But we often make different choices that deviate from your will for us . . . and we suffer for it. Help me to make good choices today so that I can enjoy your blessings tomorrow. In Jesus' name, I pray. AMEN.

February 7

Going Before You

Read: Deuteronomy 31:1–8

*Be strong and bold. . . . It is the Lord who goes before you. He will be with
you; he will not fail you or forsake you. Do not fear or be dismayed.*
DEUTERONOMY 31:7B & 8

WE OFTEN APPROACH challenging situations with a fair degree of timidity because we
fear being undone by them. We fear failure. We fear disappointment. We fear hurting someone's feelings. Our timidity is often fueled by the erroneous sense that we
are on our own—alone. But God calls us to boldness and strength, because God
goes before us into every room, every situation, and every relationship to safeguard
our well-being. With God we are never alone, and we are never forsaken.

Where do you need God to go ahead of you to prepare a way for you?

*Lord, thank you for the reminder. I am not alone. You go before me. You watch over me. In
fact, you are making preparations for me before I even begin to pack my bags for the next leg of
the journey I am on. Thank you for your presence, and allow me to draw strength and courage
from that knowledge. In your name, I pray. AMEN.*

February 8

GREAT WORK

Read: Deuteronomy 34:1–12

The Lord said to him, "This is the land of which I swore to Abraham, to
Isaac, and to Jacob, saying, 'I will give it to your descendants'; I have
let you see it with your eyes, but you shall not cross over there."
DEUTERONOMY 34:4

VERSE 10 IN this passage of scripture reads: *Never since has there arisen a prophet in Israel like Moses, whom the Lord knew face to face.* There is no bigger and more impressive life in Jewish history than that of Moses. No one could ever surpass his faithfulness, power, and personal knowledge of God. Moses will be forever remembered as the man of faith who helped to lead the Hebrew people out of captivity in Egypt and right up to the edge of the promised land. But even Moses could go only so far. There were limits. God allowed Moses to see the goal before him—from Mount Pisgah Moses surveyed the promised inheritance of his people—but he would never enter the land of Canaan. Moses died before he attained the goal that he had been striving for.

This could certainly be viewed as a rather tragic story. When you work with God, however, you quickly realize that God's dreams, visions, and goals for us are always bigger than our own. God's work—great work—always requires more than we can give. In fact, if you can accomplish in your lifetime the work before you, then it probably isn't the God-sized effort you were meant to engage in. Great works of faith require a company of people spanning multiple generations. When we work with God, the most we should hope for is being able to see on the horizon that God is calling us to. As Isaac Newton said, *"We stand on the shoulders of giants."* And if we pursue the grand work God intends for us, one day others will stand upon our shoulders, and their view of the world will be far more expansive than Moses' and our own.

What great work is God calling you toward?

— 45 —

Lord, I pray that when I come to the end of my days, my work with you will bring me to the edge of something truly grand. Like Moses, I will be more than satisfied if I can just catch a glimpse of the promised land that you have been leading me toward. Standing on the edge of your promise without being able to enter fully into it will remind me that your visions are as eternal and expansive as your life. I get to play only a small role in the cosmic drama that you have birthed me into. And yet, the view from this earthly stage is extraordinary. Thank you for including me in it all, and keep calling me toward the horizon and to new vistas. In Jesus' name, I pray. AMEN.

MANTRA

Read: Joshua 1:1–9

I hereby command you: Be strong and courageous; do not be frightened
or dismayed, for the Lord your God is with you wherever you go.
JOSHUA 1:9

HOW DOES A person take the mantle of leadership from a larger-than-life figure like Moses? How could anyone step into Moses' shoes and take the Hebrew people where Moses himself was unable to lead them? How did Joshua—who wasn't even born when the Hebrews escaped from slavery in Egypt—do it? How do any of us tackle challenges that seem far greater than the abilities we have to bring to bear on them?

In verses 6–9, God offered Joshua a specific mantra three times. God told Joshua, *"Be strong and courageous, for I am with you."* When a biblical author repeats a word or a statement, it is a clue that what is being written is of heightened importance. God wanted Joshua to have a mantra on his lips and heart and spirit that would encourage him as he led the Hebrew people across the Jordan River and into the promised land. God wanted this simple statement to run through Joshua's mind when crossing the Jordan, entering battle, and besieging Jericho. *"Be strong and courageous, for I am with you!"* The only way to fill the shoes of a great leader is to constantly be mindful that One even greater than Moses travels with you. It was God's promise to Joshua, it is God's promise to you.

"Be strong and courageous, for I am with you." Repeat that promise throughout your day today.

Lord, so often I feel as if I am on my own. I feel small. I doubt my abilities. I seem weak and uncertain. Perhaps I am, in fact, all those things. But you are not. You are everything I need, and in you, I find strength and courage. Help me to remember that as I silently whisper the mantra to myself. "Be strong. Be courageous. You are with me." In Jesus' name, I pray. AMEN.

BIBLICAL TRUTH

Read: Joshua 6:26–27 & Luke 10:13–16

Joshua then pronounced this oath, saying, "Cursed before the Lord
be anyone who tries to build this city—this Jericho!"
JOSHUA 6:26A

"Woe to you, Chorazin! Woe to you, Bethsaida! For if the deeds of
power done in you had been done in Tyre and Sidon, they would
have repented long ago, sitting in sackcloth and ashes."
LUKE 10:13

JOSHUA CURSED THE city of Jericho once the walls of that great city had fallen and the Israelites had taken possession of it. Jesus cursed three cities in Galilee that refused to respond to his message of repentance. Travel to Israel today and visit the ruins of Jericho, Chorazin, Bethsaida, and Capernaum, and you will be hard pressed to ignore that something went terribly wrong in those communities. The only semblance of a wall around Jericho are the defensive barriers the Israelis put in place to seal the Palestinians off from the rest of the country. Jericho may be one of the longest continually inhabited cities in the world, but it is also a city besieged and located among countless ruins that have never been excavated. Chorazin, Bethsaida, and Capernaum—cities that once thrived in the lush and picturesque Galilean countryside—are nothing more than crumbled ruins. Plenty of people and many scholars may doubt the historicity of events such as the walls of Jericho tumbling down to the shouts and trumpet blasts of the Hebrew people. But stand amid the ruins of Jericho, Chorazin, Bethsaida, and Capernaum and you will feel the truth of ancient curses. What Joshua cursed—what Jesus cursed—died, and in several instances, stayed dead. It may be hard to believe all the stories in the Bible, but it might be a grave mistake to discount them. Predictions, prophecies, and even certain curses made in the Bible have a way of coming true.

Do you believe in the Bible?

Lord, there is a temptation to put little or no stock in the claims and stories of the Bible. They can often feel fanciful, as if they are idle tales meant to impart lessons or instill fear. But the Bible is primarily a story about you and humankind's struggle to learn how to be in relationship with you. We fail in so many ways, but help us not to fail to take you seriously. For you are our God, and we long to be your people . . . and we need to get as serious about the relationship as you are. That is the truth! In Jesus' name, I pray. AMEN.

February 11

HEEDED

Read: Joshua 10:1–15

Joshua spoke to the Lord; and he said in the sight of Israel, "Sun, stand
still at Gibeon, and Moon, in the valley of Aijalon." And the sun stood still,
and the moon stopped. . . . There has been no day like it before or since,
when the Lord heeded a human voice; for the Lord fought for Israel.
Joshua 10:12–14

THE STORY OF Joshua asking the Lord to make the sun stand still so that the Israelites would have time to achieve victory in battle is remarkable. Most people focus on the miraculous nature of this story, wondering how the sun stood still or how the earth ceased its rotation upon Joshua's request. Such a story is certainly fodder for any skeptic who wants to take issue with the grand claims of the Bible. And yet, it may not be all that out of line with human physiology, which is something of a miracle in its own right. How many times have people found themselves in a moment of crisis, only to feel as if time slowed almost to a stop? It is amazing that when a moment calls for lightning-quick responses, our bodies and our minds process events more quickly than we ever imagined. We are able to respond with a speed that makes the event itself appear to move in slow motion. Who knows if the sun stood still for Joshua or if in the heat of battle time seemed to slow for the Israelites?

In the end, a celestial standstill is not the point of the story. The most remarkable feature of this story, according to the biblical author, is that God heeded the request of a mortal—and on a grand scale. For the writer of this story, the sun standing still wasn't nearly as impressive as God heeding Joshua's request. If you think about it, it is a remarkable claim we make as people of faith: we dare to believe that the Maker of heaven and earth pauses to consider our requests and responds to them. God pausing to consider our situation and the claim that the sun stood still for Joshua should serve to remind us of God's intense interest in our lives—individually and collectively.

What request do you want to make of God?

Lord, the sun standing still is no more remarkable than your Son stopping on the road to tend to a lost sinner. The fact that you take notice of us at all—as small as we are—is nothing short of a cosmic-sized miracle. Thank you for taking notice of us, listening to us, and heeding our requests. In Jesus' name, I pray. AMEN.

February 12

CALMING RAGE

Read: Joshua 20:1–9

Then the Lord spoke to Joshua, saying, "Say to the Israelites, 'Appoint
the cities of refuge, of which I spoke to you through Moses, so that any-
one who kills a person without intent or by mistake may flee there;
they shall be for you a refuge from the avenger of blood.'"
JOSHUA 20:1–3

THERE ARE COMMANDS in the Bible that are absolutely extraordinary. Setting aside cities of refuge was nothing short of brilliant. The concern that prompted this action was the prevalence of blood feuds. From time to time there would be an accidental death, and the family of the deceased would seek revenge even if the lethal injury occurred without malice. If revenge was successfully taken, it could spiral into a deadly cycle between families, clans, and communities. Thanks to the command of God, both Moses and Joshua recognized the need for cooler heads and clearer thinking to prevail. Therefore, sanctuary cites were set aside where an offending party could go to seek refuge until the rage that accompanied a particular death was quelled. A trial would be held and judgment would still be rendered, but rage would not be allowed to rule the day. Brilliant!

There are plenty of times when anger gets the best of us, and we act too rashly or speak too harshly. In the aftermath, we often wish we had taken a few deep breaths and paused a bit to let our rage abate before taking action or speaking our mind. Rage can prompt us to react in ways we wind up regretting. Taking time to cool down—especially when we don't want to—can safeguard our relationships, our lives, and our communities.

What do you do when you find yourself filled with anger and contemplating revenge?

Lord, your word is timeless. The commands of distant yesterdays have a way of speaking to me today. Your divine nature has a way of instructing my human nature. Thank you. And help me to pause and breathe deeply the next time anger is about to get the best of me. I don't want to be full of rage, for I desire to reflect the best of you. In Jesus' name, I pray. AMEN.

DECISION TIME

Read: Joshua 24:1–28

> *Now if you are unwilling to serve the Lord, choose this day whom*
> *you will serve, whether the gods your ancestors served in the region*
> *beyond the River or the gods of the Amorites in whose land you are liv-*
> *ing; but as for me and my household, we will serve the Lord.*
> *Joshua 24:15*

WITH FEET PLANTED firmly in the land of Canaan—the land that God had promised to Abraham's descendants generations earlier—it was time for the Israelites to decide. As a people, they had finally received the promise that had been the unrealized dream of so many of their forefathers and mothers. God had done all that God had promised to do. It had taken far longer than anyone could have imagined, but the Israelites had the promised land in their possession. The question was now at hand: who would they follow, and would they choose to remember from whom all their blessings had come? Would they follow the Lord who had been faithful to them throughout the generations, or would they begin to worship the gods of the land they had inherited?

It is a sad reality, but once the excitement and novelty of God's provision wears off, we often go back to old and less-than-inspired ways of living. God does something amazing in our lives, we swear we will never forget the blessing, and we promise that our lives will be lived better in response to God's gift . . . but time passes and our passions for holy living and faithful remembrance begin to fade. We stand in our own promised land, forgetting all that God has done to get us to where we are. Joshua told the Israelites that they would be naturally inclined to forget about God and would begin to worship lifeless idols. But Joshua swore that his family would never forget and that they would forever serve the Lord. It is a decision we all have before us each and every day—will we serve our own interests and worship every idol that attracts our eye? Or will we stand with, and serve, the God who has faithfully brought us forth into the life we now lead?

Who will you serve this day?

Lord, why do I so easily forget the many times you have saved my skin? I can scoff at the Israelites for forgetting how you led them out of Egypt. I can act astonished that they would not remember you leading them through the Red Sea. I can shake my head and wag my finger disapprovingly at the Israelites who ignored how you fed them for forty years in the desert. What halts my condemnation is the realization that I am no different from them. I forget. I become distracted. I am devoted to a thousand things other than you. O, how I long to possess the resolve of Joshua! Lord, I want to serve you, and I want my family to do the same. I have decided in favor of you, I just need your help to follow through on my intentions. For this I pray, in Jesus' name. AMEN.

February 14

DEBORAH

Read: Judges 4:1–10

At that time Deborah, a prophetess, wife of Lappidoth, was judging Israel.
She used to sit under the palm of Deborah between Ramah and Bethel in the
hill country of Ephraim; and the Israelites came up to her for judgment.
Judges 4:4–5

A JUDGE WAS a military and political leader in ancient Israel, long before the kingly leadership of the Hebrew people was established. Long before King David and King Solomon and King Hezekiah, was Deborah. Deborah was the lead arbiter and military general of her time. A woman led Israel in a day and an age when women were afforded little, if any, authority.

More than three thousand years after Deborah, our culture continues to struggle with the abilities and worth of certain individuals. We question the strength of women, we see great limitations for people with disabilities, and we malign people who appear different from ourselves. But there is no limit to what God can do with us, and who God can empower to leadership in this world. We may be slow to recognize the gifts and abilities of others, God is not. The next time you doubt your worth or ability, or the worth or ability of someone else, remember Deborah. God doesn't want you to forget.

What doubts do you have about yourself?

Lord, when I look at myself in the mirror I see a deeply flawed individual. As I work my way through life I am reminded of my limitations. As I witness the values of the culture I am a part of . . . I feel as though I am less than I should be. But time and time again, you remind me that what our world values and what you value are not the same. In Deborah, the world likely saw a dependent woman, but you saw a greater leader of people. Thank you that your vision for us prevails, just as it did for Deborah. In your name, I pray. AMEN.

February 15

JEPHTHAH'S DAUGHTER

Read: Judges 11

*Jephthah's daughter said to him, "My father, if you have opened your mouth
to the Lord, do to me according to what has gone out of your mouth, now that
the Lord has given you vengeance against your enemies, the Ammonites."*
JUDGES 11:36

JEPHTHAH WAS THE son of a prostitute, banished by his family and his community,
and forced to make a life among a band of thieves. He was an outlaw. But when the
community of Gilead needed a conquering hero, they readily invited Jephthah back
into their fold with the hope that he would lead them to victory. Victory was had,
but the price was the life of Jephthah's own daughter, who willingly accepted being
a sacrifice—a burnt offering—to the glory of God.

We might rightly cringe at the gory nature of the supposed glory of God in this
passage. This is an awful story of a vow kept against what we might consider to be
better judgment. But in the midst of this gruesome story stands the innocent faithfulness of Jephthah's daughter. She speaks through this ancient text, telling us that vows
before God should be taken seriously and kept faithfully—not discarded in moments
when they begin to cost us more than we had expected. She reminds us that more
often than not, the work of faith has to do with parting with that which is most dear
to us. And in her story, we see a foreshadowing of the story of Jesus, the only son of
God who was sacrificed to the world so that victory over sin and death might be won.

What costly vow do you need to keep?

*Lord, I don't like this story. I claim my dislike stems from a careless vow, even more care-
lessly kept. But, perhaps, it is the underlying message that most disquiets me. Vows are serious
business. Faith requires sacrifice. Vows kept and sacrifices made are a central part of your gift
to us. I do not fully understand . . . or perhaps I do not entirely want to understand, but I still
pray this all in the name of Jesus. AMEN.*

February 16

FOOLISH

Read: Judges 16:4–22

The lords of the Philistines came to Delilah and said to her, "Coax him, and find out what makes his strength so great, and how we may overpower him, so that we may bind him in order to subdue him; and we will each give you eleven hundred pieces of silver."
JUDGES 16:5

YOU CANNOT READ the story of Samson and Delilah, and not feel as if Samson got exactly what he deserved. His relationship was based on lies—he knew it, Delilah knew it, and the Philistines were counting on it. Three times Delilah tried to trick Samson into giving himself up to the Philistines, and three times Samson overlooked the transgression. His lust for Delilah overwhelmed his better judgment—assuming he had capacity for better judgment! At the end of the story, Samson looks like a bald, broken fool.

There are many reasons why we may be tempted to overlook the failings of someone we are attracted to. We may excuse the lies, hurtful words, and even the abusive actions of someone with whom we feel we are in love. But true love does not lie, nor does it abuse. And a harmful offense by a partner or spouse should not be forgiven without evidence of real repentance. We are all tempted to be fools for love and lust, but let us not be fools for life.

Do you overlook the lies and careless behavior of someone you love?

Lord, if I truly love someone, and if I believe that person loves me, then deceit should have no place in the relationship. Surely we will fail in our efforts to love to the best of our ability from time to time, but a pattern of lies and hurtful behavior are unacceptable. Help me not to allow myself to be bound up in unhelpful and unhealthy relationships. Grant me the strength to break free from people who would willingly break me down. I know I make foolish decisions now and again, but more than anything, I want to enjoy faithful relationships. For this I pray, in Jesus' name. AMEN.

RUTH AND NAOMI

Read: Ruth 1–4

But Boaz answered Ruth, "All that you have done for your mother-in-law since the death of your husband has been fully told me, and how you left your father and mother and your native land and came to a people that you did not know before."
RUTH 2:11

WE ARE ALL familiar with the touching and heartfelt vows that Ruth spoke to her mother-in-law, Naomi, on their return to Judah: *"Where you go, I will go; where you lodge, I will lodge; your people shall be my people, and your God, my God."* Ruth didn't speak those words to impress anyone, she simply spoke them out of love and loyalty. Ruth chose to take care of her mother-in-law instead of tending to her own needs in life. This good and selfless act became known in Judah, and Boaz, a relative of Naomi's, heard of Ruth's fidelity and chose to provide for both women.

Some people give to get—they make an offering, hoping to receive something in return. In fact, there is much preaching and teaching in our Christian history that asserts that the more you give, the more God will provide you. But generosity that expects something in return is false generosity. When we freely provide for others, however—when we are truly generous with all that we have—that generosity tends to inspire the generosity of others. And when the world is filled with givers, everyone will be taken care of . . . including ourselves.

Do you give to get?

Lord, help me to be more selfless in my daily living. Help me to think more of others than myself. Help me to put my needs on the back burner for a moment so that I can tend to the needs of others. Help me to be more like Ruth. In Jesus' name, I pray. AMEN.

February 18

ELI

Read: 1 Samuel 3:1–9

Then Eli perceived that the Lord was calling the boy.
1 SAMUEL 3:8

SAMUEL WAS A young boy when the Lord called him into service. God called one night saying, *"Samuel, Samuel."* But Samuel thought Eli, the chief priest of the tabernacle, was calling him, so he got up and rushed to Eli's side. Two more times God called the boy, and each time Samuel went to Eli saying, *"You called me."* Finally, Eli perceived that the Lord God was calling Samuel, and Eli instructed the boy how to respond to this divine conversation.

God calls to us every day, and yet often we are unable to hear God's voice. Without hearing God's voice, we risk living our lives apart from God's will for us. That is why it is so important for us to have an Eli—someone skilled in hearing and recognizing God's voice in our lives. Going to church, having friends who are people of faith, and getting serious about our own faith education allows us the opportunity to be both found and led by an Eli. In time, when we have become seasoned in responding to God's invitation in our own lives, we might find that we become an Eli for someone else.

Who might be an Eli for you?

Lord, lead me to someone who can help me to hear your voice. I need an Eli. I need someone to help me recognize your subtle nudging in my life. You know I don't like to ask for help, but I don't want to miss out on what you are calling me to do. I want to make the most of my life, and I am going to need some Elis to help me on my way. In Jesus' name, I pray. AMEN.

February 19

JUST LIKE EVERYBODY ELSE

Read: 1 Samuel 8:1–9

> *"Appoint for us, then, a king to govern us, like other nations."*
> *1 SAMUEL 8:5*

THE ISRAELITES REJECTED God as their king in order to be like other nations. They were tired of being different, they were fed up with being ridiculed, and they'd had enough of being "the chosen ones." They just wanted to be like everyone else. In their desire to be like other nations, however, they discarded their identity as the people of God.

Blending in, conforming, trying to be like everyone else is a basic survival instinct. Smart children try to hide their intelligence at school so they're not called a nerd, while others don't speak up in class for fear of being called stupid. The well-worn middle ground is always the safest way to survive. However, God did not create you to survive; God created you to *thrive*. And that happens when you finally decide to be exactly who God intended you to be—as different as that may be.

How has your desire to be like everyone else pulled you away from God?

Dear God, it is my natural tendency to want to fit in. I want to blend in at work, at parties, and when I go out with friends. And yet I know you have created me for the very purpose of making a unique difference in the world. I also know that when I deny who you have created me to be, I deny you. Help me to make decisions that will allow me to be more like you . . . for that is my truest desire. In your holy name, I pray. AMEN.

February 20

LOOKS GOOD

Read: 1 Samuel 9:1—10:8

There was a man of Benjamin whose name was Kish son of Abiel son of Zeror son
of Becorath son of Aphiah, a Benjaminite, a man of wealth. He had a son whose
name was Saul, a handsome young man. There was not a man among the people of
Israel more handsome than he; he stood head and shoulders above everyone else.
1 SAMUEL 9:1—2

SAUL LOOKED SO good. He was handsome, tall, commanding, and he came from a
wealthy family. What a perfect choice for Israel's first king! The Hebrew people
gave up their invisible God as their king and set in place a man who was a vision of
beauty and success. Saul appeared to be everything anyone could have hoped for
in a leader—he was the kind of person that others looked up to and dreamed of
becoming.

Yet, while Saul looked good on the outside, he had deep character flaws on the
inside. He lacked resolve, he was a fearful man, and he wound up dying amid a fever-
ish attempt to maintain his power and authority. As it turned out, Saul's servant boy
was more resolute and faithful than his master. It would likely have been better if
Samuel anointed the young boy instead of his handsome and towering master. Can it
be any surprise that once Saul's leadership unraveled, Samuel discovered the next king
not among the tall and strapping sons of Jesse but in Jesse's youngest boy, the one who
was thought worthy only to be left in the fields to tend his father's flocks? Leadership
is not about looking good on the outside but, rather, being good on the inside.

How do looks influence your decisions?

Lord, I make the same mistake that Samuel made all the time. I am captivated by out-
ward appearances and often overlook internal flaws. I make purchases, choose friends, and
assess investments based on how good they look on the outside. That kind of evaluation can
lead to disastrous results. Help me to be more discerning. In your holy name, I pray. AMEN.

February 21

Remember

Read: 1 Samuel 12

But they forgot the Lord.
1 Samuel 12:9a

WE DON'T LIKE to admit it, but we get scared sometimes. We worry that life, or the challenges life presents us, will overwhelm us, undo us, or even worse, humiliate us. We worry we won't have all we need to survive. We become anxious that somehow we will fail to provide for our loved ones in ways in which they have grown accustomed. While things seem to be going well at the moment, we are aware that fortunes can change in an instant . . . and that reality keeps us awake at night.

Throughout the biblical narrative, the Israelites' greatest failing was their forgetfulness. They had forgotten how God had delivered them from slavery in Egypt. They had forgotten how God had provided them food and water in the desert. They had forgotten how God had led them—and given them—a land flowing with milk and honey. When faced with a new challenge, they would panic as if God would somehow stop providing for them.

When we get scared, forgetfulness becomes our greatest enemy. The cure for fear is remembrance. The next time anxiety begins to take hold of your life, start remembering all the many times God has come to your rescue in the past. Remember. God will not forget you, and God will not forsake you.

Take a moment to think about a time when you thought you were done for, but God rescued you.

Lord God, forgive me my forgetfulness. Create in me a remembering and trusting spirit. Help me to cling to the truth that while I am prone to forget, you always remember. You remember me and love me for eternity, and I will endeavor to always remember to thank you. In the name of Jesus Christ, I pray. AMEN.

February 22

APPEARANCES

Read: 1 Samuel 16:1–13

*"For the Lord does not see as mortals see; they look on the out-
ward appearance, but the Lord looks on the heart."*
1 SAMUEL 16:7

WE SO OFTEN form opinions, make decisions, and take action in response to visual stimuli. We tend to hire the applicant who looks even better in person than they did on paper, we pursue and court the man or woman who is most attractive to us, and we even aggressively cut through traffic based on which lane appears to be moving the fastest. But looking primarily on the outward appearance can lead to bad choices. We often overlook the faithful and loyal heart because the long legs and seductive smile catch our eye.

God is clear. It doesn't matter if someone looks the part—they've got to have the right heart. It isn't the outward appearance that matters, it is what is inside that counts. It's not about the packaging, it's about the product. It's not about the persona, it's about the performance. When choosing a friend, when selecting a life partner, when hiring an employee . . . don't get seduced by how they look; rather, find out who they are.

Who have you overlooked lately?

Lord, I have always been confident in my sight. I look at a person, an opportunity, or a challenge, and I can quickly render a judgment. But, sometimes, looks have been deceiving. They looked good on the outside but were shallow on the inside. It appeared to be a good investment, but it had weak earnings. My new hire looked the part, but didn't have the work ethic. Lord, help me to look more deeply. Help me to see as you see. Help me to see the heart. In your Son's name, I pray. AMEN.

February 23

Music to Soothe
the Soul

Read: 1 Samuel 16:14–23

And whenever the evil spirit from God came upon Saul, David took
the lyre and played it with his hand, and Saul would be relieved
and feel better, and the evil spirit would depart from him.
1 Samuel 16:23

Music is nothing short of miraculous. Anthropologists can thoughtfully explain how music emerged in early humanoid culture. How we got from banging sticks on rocks to a Mozart concerto, however, is nothing short of astounding. The effect music has on us is just as remarkable. Music can lift our spirits and soothe our souls. Music can agitate us. Music can bring tears to our eyes as it touches deep aches in our hearts. A stirring aria, a country western ballad, or a lively guitar riff can move us in ways few other artistic expressions can. Music is both spirited and divine. It can unite people in song, it can elicit deep and profound reflection, and it can even ease the troubled heart of an evil king.

What is your favorite piece of music?

Dear Lord, thank you for music and for the way music enriches our lives. It is a gift and a blessing. The way music can affect my emotions is both miraculous and divine. Thank you for this gift. In Jesus' name, I pray. AMEN.

DAVID AND GOLIATH

Read: 1 Samuel 17

> *David said to the men who stood by him, "What shall be done for the man who kills this Philistine, and takes away the reproach from Israel? For who is this uncircumcised Philistine that he should defy the armies of the living God?"*
> *1 SAMUEL 17:26*

WE ARE TOLD that Saul and the Israelite army were paralyzed with fear as the giant Goliath taunted them from the Philistine ranks. Goliath was huge. The Philistines' iron swords were fearsome. For the Jewish army, the impending conflict seemed like mission impossible. However, what most saw as a daunting challenge, David saw as a wonderful opportunity. Upon seeing Goliath on the battlefield, the first thing David asked was what a man would receive if he killed Goliath. What was the reward for killing the Philistine?

So often in life, victory is claimed by people who see obstacles as opportunities for advancement. They believe that stumbling blocks are actually stepping-stones. In truth, challenges are always opportunities for growth and development. People who recognize this reality are the ones whose stories live on to inspire others.

What Goliath-sized opportunity is standing in front of you right now?

Lord, Goliath wants me to be scared. Goliath wants me to quake in my boots. Goliath wants me to take my little sling and handful of stones home in shame. I am tempted to do just that. I am scared when I think about stepping out onto the battlefield against such a formidable foe. I am afraid I will get killed. But what if staring down death is a pathway to life? What if facing down my fears is the key to my happiness? What if my battle with Goliath is the greatest opportunity I have to be all you created me to be? Give me courage to seize the opportunity in every challenge. In Jesus' name, I pray. AMEN.

February 25

JEALOUSY

Read: 1 Samuel 18:1–8

And the women sang to one another as they made merry, "Saul has killed his thousands, and David his tens of thousands." Saul was very angry, for this saying displeased him. He said, "They have ascribed to David ten thousands, and to me they have ascribe thousands; what more can he have but the kingdom?"
1 SAMUEL 18:7–8

WHEN IS BEING a king not enough? When is having a loyal and successful servant such as David not enough? When are your own impressive accomplishments not enough? Apparently, when you are filled with jealousy and rage. Saul was the first king of Israel. He had led numerous successful military campaigns. He commanded the respect and devotion of men like David who would have willingly given their lives for their king. But Saul became incensed when he heard the cheers of his people—and the recognition that David's triumphs on the battlefield were greater than his own. Somehow, Saul could not appreciate people cheering his own accomplishments, because they seemed less than David's. For some reason, Saul missed the fact that David's victories were his own as commander and chief. Saul was jealous, and jealousy wound up eroding his common sense.

Everyone will discover that there is someone in the world with more impressive accomplishments or greater possessions or better looks. There is always someone greater than ourselves. We can either become jealous of that reality or we can be thankful for who we are and what God has allowed us to do in life. Life is not a competition, and it is best when there is cooperation. How different our communal existence would be if we celebrated all the accomplishments within our human family as if they were our own. When one of us does well, the entire family is blessed! The good deeds of others should fill us with joy, not jealousy.

Are you a jealous person?

Lord, it is an embarrassing truth, but there are times when the accomplishments of others perturb me. In fact, I can feel more satisfied with someone's failure than with their success. It is because I am jealous. When someone does something great, it makes me feel oddly diminished. I know this is wrong. I should not begrudge the success of others—I should celebrate it. You have given me thousands of reasons to be thankful in this life—it makes no sense to be jealous of those people who appear to have tens of thousands of things to be thankful for! Help me to gain perspective. Calm my jealous heart. Remind me that my worth is not calculated against the achievements of others. In the name of Jesus Christ, I pray. AMEN.

February 26

BOUNDLESS JOY

Read: 2 Samuel 6:12–19

> *As the ark of the Lord came into the city of David, Michal daugh-*
> *ter of Saul looked out of the window, and saw King David leaping*
> *and dancing before the Lord; and she despised him in her heart.*
> 2 SAMUEL 6:16

THERE ARE MOMENTS, as infrequent as they may be, when we are so caught up in joy that we could literally dance in the streets. A prayer has been answered or a burden has been lifted or an opportunity has opened up for us that made our spirit leap with gratitude, and our bodies were willing to follow in the celebration! That was David's response when he brought the Ark of the Covenant—the symbolic presence of God—into Jerusalem. David danced wildly, and half naked before the Ark, in the sight of all his people. His wife, Michal, was horrified by what seemed to her to be a vulgar display of emotionalism. However, when the Spirit of the Lord seizes you, when abounding joy captivates your life, you just can't help yourself!

When was the last time you were completely filled with joy?

Lord, it is not often when I am entirely and joyfully enraptured by your presence. There have certainly been moments when your presence in my life has prompted within me an irrepressible joy. I may not have danced in the streets, but my heart certainly leapt with gratitude. I wish this were a more common occurrence for me. Maybe, like David, I have to usher you into my life, as he ushered you into Jerusalem, if I want to experience that kind of ecstatic and joyous reunion. I open my life up to you anew today. Enter in. I am ready to dance! In the name of Jesus Christ, I pray. AMEN.

DEEPEST SORROW

Read: 2 Samuel 18:33—19:8

The king was deeply moved, and went up to the chamber over the gate, and
wept; and as he went, he said, "O my son Absalom, my son, my son Absalom!
Would that I had died instead of you, O Absalom, my son, my son!"
2 SAMUEL 18:33

WE SAY THAT the deepest sorrow a person can experience is the loss of a child. While this is true, the experience can vary widely. Sometimes children die due to tragically unfortunate events beyond anyone's control, and other times children die as a result of their own harmful choices. To read David's lament, one might assume that the loss of his son Absalom was a misfortune beyond compare. Absalom's death, however, occurred during his attempt to overthrow his father and assume control of the kingdom of Israel. Absalom was David's son, but he had also made himself David's enemy. If ever there was a reason not to lament the loss of a child, David had it. And yet, David wept for his son, wishing that he could have died in Absalom's place.

A parent's love never really dies. No matter how challenging the relationship, most parents would choose to take away their child's pain if they could. The parental desire to trade places with children when they are imperiled is irrepressible. Absalom's offense was great, but David's love was even greater. Parents know that feeling. We can only assume that God, the parent of us all, finds our lives and our plight equally compelling.

Can you imagine how much your Father in heaven loves you?

Lord, you must grieve every time one of your children is injured. Even when injury is
self-inflicted, your heart must break. Perhaps that is why you were not contented to stand at a
distance from us, but chose to join us in the person of Jesus. You love us more than anyone ever
could, even when we act in less than loving ways. Thank you for that grace. In Jesus' name, I
pray. AMEN.

February 28

DAVID AND BATHSHEBA

Read: 2 Samuel 11—12:23

David said to Nathan, "I have sinned against the Lord." Nathan said to David, "Now
the Lord has put away your sin; you shall not die. Nevertheless, because by this
deed you have utterly scorned the Lord, the child that is born to you shall die."
2 SAMUEL 12:13–14

THE STORY OF David and Bathsheba is possibly one of the most disturbing abuses of power in the entire Bible. This story is not merely troubling because of the gruesome nature of the crime but because the offense was committed by a man who was beloved by God and who certainly knew better. Lust overcame David, and when Bathsheba became pregnant, murder turned out to be David's exit plan. The story came to an end when David confessed his sin to the prophet Nathan. God forgave David, but David and his family were forced to bear the consequences of the sin.

That may be exactly the way God deals with people of faith. We sin, we confess, we are forgiven, but we must live with the consequences of our actions. Sin does not limit God's love for us. And yet, God's love for us does not limit the consequences of our behavior.

Can you accept love that requires you to accept consequences?

Lord, I have sinned. That is David's confession, and it is mine as well. We are sinful
creatures who do not deserve your love. And yet, you love us all the same, and you forgive us
when we ask. That does not mean we don't have to pay the price for our bad behavior. Help
me to embrace your love and your forgiveness while accepting the consequences of my actions.
In Jesus' name, I pray. AMEN.

February 29 (Leap Year)

Wisdom of Solomon

Read: 1 Kings 3:1–28

All Israel heard of the judgment that the king had rendered; and they stood in awe of
the king, because they perceived that the wisdom of God was in him, to execute justice.
1 Kings 3:28

IT IS A story that is familiar to many of us: God allowed Solomon to request anything
the young king wanted in life, and Solomon requested wisdom to rule the Hebrew
people. Solomon could have asked for anything in the world—anything and everything he might have desired for himself—but, instead, he asked for something that
would benefit others, and God enthusiastically honored Solomon's request.

Solomon's request was deeply pleasing to God, because Solomon thought first
of others when presented with the opportunity to have whatever his heart desired.
As a result, Solomon's wisdom became legendary, and God blessed Solomon's life
beyond measure. When we put others' needs before our own, God is pleased, and
out of that pleasure flows immense blessing.

If you could have anything in the world, what would you ask for?

Lord, I don't like to admit this . . . but I am in the habit of thinking first of myself. When
I do think of others, it is only when I have carefully weighed and considered the cost to myself.
This is not the way you want life to be—it is not the way I want my life to be. Grant me
wisdom, for I need it dearly. In Jesus' name, I pray. AMEN.

March 1

DOWN, BUT NOT OUT

Read: 1 Kings 19:1–18

"What are you doing here, Elijah?"
1 KINGS 19:9 & 13

ELIJAH, ONE OF the greatest and most renowned prophets in the history of Israel, ran into the wilderness and away from his God-given mission, because Queen Jezebel had threatened to kill him. Even though God had worked powerfully throughout Elijah's life, when the queen threatened his life, he ran for the hills in fear. Elijah ran to Mount Horeb, the mountain of God—Mount Sinai—the very mountain upon which God gave Moses the Ten Commandments.

On the mountaintop, God spoke to Elijah saying, *"What are you doing here, Elijah?"* Then, just to ensure that God had Elijah's attention, God had wind and an earthquake and fire blast the mountainside. After that fantastic display, God asked again, *"What are you doing here, Elijah?"* That was God's way of saying, *"You shouldn't be here."* God continued and said, *"Go, return on your way . . . you shall anoint Hazael as king, . . . you shall anoint Jehu . . . as king . . . ; and you shall anoint Elisha . . . as prophet in your place."* That was God's way of saying, *"You might be done, Elijah, but I've just begun. You might be down, but don't ever count me out. You may have run away in fear, but I am going to send you back in faith."*

There are times when we are tempted to run away from distressing situations—a strained relationship, a difficult conversation, a challenge that seems too daunting for us to handle. Sometimes, even though we are reluctant to admit it, we feel lonely and afraid. Through this story, God wants you to know that you may be down but you are not out. God has more work to do with you and through you. It is time for you to head back into the fray.

What challenges are you tempted to flee from that God wants you to return to?

Lord, I confess that there are times when fear prompts me to flee. There are moments when I feel like I am bearing the burdens of life alone, and I am afraid I will be undone by them. Help me to shed my fear, and allow me to reenter the fray with the faith that you will never abandon me to face my fears alone. In Jesus' name, I pray. AMEN.

March 2

DELIVERED

Read: 2 Kings 19:1–7

It may be that the Lord your God heard all the words of the Rabshakeh, whom his mas-
ter the king of Assyria has sent to mock the living God, and will rebuke the words that
the Lord your God has heard; therefore lift up your prayer for the remnant that is left.
2 KINGS 19:4

IT HAS BEEN said that Hezekiah would have made a better priest than a king. He certainly was a ruler who allowed his faith to govern his political decisions. King Hezekiah led a national effort to restore the proper worship of Yahweh in the kingdom of Judah. Whatever Hezekiah's faults and failings might have been, he tried his best to be faithful to God, and to trust in God's provision even when the odds seemed stacked against him and his people.

After the Assyrians had conquered the Northern Kingdom of Israel, the invading army moved south and besieged Jerusalem. The leader of the Assyrian armies taunted the Jews who had taken refuge behind the walls of Jerusalem, and he derided Hezekiah's belief in Yahweh's deliverance. This story is one of a battle between Hezekiah's faithfulness and Assyria's sheer force. While we may be tempted to question the theology behind the event, history is quite clear about what happened next: the Assyrians inexplicably retreated, never to return to the kingdom of Judah. Hezekiah and his people were delivered, and they firmly believed that their deliverance came from God. Questions abound, of course, for all people of faith have experienced moments when prayers have not been answered, and bad things have befallen good people. But the teaching of this story is one that is echoed throughout the entire Bible: in the end, faith triumphs over force.

Do you believe in God's deliverance?

Lord, scripture attests to the fact that you shower your blessings on faithful people and
unfaithful people alike. That means your provision is offered to the Hezekiahs of the world as

well as the Rabshakehs of the world. Therefore, it may be futile to try to figure out whose side you are on . . . perhaps because you love all sides involved in every dispute, disagreement, and conflict. So, what use is prayer? How can faith claim to triumph over force? How can we believe that good will eventually win over evil . . . when we are not always able to tell the difference between the two? There is so much we just do not know or understand. So, we will continue to pray for deliverance, and for the wisdom to know what is right . . . and we entrust the rest to you. In Jesus' name, we pray. AMEN.

March 3

BUILDERS

Read: 1 Chronicles 22:6–16

> *David said to Solomon, "My son, I had planned to build a house to the name*
> *of the Lord my God. But the word of the Lord came to me, saying, 'You have*
> *shed much blood and have waged great wars; you shall not build a house to*
> *my name, because you have shed so much blood in my sight on the earth.'"*
> 1 CHRONICLES 22:7–8

TO THIS DAY, the most sacred physical location in Jewish tradition is the Western Wall. The wall consists of enormous stones that served as the retaining wall for the Temple Mount. Those stones are all that remain of the temple complex that was expanded under the leadership of King Herod in the time of Jesus. The original temple was built by King Solomon after the death of his father, David. The great desire of David's life was to build a temple in which the Ark of the Covenant could reside. But, by the word of God, David was not allowed to construct the temple. David was a warrior who had spilled much blood, and such a person would not be allowed to build the most holy and sacred of places. Only a man who reflected the peace and love of God would be allowed to construct the temple.

David was a man of war, and Solomon was to be a man of peace. Warriors know how to tear down, peacemakers know how to build up. David had crafted a kingdom by use of force, Solomon built the most beautiful monument to God carefully and peaceably. There are questions about how peace-loving Solomon actually was, but under his reign Israel remained uncommonly safe and secure. This story does, however, witness to an important truth: conflict is destructive, peacemaking is constructive.

Are you a peaceful person?

Lord, I am not always peaceable. I am are more than willing to pick a fight. Family squabbles, office disagreements, and neighborhood strife are evidence of my warring tendencies.

And yet, like David, I long to be a builder, to be constructive, to leave behind a glorious legacy. You remind me that peace is the pathway to constructive living. I may be inclined to fight, but my deepest longing is for peace. Help me to live out my best intentions and better nature. Help me to build temples of grace and peace that reflect who you truly are. In Jesus' name, I pray. AMEN.

Supporting Role

Read: 1 Chronicles 29:1–5

> *"So I have provided for the house of my God, so far as I was able, the gold for the things of gold, the silver for the things of silver, and the bronze for the things of bronze, the iron for the things of iron, and wood for the things of wood, besides great quantities of onyx and stones for setting, antimony, colored stones, all sorts of precious stones, and marble in abundance."*
>
> *1 Chronicles 29:2*

KING DAVID WAS not allowed to build the temple in Jerusalem. The honor of temple construction was offered to David's son, Solomon. God chose Solomon over David for the project, and while that may have been a disappointment for David, it did not stifle David's desire to help make the temple a reality. David loved God with his whole heart, and even though David was a deeply flawed man, he desired to offer his very best to his Lord. While David was not chosen to be the builder, he was committed to supplying everything needed for the task. David might not have been the leader of the project, but that didn't mean he couldn't play a significant supporting role.

Sometimes we don't get to do what we want—we get passed over for promotion or someone else is tapped for a leadership role we desired or a project goes in a different direction than we had hoped. In response, we are tempted to walk away feeling frustrated and perhaps, even a bit vindictive. How amazing to see the way David chose to respond to rejection! He didn't get to do what he wanted to do, but he chose to play a major supporting role in the project all the same. Solomon might have built the temple, but David provided all the materials to make it happen.

Is there a person or a project than needs your support?

Lord, when things don't go my way, I am tempted to "take my ball and go home." I am happy to take a leading and visible role in different projects and activities, but if I am somehow overlooked or underappreciated, I find it difficult to be of service. Why am I reluctant to take on supporting roles? Why can't I celebrate and be a part of great works, even when I am not in charge of them? If David could swallow his pride and get over his disappointment, why can't I? All I know is that I should gratefully and enthusiastically support your work in the world. I should simply celebrate the fact that I am allowed to be involved in it at all. In Jesus' name, I pray. AMEN.

DIVINE AGENT

Read: 2 Chronicles 36:22–23

> *"Thus says King Cyrus of Persia: The Lord, the God of heaven, has given*
> *me all the kingdoms of the earth, and he has charged me to build him*
> *a house at Jerusalem, which is in Judah. Whoever is among you of all*
> *his people, may the Lord his God be with him! Let him go up."*
> *2 CHRONICLES 36:23*

YOU NEVER KNOW whom God will work through on your behalf. Or perhaps, God can work through anyone; therefore, we should not be surprised when, how, and through whom our deliverance arrives. The list of Hebrew adversaries was long. The Egyptians, the Philistines, all kingdoms in and around the region of Canaan, the Assyrians, and the Babylonians had all taken up arms against the Hebrew people at one time or another. And Babylon's conquest had led to a spirit-crushing exile for the Jews of Judea. There was no reason to assume that life under Cyrus would be any better. When the Persians conquered the Babylonians, the Jews exiled in Babylon must have assumed that the Persians would be another occupying and oppressive force with whom they would have to contend. But Cyrus, to everyone's surprise, and to the Jews' great joy, released the captive Hebrews so they could return to Judea and rebuild their country. It was as if Cyrus was an instrument of God, making good on the promises of the prophet Jeremiah, that the Hebrew people would one day be returned to their land. It was nothing short of a miracle that a Persian king served as a divine and delivering agent for the Jewish people. But that is how God works—our deliverance arrives through the most unexpected of people and from the least expected of places. Divine agents can be anyone, even us.

Who has served as a deliverer in your life?

Lord, there are times when I fear that deliverance will never come. Or I look at my situation—I consider the challenges before me—and I just cannot imagine a way out. I cannot imagine who could come to my aid and bring me through the difficulties I face. Yet scripture attests to the fact that you are working in and through all people. You can bring salvation and deliverance from any corner of the world. I long to believe that, Lord. Help me to look for it, too. In Jesus' name, I pray. AMEN.

March 6

CLEARLY CALLED

Read: Ezra 7:1–10

> *For Ezra had set his heart to study the law of the Lord, and to*
> *do it, and to teach the statutes and ordinances in Israel.*
> *EZRA 7:10*

EZRA KNEW WHAT he was supposed to do with his life. He was trained as a scribe during the Hebrew exile in Babylon, and his dream was to return to Jerusalem to teach and preach in the land of his ancestors. His dream was realized when King Artaxerxes allowed the Hebrew people to rebuild the temple in Jerusalem and reestablish a worshiping community in Judah.

Most of us would long to have such clarity when it comes to our purpose in life, but clarity is often illusive. As a Hebrew scribe, Ezra would have been a person of prayer, a student of scripture, and part of a community of discernment. When we regularly engage in faith practices, God's will for us can be most readily revealed. Spending time in prayer, studying the Bible, and gathering with people who are intent on discerning God's will for their lives can be the best path toward clarity in your own life.

What are you being called to do with the rest of your life?

Lord, I so desire clarity. I want to know your will for my life. I want to know what I am supposed to be doing with the gifts and abilities you have given me. Speak to me in this time of prayer or in the scripture I read or in the people who gather around me and care for me. In your name, I pray. AMEN.

March 7

Rebuilding

Read: Nehemiah 1 & 2

Then I said to the king, ". . . I ask that you send me to Judah, to
the city of my ancestors' graves, so that I may rebuild it."
Nehemiah 2:5

Nehemiah was the cupbearer to the King Artaxerxes of Persia. Nehemiah learned that his native city of Jerusalem was in ruins with its great wall no more than a heap of rubble. With an aggrieved heart, Nehemiah prayed to God, and in prayer he was moved by God to ask the king for permission to rebuild the walls of Jerusalem. Nehemiah was not a mason, he was not a leader, he was not even living in Jerusalem—he was simply the person who brought the king his wine cup when it was requested. Nehemiah may not have had the skill set to rebuild much of anything, but he was in the position to make it happen. Nehemiah made his request, permission was granted, and rebuilding ensued.

God is a building and rebuilding God. Even when God breaks something or someone down, it is with a mind to rebuilding stronger and better. We, too, are called to be builders and rebuilders. We may not have the skill set of a master mason, but sometimes that does not matter as much as being in the right place and having the right relationship to facilitate a reconstruction project. Opportunity is often more important than ability. You may be the family member who is best positioned to mend estrangements. You may be the employee who is perfectly positioned to suggest paths to integrity and prosperity. In an uncertain economic time, you may be well positioned in your town to encourage community-building activities. We live in a broken world, and God calls each of us to use our position to rebuild our lives together.

What brokenness can you begin to mend in the lives and world around you?

Lord, there is brokenness all around me. I see it. I hear of it. I feel it. Most of the time, I do not feel I have the abilities needed to mend the rifts and rebuild the relationships that cry out for healing. But, you have put me in a position to effect changes if I am simply willing to make the effort. Lord, you are a builder and rebuilder. I am ready to join you in your work. In your name, I pray. AMEN.

March 8

SIDE BY SIDE

Read: Nehemiah 2:17—3:32

Then they said, "Let us start building!" So they com-
mitted themselves to the common good.
NEHEMIAH 2:18

THROUGHOUT HUMAN HISTORY God calls humankind to work side by side in the building of a just, peaceful, and reverent world. God is both a builder and a uniter, and
God's purposes are fulfilled when we come together to labor for the common
good. Like a parent's pride and love swelling when the children are playing peace-
fully together, God's love and pride swells when we live and work and play together
in unity.

For fifty-two days the Jews of Jerusalem set aside their individual pursuits.
For fifty-two days they set aside the work they would typically do to sustain their
own families. For fifty-two days the Jews of Jerusalem worked for the good of
the whole, instead of pursuing individual interests. Of all the many things those
individual Jews must have done in their lives, what they are remembered for is how
they came together to build a wall. It is a miracle they are remembered at all. Their
names are listed and immortalized in this passage of the Bible for a moment when
they labored side by side to accomplish a common purpose—and their efforts are
remembered eternally by God. Coming together to build a wall for fifty-two days
of their lives is their holy legacy.

How will you be remembered?

Lord, I spend most of my life working for my own good. The common good, the common-
wealth, the welfare of others is not something I spend much time considering . . . As a result,
I am likely living an entirely forgettable life. Help me to focus on the common good. I want
to be remembered for the works I have done to your glory. I want to be remembered by you. In
Jesus' name, I pray. AMEN.

March 9

INTERPRETING RESISTANCE

Read: Nehemiah 4

The burden bearers . . . each labored on the work with one
hand and with the other held a weapon. And each of the build-
ers had his sword strapped at his side while he built.
NEHEMIAH 4:17 & 18

WHEN FACED WITH resistance, when our hopes for our lives or our relationships hang in the balance, when we finally desire to release ourselves from the
anxiety of waiting for what either will be or will not be, we are often tempted
to exclaim, *"If it is meant to be, it will be."* We often associate *ease* with God's
will. If something is God's will for us, then we assume that everything will
just magically fall in place. Somehow we believe that if we are really doing
what we are supposed to be doing, then there shouldn't be any obstacles to
our progress.

Nothing happens easily in the Bible. Nehemiah was called by God to rebuild
the walls of Jerusalem that had been laid waste for generations. Nehemiah believed
the rebuilding was God's desire for his life, Nehemiah had permission from the
king to begin construction, and yet Nehemiah encountered constant resistance.
His laborers had to wear weapons as they worked in anticipation of a possible
attack. Throughout the Bible, God's people always encounter resistance to their
pursuits—and God always seems to encounter resistance from those same people!
Resistance isn't a sign that you are doing something you are not meant to be doing.
Resistance itself might be the indication that you are doing exactly what God
intends.

How do you interpret the resistance you encounter in your life?

Lord, my resolve tends to be rather weak. If I try to do something and encounter
obstacles, I find I am tempted to assume that I am doing something that I am not meant

to be doing. I somehow erroneously assume that if I am following you, my life and pursuits should be less labored. Perhaps instead, I should consider the possibility that the crosses I encounter are actually signposts that confirm that I am, in fact, on the right road. Lord, help me to respond to the resistance I encounter with resolve instead of resignation. In your name, I pray. AMEN.

March 10

FOR SUCH A TIME AS THIS

Read: Esther 4:1–17

> For if you keep silence at such a time as this, relief and deliverance will rise for the Jews from another quarter, but you and your father's family will perish. Who knows? Perhaps you have come to royal dignity for just such a time as this.
> ESTHER 4:14

THE BIBLE TELLS us that Esther was the Jewish queen of the Persian king Ahasuerus. During Ahasuerus's reign there was a plot hatched to exterminate the Jewish people from the Persian Empire. The only chance the Jews had for survival was the advocacy of Queen Esther. But no one was supposed to approach the king unless summoned. The punishment for making an unrequested advance toward the king was death—even for a queen! Therefore, for Esther to save her people, she had to risk her own life. As Esther weighed the decision before her, her uncle Mordecai encouraged her with the thought that God might have made her queen *"for just such a time as this."*

There are moments in life when we have the opportunity to be advocates for someone or something important, but that advocacy could somehow put us in a difficult or unpleasant situation. We would like to help, but we worry that the personal cost might be too high for us to bear. It is in moments like those when we must consider, as Esther did, that the position we hold we have for the very purpose of that advocacy. The only reason we may be where we are is to step up and step forward in a particular moment of trial. The challenge before you might be the very reason you are where you are. You have been positioned not for comfort but to face an important challenge that can define your life and the lives of others. It might be for such a time as this that you have been placed right where you are.

How have you been positioned to help others?

Lord, for some reason I believe that the positions I aspire to will allow me a degree of comfort and stability. I somehow think that the more authority I acquire will allow me greater ability to chart my own course and set my own agenda. But what if the position I have been afforded is not for my benefit but for the well-being of others? What if I am where I am so that I can step forward and step into a particularly challenging situation that could use my advocacy and presence? What if my position in life has been orchestrated by you for the accomplishment of your will? As unsettling a prospect as that may be . . . it lines up well with the stories of the Bible. You place people where they will be needed, not where they will be comfortable. Help me to not shrink from that important reality. In your name, I pray. AMEN.

March 11

WHEN BAD THINGS HAPPEN

Read: Job 38—40:5

> *Then the Lord answered Job out of the whirlwind:"Who is this that dark-*
> *ens counsel by words without knowledge? Gird up your loins like a man, I*
> *will question you, and you shall declare to me.Where were you when I*
> *laid the foundation of the earth? Tell me, if you have understanding."*
>
> JOB 38:1—4

HARD WORDS. THAT is what Job received after lamenting his misfortune. Job had been as faithful as a person could be. His devotion to goodness and to God seemed to result in a life of blessing and abundance. But then his life was shattered. His family, his home, his possessions, and even the health of his body were taken away from him for no apparent reason. In the midst of his physical suffering and his personal anguish, Job asked that age-old question of those who have ever suffered needlessly: *"Why?"*

God's answer to the suffering of people who are good or evil is less than com-forting. Through the story of Job, we learn that we don't even have the right to ask the question *"Why?"*We best not even try to contend with God, because we cannot even begin to count ourselves as equal with God. God's will, God's wisdom, and God's work in the world are simply beyond our comprehension. Whether we like it or not, we are creatures who exist for no other reason than for the pleasure and purposes of God . . . and creatures have no right to question their Creator. Our best response to the good and bad of life should sound something like Job's response to God's challenge: *"See, I am of small account; what shall I answer you? I lay my hand on my mouth. I have spoken once, and I will not answer; twice, but will proceed no further."*The teaching is hard but true: rather than questioning God about our life, we should simply thank God for it.

Do you blame God or someone else for the challenges of life?

Lord, I don't like this teaching in Job. I want to be in conversation with you. I want to share my pain and frustration with you. I know I cannot claim equality with you, but I don't want to be an insignificant creature in your cosmic creation either. Perhaps, I should be satisfied with the fact that I exist, and you exist, and whatever good or ill happens in life, we share in it together. Instead of complaining about misfortune, I can spend time giving you thanks for the life I have been given. Your words can be hard, Lord, but they help me to gain much-needed perspective. Thank you. In your name, I pray. AMEN.

Planted

Read: Psalm 1

Happy are those whose . . . delight is in the law of the Lord. . . . They are like trees planted by streams of water, which yield their fruit in its season, and their leaves do not wither. In all that they do, they prosper.
PSALM 1:1A, 2A, & 3

PEOPLE WHO CLEAVE to the will and way of God are like trees planted and rooted by streams of life-giving water. Those who pin the hopes of their lives on other pursuits and relationships *"are like chaff that the wind drives away."*

You can tell a person of faith by their depth. There is something about them. They may bend, but they don't ever seem to break. They remain grounded when others seem to always flit about. They do not succumb to the whims and worries of the world. They stand firm—planted and strong in the word of God. They prosper.

Are you well rooted?

Lord, I want to be grounded in you. I want your word, your presence, and your law to be the source of my nourishment in life. Help me to find the stream that runs to you and from you. In Jesus' name, I pray. AMEN.

March 13

REQUEST FOR PROPOSALS

Read: Psalm 2

Ask of me, and I will make the nations your heri-
tage, and the ends of the earth your possession.
PSALM 2:8

EVERYONE WHO PRAYS has had an experience of asking God for something and not receiving it. People of faith often respond to the experience of unanswered prayers by asserting that while God doesn't always give us what we want, God never fails to provide us what we need. That may be the way God works. But it may be even more helpful to think of God as a grantor. God says, *"Ask.""Make your requests.""Submit to me your proposals...and I will evaluate them and render a decision."* Like any grantor, not every proposal will meet with approval, but there will be no movement whatsoever if a request has not been made. It is very possible that God will only respond to our desires if we have taken the time to make a request. While there is no guarantee that God will grant our wishes, if we don't ask...we surely won't receive.

Do you submit your proposals to God?

Lord, I should make all my requests known to you. If I don't ask, why should I expect to receive? You may be all-knowing, but why would you act in the absence of a direct petition? If I want something from you, I need to be in conversation with you about it. That makes all the sense in the world. I, therefore, make a request that you help me to both live and pray that sensibly. In Jesus' name, I pray. AMEN.

March 14

In Charge

Read: Psalm 3

Deliverance belongs to the Lord; may your blessing be on your people!
Psalm 3:8

At some point, each one of us has to decide who is in charge. Who orders our lives? Are we the sole directors of our circumstance? Or does a boss or a spouse or a teacher rule our days? Are we marionettes manipulated by people who can pull strings in our lives? Or were we created for something more?

We all choose who orchestrates our situation in life. We can allow others to unduly influence our direction, or we can seize control ourselves and run our lives in any way that pleases us. Both of these courses, however, can often lead to our ruin. Perhaps we should entrust our lives to the One who watches over us when we sleep, who wakes us up in the morning, and who sustains us throughout the day.

How can you allow God to take a leading role in your life?

Lord, it must look like a train wreck to you at times. Our lives are piled up in a cascading collision of bad decisions, poor timing, and lack of foresight. We choose to follow our own whims, or we let someone other than you guide our lives . . . and we wonder why we find ourselves in so many predicaments. Lord, help me to put you first, and let me know what that actually means. In Jesus' name, I pray. AMEN.

March 15

ATTENTIVE

Read: Psalm 4

Be gracious to me, and hear my prayer.
PSALM 4:1

WHAT AN AMAZING claim—that God Almighty, Creator of heaven and earth, the Alpha and the Omega, the beginning and the end hears our prayers and responds to them. The idea that God even notices the puny speck of humanity we are is mind boggling. In fact, given our miniscule standing in the universe, it is worth questioning God's attentiveness to us. In the great swirl and expanse of the cosmos, how is it possible that God cares for me?

You can hear cries of doubt in the Psalms. Psalms are ancient prayers of both doubt and praise, worry and worship, deep questioning, and yet, even deeper trust. The ancient Hebrews were at times wary of God's absence while hopeful of experiencing God's presence. There are many times in our lives when it feels as if God's gaze is far off, and we cry out for God's presence, not fully believing we are deserving of God's attention. And yet, God is there listening, responding, and heeding our cries. With all the doubt and anxiety that is present in the Psalms, the final notes of these sacred hymns tend to be hopeful. *"I will both lie down and sleep in peace; for you alone, O Lord, make me lie down in safety."*

Have you given thanks lately for God's presence in and attentiveness to your life?

Lord, I confess that I often doubt that you care for me. You are so silent. You are so unsearchable. You are so far beyond my ability to comprehend. And yet, I trust that you are there. Somehow, deep inside, I sense your presence. And when push comes to shove, I trust in your leading. I thank you for your continual attention and presence in my life. In your name, I pray. AMEN.

BOWING

Read: Psalm 5

> *I will bow down toward your holy temple in awe of you. Lead me, O*
> *Lord, in your righteousness . . . ; make your way straight before me.*
> *PSALM 5:7 & 8*

ANYONE CAN GIVE thanks to God when times are good—though we often don't. We might remember to count our blessings around a Thanksgiving table, but more often than not, when we feel well, we forget God. It is when our hearts ache or when our disappointments pile up or when we have fallen into difficult circumstances that we turn to God and plead. There is no question that God receives more pleading than praise from our hearts and our lips.

It is in moments of trial that we are reminded of the undeniable truth that God is the one we turn to in times of trouble. God is the one we search for when we feel lost. God is the one we bow to when we have been broken in pieces. Often humbled by the demands of our lives, we turn to God trusting—as much as we are able—that God rewards righteousness and condemns wickedness. We trust that if we turn from our sin and bow our lives before the God of all creation, we will be led down the right road, and our crooked little lives will be made straight.

How can you bow and bend your will to God today?

Lord, I like to stand straight up, confident in my own abilities, trusting in my own insight, and ready to exercise my freedom by doing whatever I choose. As a result, I live a sin-stained life and I know it. Lord God, you love right living and you abhor wickedness. Help me to bow to you and your will for me today, so that I can experience blessing and live a life that is pleasing to you. In Jesus' name, I pray. AMEN.

March 17

PLEADING

Read: Psalm 6

O Lord, do not rebuke me in your anger, or discipline me in your wrath.
PSALM 6:1

THE HARD TRUTH is that each and every one of us deserves punishment. We don't like to think it, speak it, or confess it in any way, shape, or form, but we are depraved sinners who deserve divine rebuke. We have failed to love both God and neighbor. In fact, we have done far worse than merely withhold love from those who need it. We can be hostile, hateful, and utterly hard-hearted. We more than deserve the lumps we get in life.

It is because we know we have done wrong that we cry to God for mercy. There is a lingering hope buried deep in our spirit that prompts us to believe that God might relent. We plead for God's mercy, peace, and presence knowing we don't deserve it, but praying we receive it all the same. Thankfully, God's love runs deeper than ours, God's compassion has no limits, and God's willingness to forgive eclipses our ability to sin. We plead, and we discover in our petitioning that truly nothing can separate us from the love we have found in Christ Jesus. God hears our weeping. God responds to our cry. God forgives us when we repent.

What is the pleading of your heart today?

Lord, your silence may be an indication that you are listening, which would mean that my rantings and ravings are all known to you. You know my guilt. You know my sin. You have heard how I cry out for your presence and mercy, though I have done nothing to deserve it. Forgive me, Lord. Draw me up from the pit. Set me on level ground. Allow me yet another chance to try to walk in your way. In Jesus' name, I pray. AMEN.

March 18

JUDGING GOD

Read: Psalm 7

God is a righteous judge.
PSALM 7:11A

IT IS OUR hope and our prayer that God will reward the righteous and condemn the wicked. When we pray that prayer or speak that hope, we do so assuming we are in the right. When we feel someone has wronged us, or we have been injured unjustly, or we have suffered as a result of malicious intent, we want the gavel of God to pound out a conviction that will satisfy us.

But it is tenuous business claiming righteousness and making assumptions about judgment. Are we not the ones often in the wrong? Can we unflinchingly claim inherent goodness? And if we are momentarily in the right, does it take long for us to fall short of God's expectations of us? I suspect what we really need is for God to condemn and cast away our own wickedness while encouraging our better nature. Thank God, that is exactly what the Lord does.

Do you judge others more rigorously than you judge yourself?

Lord, I fume when I feel I am in the right and yet have been wronged. I shudder to think what it would be like if you were as furious with me in regard to my sins and failures! Thankfully, you love unconditionally and forgive unflinchingly. Teach me to be more like you. In Jesus' name, I pray. AMEN.

March 19

SMALL, BUT SPECIAL

Read: Psalm 8

> *When I look at your heavens, the work of your fingers, the moon*
> *and the stars that you have established; what are human beings that*
> *you are mindful of them, mortals that you care for them?*
> PSALM 8:3–4

THE EARTH IS a speck of dust swirling in the midst of a luminescent universe. Human activity throughout our entire history isn't loud or expansive enough to cause the slightest ripple in the cosmos. We are small creatures. Our lives are a brief flicker of enmeshing energy and matter. We are entirely forgettable life forms.

Yet God has taken note of us. Scripture attests that creation was birthed in order to produce us. The whole cosmic plan was designed for God to be in relationship to us. How amazing and wonderful is that? We are small creatures who are very special to God.

Can you feel both small and special?

Lord, if I think too much about it, my cosmic insignificance deeply unsettles me. I don't like to think of myself as insignificant and forgettable. I want my life to be as significant to you as it feels to me. I struggle to believe and understand why in your grandeur and majesty, you would take an interest in my tiny mortal life. I don't understand it . . . but I dare to believe that it is so. In Jesus' name, I pray. AMEN.

THE GOOD LIFE

Read: Psalm 15

> *O Lord, who may abide in your tent? Who may dwell on your holy*
> *hill? Those who walk blamelessly, and do what is right.*
> PSALM 15:1 & 2A

WE ALL HAVE an image in mind of the good life. It is different for each of us, of course, but the pursuit of that life is quite similar. We have an image of what a pleasant, peaceful, stress-free life would look like for us. The picture often includes more money and fewer financial pressures, more time playing and less time in the office, more free time and fewer standing obligations. Our image of the good life is something like an idealized heaven on earth that we strive for with every ounce of our being and yet never fully attain.

The psalmist assumes that a good life is rewarded by an experience of an *eternally* good life with God. *"O Lord, who may abide in your tent?"* The answer? Those who walk blamelessly. Those who speak truthfully. Those who do not slander with their tongue. Those who stand by their oath even when it is inconvenient to do so. God does not call us to a life full of pleasure; the Lord encourages us to take a longer view—to live in faithful ways *today* so that we may dwell in paradise with God *forever*.

What is the difference between enjoying *the good life* and living a *good life?*

Lord, I am often obsessed with living well now. I want the trappings of paradise today. And yet, I never quite get there. Help me to focus on living a good life every single day, rather than striving for some idyllic existence that can only be had with you. In Jesus' name, I pray. AMEN.

March 21

GOODLY HERITAGE

Read: Psalm 16

> *The Lord is my chosen portion and my cup. . . . The boundary lines*
> *have fallen for me in pleasant places; I have a goodly heritage.*
> *PSALM 16:5–6*

LIFE IS GOOD. Life may not be perfect, we may not always get exactly what we want, and we might be able to envision an even more idyllic existence for ourselves, . . . but the life we have been given is undeniably good. We have a goodly heritage. When we make God the center of our lives, life has a way of unfolding in very pleasant and pleasing ways. When we *"keep the Lord always before [us],"* we are led down *"the path of life."* We are promised that there is joy and fullness of life when we seek to enter into the presence and purposes of God. This does not mean that with God life becomes an unending series of glorious and joyful experiences, but when the joys and sorrows of a given day are tabulated, the verdict is simply this—life is good, God is good and well deserving of our continual praise.

How is your life good?

Lord, it is a constant refrain in my life—thank you. Even when I feel as if the world has turned against me, even when my relationships become strained, even when my hopes and dreams for my life do not entirely come to fruition . . . I know in the very core of my being that life is as good as you are. Life is a blessing, and life with you is a joy. Thank you for all the gifts. In Jesus' name, I pray. AMEN.

March 22

REMINDERS OF GOD

Read: Psalm 19

> *The heavens are telling the glory of God; and the firmament proclaims his handiwork.*
> *PSALM 19:1*

WE OFTEN FORGET about God, or rather, we are fairly unmindful of God. We keep our heads down, our noses to the grindstone, and our focus fixed firmly on the tasks at hand. As a result, our view is limited, and we miss out on the expansive goodness, the majestic glory, and the awe-inspiring grandeur of God and the created order.

The good news is that the heavens themselves speak to the presence of God. Step outside on a starlit night, take a walk in the woods, wake up in time to witness the brilliant hues of color in a sunrise. Take time to take in the beauty of creation . . . and be reminded of God.

When was the last time you stopped to admire the handiwork of God?

Lord, remind me to look up. I keep my head down far too long, absorbed in whatever I am doing. Elevate my sight and my spirit so that I can go through my days mindful of your presence and your purpose for me. In your name, I pray. AMEN.

REAL SIMPLE

Read: Psalm 23

The Lord is my shepherd, I shall not want.
PSALM 23:1

IF KING DAVID wrote this beloved psalm as the text suggests, then this reflection is of a simpler time when his worries did not include the flood of demands placed upon him by his position of leadership. In this psalm, David reflected on his early years when he shepherded his father's flocks in the field. There was something divine about the simplicity of a shepherd guiding, protecting, and sustaining sheep. Could the cosmic relationship between God and God's people be accurately captured in such an image? Could God be trusted as sheep trust the one who watches over them? Could the multiplicity of fears that lurk in the valleys and shadows of our lives be dismissed in favor of trusting the One who walks by our side? Could life and leadership be that simple? Psalm 23 offers us a resounding and poetic *"Yes!"*

In what ways do you need to simplify your life?

Lord, my life has become too complicated. I have too much stuff. I keep too many commitments. I have more worries than I know what to do with. I want life to be simpler. I want to live less encumbered by the demands that assail me. I want to live essentially, which means I want to live by your direction. You are my shepherd, I am your sheep. Lead me so that I may not want. In Jesus' name, I pray. AMEN

A PASSING GUEST

Read: Psalm 39

Lord, let me know my end, and what is the measure of my days; let me know how fleeting my life is. . . . For I am your passing guest, an alien, like all my forebears.
PSALM 39:4 & 12c

WHENEVER WE FIND ourselves in a place that fills us with peace, contentment, and joy, we can find ourselves imagining how we can own the moment or that place. Could we buy a home there? How could we get there more frequently? Can we find a way to make sure each of the days of our lives are that blissful? Essentially, we want to figure out how to recreate that moment and place instead of just enjoying it for what it is . . . a wonderfully fragile moment to be savored.

This scripture reminds us that we own nothing. *"You have made my days a few handbreadths. . . . Surely everyone stands as a mere breath. Surely everyone goes about like a shadow."* God owns everything; we are only *"passing guests"* in this world. When we grasp that truth, we are free to stop our anxious striving for more, for euphoric fulfillment, and for ownership of life. As God's guests in life, we are free to accept God's care, trust in God's provision, and be respectful of God's creation. What a wonderful way to live! Like our ancestors before us, if we can come to terms with the brevity of life—if we can let go of our restless desire for permanence in this world—then, perhaps, we can get on with living it to the fullest.

As a "passing guest" in God's world, what can you let go of in order to live more fully and freely?

Lord, I say I want it all. I act like I want it all. I anxiously strive to own everything I can—even life itself. Help me to let go of those fruitless pursuits. Help me to claim my role as your guest in this world. Forgive me for my anxious overreaching, and help me to live fully in the blessing of this moment. In Jesus' name, I pray. AMEN.

March 25

CHANGING WORLD

Read: Psalm 46:1–7

Therefore we will not fear, though the earth should change,
though the mountains shake in the heart of the sea.
PSALM 46:2

CHANGE CONCERNS US. Global, environmental, or personal change is often an unwelcome visitor in our lives. The world becomes unsettled when the political landscape of a country destabilizes, even if the former regime was oppressive or abusive. As the earth warms and the seas rise, we try to stave off floods by creating more effective barriers against the rising tides. When there is a management change in our company, when there is a divorce or death in our family, or when the rhythm of our day or the pattern of our life is interrupted, we feel deeply unsettled and resistant to the adjustment.

The Bible tells us that all things change. The earth changes. Nations change. Families change. Change is part of God's plan. We should not fear it, nor should we try to fight against it. Change allows for opportunity and growth, both of which God can use to mold us into the very best people we can be. God is our refuge, and change is God's method of renewal.

What change in your life or in the world has you concerned?

Lord, help me to embrace the changes that unfold before me today. Instead of being resistant to change, help me to embrace it as an opportunity for you to reshape and renew my life in important ways. In Jesus' name, I pray. AMEN.

March 26

STILLNESS

Read: Psalm 46:8–11

Be still, and know that I am God!
PSALM 46:10A

DON'T MOVE. PAUSE. Cease all motion for a moment. That is the command of God as related by the psalmist. The command for stillness is a call to recognize that God is at work in the world so that we don't always need to be. Be still, and watch for God at work. Be still, and become newly aware that God acts on our behalf. Be still, and take note of the fact that life continues uninterrupted without our assistance.

Stillness is a form of sabbath. Stillness requires that we rest from our labor. Stillness quiets our activity long enough for us to take notice of all the remarkable happenings going on around us. In fact, our over activity may blur our vision in ways that prevent us from seeing how God is at work in the world and in the lives around us. The command is beautiful and simple: Be still, and know God!

Can you take some time to be still and observant today?

Lord, I keep myself in perpetual motion. I am not entirely sure why. Perhaps my busyness is a way of coping with the deep questions about my existence that I would rather not take time to ponder. Questions of life and death are simply beyond my ability to comprehend, so I would rather ignore them by pressing on and working hard. But if I don't stop to contemplate who I really am, what I am doing in the world, and who you call me to be, I will likely miss out on the most important part of my existence . . . my relationship with you. I will pause today to look for you. Please reveal yourself to me. In Jesus' name, I pray. AMEN.

March 27

PENITENT

Read: Psalm 51

Create in me a clean heart, O God, and put a new and right spirit within me.
PSALM 51:10

THE BIBLE INDICATES that the fifty-first psalm is the prayer King David offered after the prophet Nathan confronted David with his most egregious sin. While Uriah the Hittite was fighting in David's army, David took Uriah's wife, Bathsheba, and had an affair with her. To cover up his indiscretion, David had Uriah killed during a military operation, and then took Bathsheba as one of his wives. This was a shocking abuse of power by one of the most beloved and revered figures in Jewish history. If there is anything redeeming about this story—and one has to look hard to find anything at all—it is David's willingness to admit his sin when confronted with it. Unlike so many political leaders caught in scandal, David acknowledged his guilt and immediately began to repent. David asked God for a new beginning, a clean heart, and a spirit that would no longer do wrong. David requested to be made a new man.

We may not abuse power, commit adultery, or murder to cover up our failings, but that does not mean our own hearts are as white as snow. Each one of us has dark corners of our lives we would prefer that no one see or know about. But God sees and God knows, as do we. Repentance from our sinful thoughts and impulses is an essential way of making sure they do not evolve into sinful actions. If David had prayed Psalm 51 the moment he laid his eyes on Bathsheba, perhaps that cruel and gruesome chapter of David's life would not have been written. A daily request for forgiveness can be the best defense against egregious sin.

Do you need to ask God for forgiveness today?

Lord, I do sin in thought, word, and deed. I sin in ways that are both known and unknown to me. I need your forgiveness if I am going to have a chance at living faithfully. "Purge me with hyssop, and I shall be clean; wash me, and I shall be whiter than snow." For the cleansing of my life, I pray in your name. AMEN.

March 28

Yearning for God's Presence

Read: Psalm 84

> *How lovely is your dwelling place, O Lord of hosts! My soul longs,*
> *indeed it faints for the courts of the Lord. . . . For a day in your courts*
> *is better than a thousand elsewhere. I would rather be a doorkeeper*
> *in the house of my God than live in the tents of wickedness.*
> PSALM 84:1–2, 10

THERE IS A deep hunger within us that only God can satisfy. We spend our lives pursuing relationships, jobs, and different forms of recognition and approval in order to fill the emptiness we sense within us. We would willingly mortgage our soul for a down payment on happiness if we thought it would last a lifetime. But God calls us to a relationship that spans eternity, and that relationship begins when we stop frantically looking for fulfillment in all the wrong places and start enjoying the restful and confident presence of God.

What position would you long for in the court of the Lord?

Lord, to set my burdens aside and walk in your presence is my heart's desire. I would be glad to man the door or sweep the floors of your courts just to have the opportunity to be with you. Nothing more do I long for but you. I love you. In your name, I pray. AMEN.

March 29

Sheltered

Read: Psalm 91

You who live in the shelter of the Most High, who abide in the shadow of the Almighty, will say to the Lord, "My refuge and my fortress; my God, in whom I trust."
Psalm 91:1

Being sheltered is often viewed as a liability. When we say someone has lived a sheltered life, it is an indication that we believed they really haven't been living at all. The desire to play it safe has not allowed them the joy of adventure and discovery. A sheltered existence is a sure way to miss out on so many of the pleasures of life. We are equally skeptical that a life can be sheltered or protected by God. The promise that God will safeguard people who are obedient to God's will is objectionable because of the many examples we have of bad events befalling good people. A person can be as faithful as they want, and yet they will still have to suffer all the pains and losses that accompany life.

But the biblical idea of being sheltered may be more dynamic that we tend to imagine. Shelter offers respite from the storm—it does not prevent the storm from brewing and unleashing its power and fury on the world. Shelter offers a momentary reprieve from the harsh conditions of the environment in which we live. God offers us shelter, not as a way of eliminating all harm that might befall us but as a means of letting us know that God is with us in the midst of all the trials of life. Being sheltered by God is not about living safely, it is about being afforded some respite and reprieve when one is fully engaged in the world as God desires. Being sheltered is not about living less, but living more, as indicated in the final two verses of this psalm: *"Those who love me, I will deliver; I will protect those who know my name. When they call to me, I will answer them; I will be with them in trouble, I will rescue them and honor them. With long life I will satisfy them, and show them my salvation."*

Have you been sheltered?

Lord, I do long for safekeeping. But that is not what you offer us. You ask us to fully engage the world and the people around us. You ask us to trust that if we follow your will and way, in the end all will be well. Storms and challenges and trials may assail us, but there will be glorious moments when we experience your saving presence. Lord, shelter me long enough today so that I am prepared for the demands of tomorrow. In your name, I pray. AMEN.

March 30

OUR KEEPER

Read: Psalm 121

The Lord is your keeper; the Lord is your shade at your right hand. . . . The Lord
will keep your going out and your coming in from this time on and forevermore.
PSALM 121:5, 8

TO BE KEPT is the opposite of being discarded. God is a keeper. God does not discard those who turn to God for help. There are indeed times when we look to the hills to see if our deliverance will arrive, only to see nothing of particular note on the horizon. It is true that God is silent so much of the time, and that God is not clearly visible in most circumstances. This can lead us to assume that God is absent, as if God set our world and our lives in motion and then somehow lost interest in us.

Scripture, however, insists that God is present, that God loves creation, and that God does not intend to lose any of what God has made. God intends to preserve life. For God, preservation of life is not merely an earthly hope, it is an eternal reality. God's plan is to keep us *forevermore*. We may not be able to see God appear on the mountaintop bringing us deliverance, because God's deliverance expands beyond all human vision—God saves us and promises to keep us for *eternity*.

What does it mean for God to be your keeper?

Lord, I wish I had a clearer vision of you, or had a more concrete faith in you. It is very easy to mistake your silence and invisibility for absence. Help me to believe that you are indeed present in the world, and that you intend to preserve life, and keep my life forever. In your name, I hope and pray. AMEN.

March 31

HAPPY

Read: Psalm 128

Happy is everyone who fears the Lord, who walks in his ways. Your wife will be
like a fruitful vine within your house; your children will be like olive shoots
around your table. Thus shall the man be blessed who fears the Lord.
PSALM *128: 1, 3 & 4*

FEAR DOES NOT initially sound like a way to happiness, but the fear that the psalmist writes about is not the kind of fear and trembling we felt when we were children. *"Fear of the Lord"* is mentioned often in the Bible. *Fear* is a biblical word for reverence and respect. When we honor God more than ourselves, when we revere and respect God, when we look to God for insight instead of relying solely on our own wits to get us through, life goes well for us. Life in union with God is a way to happiness; life in discord with God can be a jumbled and disconcerting mess. The psalmist entreats people to observe the ways of God, promising that if we seek to live holy lives, we will prosper, and our families with us.

It is a parent's greatest joy to see his or her children grow up to become fine men and women. It should also be our great joy to see our spouses develop into the vital and fruitful people God created them to be. How wonderful it would be to *"see our children's children,"* grow, thrive, and succeed! The Bible asserts that it all starts with our *fear*, or reverence, of God. Our family's blessing relies heavily on our fidelity to God.

What would make you truly happy today?

Lord, I do not want to live scared of you, and I know that is not what you intend. I do,
however, long to live happily. I long for my spouse and children and grandchildren to live
blessed. If my fidelity and fearful reverence of you is the key to unlocking that kind of blessing
for those whom I care about most, then I will pursue it with passion and persistence. I just ask
that you pick me up when I falter, inspire me when I lag behind, and encourage me to do my
best every step of the way. In Jesus' name, I pray. AMEN.

April 1

CONTENTED

Read: Psalm 131

> *O Lord, my heart is not lifted up, my eyes are not raised too high;*
> *I do not occupy myself with things too great and too marvelous for*
> *me. But I have calmed and quieted my soul, like a weaned child with*
> *its mother; my soul is like the weaned child that is with me.*
> *PSALM 131:1—2*

THIS PSALM BEAUTIFULLY expresses what it means and feels like to fully rest in the presence of God. It is like being an infant in a mother's arms, just after being fed. It is as if a person has been blanketed in a warmth and care that washes away all concerns and quiets all anxiety. It is a sense of contentment that completely settles one's soul.

The Bible so often refers to God as a father, but there are some wonderful images in the biblical canon that evoke the divinity and sacred care that exist between a mother and a child. If you have ever cried out for your mother and have been readily enfolded in her warmth, care, and love, you have experienced something akin to being in the presence of God. You suddenly find you are contented, without a care in the world.

When was the last time you felt truly contented?

Lord, I long for the kind of contentment described in this psalm. As old as I am, I still long to crawl up into your lap so that I can rest secure in your presence and care. How I long to live surrounded by your warmth, love, provision, and care. Take me in up into your arms today, so that I can experience what it means to rest in you. In your name, I pray. AMEN.

April 2

BLESSING OF UNITY

Read: Psalm 133

How very good and pleasant it is when kindred live together in unity!
PSALM 133:1

NOTHING IS MORE pleasing than when families live together in peace, love, and harmony. Family unity is nothing short of a blessing from God. It is often easier to live peaceably with friends and colleagues and neighbors than it is with family. Families live in close range to one another, and that kind of intimacy inevitably leads to a fair amount of relational bruising. Families can have such painful and long-running histories and hostilities that the slightest offense can set off explosive confrontations. There isn't a family in the world—God's family included—that doesn't struggle to get along. In the midst of family squabbles and tension, unity can seem like nothing more than a pipedream. But unity is possible, and it should be highly prized and pursued at all costs. Like a holy and priestly blessing, like the life-giving morning dew, unity among family is not only refreshing, it is also life affirming and life enriching. Nothing is better than the loving embrace of family—God knows it and we know it too.

Is there unity within your family?

Lord, it is true that is it often easier to get along with total strangers than with family. It is also true that familial embrace and love are joys that surpass all others. You want unity within families—you desire unity within your family. Help me work for those harmonious and pleasing relationships today. In Jesus' name, I pray. AMEN.

April 3

LIGHT POLLUTION

Read: Psalm 139:1–18

Such knowledge is too wonderful for me; it is so high I cannot attain it.

PSALMS 139:6

IF YOU HAVE the opportunity to view the night sky in its expansive majesty, it is difficult not to be overwhelmed by the grandeur of creation and the awesome nature of God. In fact, if you are able to see the banding milky clusters of countless stars stretching out into infinite space, you realize that your finite mind cannot grasp the expansive presence of God, and all that God has made. Creation is both wonderful and terrifying, intimate and infinite, awe-inspiring and mind-boggling.

It cannot be all that surprising that less advanced societies are often the ones who are most reverential to the divine mysteries of life—their light has not crowded out God's light. For the rest of us, streetlights, traffic lights, city lights pollute the evening sky. We cannot see beyond our existence. We are blind to the magnificence of God.

When was the last time you caught a glimpse of the awesome and expansive nature of God?

Lord, I often get so caught up in my own business and busyness, that I miss out on the astounding beauty and mind-bending extravagance of your creation of which I am but a small part. Perhaps, I don't want to see it. If I avert my eyes, I can pretend to be God for a day. I can ignore your presence and shirk the call to reverence. But I know that is no way to live— divorced from myself and from you. Break into my life with a vision of your grandeur that I cannot dismiss. Help me to grow more comfortable with the fact there are things in heaven and on earth that I will never be able to understand or explain. In Jesus' name, I pray. AMEN.

April 4

PRAISE!

Read: Psalm 150

Let everything that breathes praise the Lord! Praise the Lord!
PSALM 150:6

THE FINAL VERSE of the final psalm in the Bible is an encouragement for all creation to praise God. In fact, the entire psalm is a call to praise. If you read through the psalms, you quickly realize that they are filled with every human emotion imaginable: gratitude, anger, joy, anguish, faith, doubt, hope, and despair. There are songs of thanksgiving for God's presence alongside heartbreaking cries of lament in response to God's absence. These ancient hymns are as emotionally varied and convulsive as the experience of the Hebrew people. And yet the final note of the final verse of the final hymn is a call to praise.

No matter how difficult and demanding life is, it is a gift from God. No matter how chaotic and uncertain creation is, it is a gift from God. Whether viewing the world from an emotional mountaintop or from the deepest and darkest valley, the experience of seeing and witnessing and participating in the unfolding of life is a gift from God worthy of our praise. If we were to utter only one sentence in our entire lives, it would be best if it were that of the final psalm: *"Praise the Lord!"*

How do you offer God praise?

Lord, thank you. Thank you. You have given us everything—you have given us the world. The only appropriate response is to praise you and thank you. And I will praise you until my very last breath. I want the last sentence of my life to be an acknowledgment of my gratitude. In Jesus' name, I pray. AMEN.

April 5

ACKNOWLEDGE THE LORD

Read: Proverbs 3:1–12

Trust in the Lord with all your heart, and do not rely on your own insight. In all your ways acknowledge the Lord, and he will make straight your paths.
PROVERBS 3:5–6

WE OFTEN FEEL that we're supposed to have all the answers. We tell ourselves that we don't need directions because we should instinctively know the way. We don't ask for help because we feel should be able to do it on our own. Lack of knowledge and the need for direction or assistance are viewed as intolerable expressions of weakness in our culture. We would rather be wrong than unsure; we would rather be lost than ask for guidance; we would rather fall on our face than reach for a helping hand. No wonder we often feel so alone and helpless. But who can we turn to in our time of need?

Speak to Jesus—refuse to go it alone. Open your heart to the Lord. Share your frustrations and anxieties and hopes with God. Allow scripture, prayer, and worship to be the guiding light in your life. Lean on God, and the Lord will make your paths straight, the load lighter, and your life more joyous.

When was the last time you talked to God for five straight minutes?

Lord, my life can feel overwhelming at times, and at other moments, life can be absolutely grand. But underneath—deep down—you know the constant pressure I feel. Will I succeed? Will I understand? Will I know the way? Help me to lean on you. Help me to find time to talk with you. Help me to share with you that which no one else knows. Lead, and I will follow. In Jesus' name, I pray. AMEN.

April 6

TIME

Read: Ecclesiastes 3:1–8

For everything there is a season, and a time for every matter under heaven: a time to
be born, and a time to die; a time to plant, and a time to pluck up what is planted.
ECCLESIASTES 3:1–2

TIME IS POSSIBLY the greatest gift we have been given. There is a fullness to time that
allows for every experience under heaven to take place. Some of those experiences
will be euphoric, others will be banal, and still others will be painfully difficult.
Unfortunately, we often wish away time. We look out at our daily task, or at a particularly busy stretch of time, and we say, *"If I can just get through this next week, if I can*
just get through this upcoming project or assignment, if I can just get through the holidays!"
Then what? Do we believe we will find ourselves in a more pleasant moment in
time? Perhaps. But the next challenge will present itself to us soon enough, and
we will once again be confronted with a choice: we can choose yet again to wish
ourselves through the moment, or we can embrace the moment for the gift that it
is. Time is a gift to be savored, not an experience to be endured—either you make
the most of it or you lose it.

How much time have you wished away in your life?

Lord, I often treat the time I have been given as a chore I need to get through. Life is
work—hard work at times. But time is also a gift filled with enough richness and complexity
to provide a lifetime worth of discovery. Help me to receive the time I have been allotted for
the gift that it is. In your name, I pray. AMEN.

April 7

HIGHS AND LOWS

Read: Song of Solomon 1:1–4 & Lamentations 1:1–6

> *Let him kiss me with the kisses of his mouth! For your love is bet-*
> *ter than wine, your anointing oils are fragrant, your name is per-*
> *fume poured out; therefore the maidens love you.*
> SONG OF SOLOMON 1:2–3

> *How lonely sits the city that once was full of people! How like a*
> *widow she has become, she that was great among the nations!*
> LAMENTATIONS 1:1A

THERE ARE PLENTY of people who doubt the truth of the Bible. They question its historicity, and they call into question its miraculous claims. However, the Bible is a supremely truthful and honest book. It does not shy away from the devastating tragedy of life, nor does it mute the exuberant passions that human beings have for one another. One book of the Bible can be filled with a vigorous lust for life, while the next book can tap into the deep lament of communal misfortune. No topic is off limits in the Bible, and stories that are too painful to tell are unhesitatingly shared. The Bible is not religious propaganda that attempts to get people to believe outrageous claims . . . the Bible is a living testimony to the challenges and joys of life and the God who has chosen to be with us in and through it all. Life is love and lament intertwined, with God calling us forward into ever more faithful ways of being in relationship. The Bible presents life *as it is*, and it has a way of opening up for us life *as it could be*.

What was a high point and a low point of your last week?

Lord, I thank you that the Bible is such an honest book. It is far more faithful than preachers who encourage me to believe in five steps to fulfillment, or seven steps for success, or ten steps to triumphant living. The Bible tells us that life can be blissful in one moment and crushingly disappointing in the next. The Bible attests to the joys and challenges of life and your desire to experience every moment of it with us. Thank you for that witness . . . and for your presence. In Jesus' name, I pray. AMEN.

— 120 —

April 8

Plowshares and Pruning Hooks

Read: Isaiah 2:1–4

He shall judge between the nations, and shall arbitrate for many peoples; they shall beat their swords into plowshares, and their spears into pruning hooks; nation shall not lift up sword against nation, neither shall they learn war any more.
Isaiah 2:4

GIVEN THE VIOLENCE, carelessness, and greed that seem to permeate our lives and our world, it is difficult to believe that a day will come when wars will cease, abuses will end, and all wrongs will be made right. Such claims seem more akin to fanciful thinking than a future promise. But the Bible doggedly asserts that the world will not cease its turning before our destructive instincts are transformed into productive impulses. Instead of making war, we will choose to make peace. Instead of striking people down with swords, we will choose to plow fields together in anticipation of future harvests. Instead of training spears in the direction of our enemies, we will train vines and trees and flowering bushes so that they produce in abundance. Such a way of living and such a world seem to be an unreachable reality. Yet, every time we choose to be productive instead of destructive, that reality begins to take shape. With every good deed and generous act, a spear is set down and sword is sheathed . . . and God's vision for our world is further revealed.

Are you more comfortable wielding a sword or using pruning shears?

Lord, I am more than willing to lash out at others with sharp words and cutting critiques. I may not go into physical battle, but I can certainly be rough with others. I am not proud of my impulses. I admit that I have destructive tendencies that stand in opposition to your productive desires for me. Help me to realize that the peace I long for in my own life and the harmony you desire to see among your people take shape when the sharp tools I choose to use are the ones that aid in the cultivation of the world as you created it to be. In Jesus' name, I pray. AMEN.

April 9

HERE I AM

Read: Isaiah 6:1–13

> *Then I heard the voice of the Lord saying, "Whom shall I send,*
> *and who will go for us?" And I said, "Here am I; send me!"*
> *ISAIAH 6:8*

ISAIAH FOUND HIMSELF in the presence of the Lord, and amid that presence, Isaiah was painfully aware of his inadequacies as a person. He was sinful. His lips were unclean. He was frail. And yet, for Isaiah, there was an even deeper desire to offer his life—as imperfect as it was—to God. As soon as he felt cleansed by God, his heart leapt and he eagerly responded to God's call to service.

There are at least two conflicting impulses within each of us. The first is a deep sense of inadequacy. We are painfully aware of our shortcomings. Our secrets, sins, and public mistakes weigh heavily on us. We struggle to shake our inherent sense that we are deeply flawed creatures. And yet there is a second, perhaps even more powerful impulse that propels us in God's direction. When we sense God's presence—or hear God's call on our lives—our hearts leap and our spirits soar and we feel ready to do whatever the Lord asks of us. We know we are sinful people, but that doesn't negate our even deeper desire to respond exuberantly to God's commands. The awareness of our sin can keep us silent in the presence of God, but the irrepressible desire of our spirit is to jump up and say to our Lord, *"Here I am! Send me! Call on me! I am ready to do what you ask!"*

Do you recognize in your human nature a divine impulse to serve God?

Lord, like Isaiah, without your help I am not worthy to stand in your presence. Perhaps my selfish living has something to do with my sense that I cannot be more than my sinful nature dictates. But there is an even greater desire within me to serve you. If you would just call on me, if you would just choose me, if you believed I was able to do work on your behalf . . . I know I could do nothing other than exuberantly leap into action. Here I am, Lord. I am ready. Send me! In your name, I pray. AMEN.

April 10

THE PROMISE OF A CHILD

Read: Isaiah 9:1–7

For a child has been born for us, a son given to us; authority rests upon his shoulders;
and he is named Wonderful Counselor, Mighty God, Everlasting Father, Prince of Peace.
ISAIAH 9:6

MUCH OF ANCIENT Israel's history was defined by war, persecution, occupation, and exile. Throughout history, the land of Israel has sat at an unfortunate intersection between major world powers. When the Egyptian Empire wanted to conquer the world, they marched troops over Israel. When the Assyrians were bent on world domination, they charged through Israel. When the Babylonians wanted to expand their empire, they plowed right over the land of Israel. The Greeks, the Romans, and the Ottomans all did the same. Israel was never the primary target of imperial aggression, it was just a frequent casualty in the continually shifting balance of world powers. Into this volatile land, a promise was made through the prophet Isaiah that a child would be born in Israel who would herald an everlasting age of peace and righteousness.

It is a wildly presumptuous promise to be sure. How can a child change the world for the better? What can an infant do to affect regional events? How can a new birth herald a new age? The answer is found in our experience with our own children. Children change everything! New parents find that the moment they see their newborn child, life becomes a more earnest endeavor. Self-interest is readily set aside in favor of taking care of another. Individual hopes and aspirations are no longer as significant as making sure that offspring have a chance to succeed. An infant born signals a new reality and new opportunities for everyone who comes in contact with that new life. How does the world and the power structures of our human family change? One life at a time, one child at a time, one new birth or rebirth at a time. Who could have ever imagined that the great Roman Empire would one day come under the authority of a religious movement focused on the life and ministry of a man who was born in a stable in the little town of Bethlehem in Judea? Roughly eight hundred years before the birth of Jesus, Isaiah prophesied just that!

How has an infant changed your life?

Lord, you have told us that faith the size of a mustard seed can move mountains. You have chosen to reveal yourself to the world through the Hebrew people who have spent much of their existence as slaves, exiles, and scapegoats. You challenge us to believe that a world full of peace can begin with a baby in a manger. We struggle to understand how great movements of faith have their genesis in seemingly insignificant daily events. But that is how you work, and your work is wonderful, mighty, and everlastingly peaceful. In your name, I pray. AMEN.

April 11

LONGING

Read: Isaiah 11:1–10 & Psalm 72:1–7

The wolf will live with the lamb, the leopard will lie down with the kid, the calf and the lion and the fatling together, and a little child shall lead them.
ISAIAH 11:6

May he be like rain that falls on the mown grass, like showers that water the earth.
PSALM 72:6

THERE IS A deep longing within us that can only be met and satisfied by God. Longing for love. Longing for peace. Longing to live with meaning. Longing for the feeling of barrenness to be quenched by holy waters. This is a longing, a sense of incompleteness, that has been witnessed for thousands of years. It is the creation longing to be reunited with its Creator. And while lions and lambs do not yet lie down together, we dare to believe that in Jesus Christ, the longing for unity and harmony and renewal in our lives and in our world can be satisfied.

What do you long for?

Lord, I invite you into the barren places in my life so that long dormant growth might be possible. Be water to my life, and bring peace to the earth. In Jesus' name, I pray. AMEN.

April 12

Going Naked

Read: Isaiah 20:1–6

Then the Lord said, "Just as my servant Isaiah has walked naked . . . for
three years as a sign and a portent against Egypt and Ethiopia."
ISAIAH 20:3

SOMETIMES GOD ASKS us to do crazy things, humiliating things, and God asks us to do them for quite some time. Isaiah was not an eccentric wandering prophet. He was a councilor to the king and a spokesperson for the Most High God. Isaiah was a highly respected religious leader in Israel. Which makes this story all the more unsettling!

God asked Isaiah—a member of the king's court—to take off his clothes and walk around naked and barefoot as a way of demonstrating the humiliation that was to befall the Egyptians and Ethiopians, who at times were enemies of Israel. What is even more shocking is the fact that God had Isaiah do this for *three years.* This wasn't a one-time publicity stunt; this was a three-year project for Isaiah. God used Isaiah to speak to a whole nation, and Isaiah was honored to be in God's service. But that service required Isaiah to do things and act in ways that must have been terribly uncomfortable.

To serve God means that sometimes we have to be willing to do unpopular, unconventional, and even humiliating things. We may have to silently take the blame for an error we did not commit in order to safeguard others. We may have to speak up and out about harmful practices within our company when everyone else is afraid to raise their voices. At a town meeting, at church, or in the boardroom we may have to make a public display of ourselves in order to make a point we believe God is calling us to make. Sometimes God asks us to do crazy things—humiliating things—and God asks us to do them for quite some time. Being in God's employ can be costly, but there is no better place in the world to be!

Has your faith cost you anything in the last year?

Lord, I don't want to have to make a spectacle of myself for you. If I were Isaiah, I probably would have quit before stripping down. I say I am willing to follow you, but I know I have my limits. Lord, I am no Isaiah. It is unlikely I will be your spokesperson to a national audience. I know I will put more limits on our relationship than you will. Still, work with me. Stretch me. Help me to be more useful, more courageous, and more dutiful to your wishes. In your name, I pray. AMEN.

April 13

WAITING FOR RENEWAL

Read: Isaiah 40:1–8, 31

But those who wait for the Lord shall renew their strength, they shall mount up with wings like eagles, they shall run and not be weary, they shall walk and not faint.
ISAIAH 40:31

WAITING IS FRUSTRATING business. Few people enjoy waiting, and plenty of people are undone by it. Waiting for test results from a doctor, waiting to hear back from a potential employer after a job interview, waiting for a family member to arrive home after an extended absence can seem excruciatingly difficult. We prefer quick results, responses, and returns. But the Bible continually recognizes that times of waiting are central to the experience of faith. For God, apparently, waiting has value. The passage of time is an important component in our development as people of faith. Somehow, the waiting itself has a way of producing renewal in our lives.

When we are forced to wait, we are forced to recognize that certain situations and processes are simply out of our control. And while that reality unsettles us, it can be helpful to have to come to terms with life as it truly is. We are not in charge, and we have precious little influence over the course of our lives and the fate of our world. That is just the way life is. At some point in our waiting hours—if we are faithful to the experience—we are prompted to surrender our desire for control, and we entrust ourselves anew to God. When we finally admit to ourselves that there is nothing we can do but wait, we unconsciously make room for God to act in our lives. When God has room to work within us, that is often when we find ourselves renewed. The weariness of propelling ourselves by our own steam is replaced by the joy that can be experienced when we are carried on the wings and winds of God.

What do you do when you are waiting?

Lord, I am not a fan of waiting. I struggle to find value in what seems to me to be idle time. I am very much in lockstep with a culture that prefers instant gratification, immediate results, and the rapid exchange of information and communication. However, I know that fast-paced living is wearying. The ever-increasing speed of life outpaces my ability to keep up. In fact, efforts to reduce waiting time might crowd out important moments when you try to catch my attention. Lord, the next time I find myself waiting, help me to consider that moment as a time of critical communication between you and me. Help me to realize that renewal and waiting go hand in hand. In your name, I pray. AMEN.

April 14

Suffering Servant

Read: Isaiah 52:13—53:12

He poured out himself to death, and was numbered with the transgressors;
yet he bore the sin of many, and made intercession for the transgressors.
Isaiah 53:12b

The story of the Suffering Servant in the book of Isaiah does not fit nicely and neatly into the progression of the book. It can seem out of context—not particularly well connected to the material that comes before and after. This story gained new meaning and drew renewed attention generations after its composition, as the first followers of Jesus struggled to understand who Jesus was. Jesus' followers had believed that he was the Messiah—the soon to be crowned king of Israel and redeemer of God's chosen people. However, upon Jesus' death, that belief was called into question. How could there be a crucified Messiah? Even if one were to believe in Jesus' miraculous resurrection, there seemed to be no biblical model for a suffering and dying heavenly king.

That is when the odd and seemingly disconnected story of the Suffering Servant gained power and recognition. The plight of the Suffering Servant seemed to match Jesus' life and ministry exactly. It is nearly impossible to read Isaiah 53, and not feel as if Jesus is the complete fulfillment of that passage of scripture. Jesus may not have fit the model of the Messiah the Jewish people had hoped for, but he appears to be the complete fulfillment of the self-sacrificing leader God promised in the book of Isaiah.

Can you see Jesus as the Suffering Servant prophesied in the book of Isaiah?

Lord, I find when I look for you, it is often in the wrong places. I seek to witness you in power and majesty, and therefore I can easily miss you in moments of suffering and service. Help me to be attentive to the unique and unexpected places you reveal yourself. I thank you for the many scriptures that can refocus me on where and how you choose to encounter us. In Jesus' name, I pray. AMEN.

April 15

Obeying the Rules

Read: Isaiah 58:9–14

> *If you refrain from trampling the sabbath, . . . I will make you ride*
> *upon the heights of the earth; I will feed you with the heritage of*
> *your ancestor Jacob, for the mouth of the Lord has spoken.*
> *Isaiah 58:13–14*

WHAT IF WE just obeyed the rules? What if we actually followed the commands of God? What if we began to live our lives as if God does indeed know what is best for us? What if the rules in the Bible are not arbitrary restrictions, but essential keys to healthy living? What if the rules are in place for our safety and success? Imagine that! For instance, if we observe the Sabbath, we are promised the world!

Why do we recoil from God's commands and treat them as if they mattered little?

Lord, I am a rule breaker. I view your commands as optional. I do not consider that your direction has been given so that I can more fully enjoy life. Teach me how to be an obedient child of yours. In Jesus' name, I pray. AMEN.

April 16

GOOD NEWS!

Read: Isaiah 61:1–11

The spirit of the Lord God is upon me, because the Lord has anointed me;
he has sent me to bring good news to the oppressed, to bind up the broken-
hearted, to proclaim liberty to the captives, and release to the prisoners.
ISAIAH 61:1

WE LIVE IN a world that thrives on bad news. We publically bemoan the intense media focus on stories of death, destruction, and despair, but like rubbernecking on the highway when passing an accident scene, we find ourselves engrossed by it. For some reason, bad news can be more absorbing than the uplifting human interest stories we say we would like to see more of but never actually read or watch.

As Christians, as people of faith, as heirs to a tradition grounded in prophetic works like the book of Isaiah, we are called—anointed—to speak good news in a bad news world. Where some see death, we proclaim life. Where some witness despair, we speak hope. Where some fear destruction, we announce opportunities for rebuilding. There are certainly reasons for fear and uncertainty in our world, but we dare to believe in a good God whose design is for all creation to be saved and loved for all eternity. When we believe that the world was created in goodness and that the age to come will be filled with righteousness, how can we preach anything other than good news!

Does good news or bad news most readily capture your attention?

Lord, I confess that bad news can grab hold of me in ways that make it difficult to feel hopeful, let alone share optimistic words with others. Turning on the television, going online, or opening up the morning paper releases a flood of disturbing news that can make even the most cheerful of people blue and despondent. And yet, you encourage us to look past the headlines to look more deeply at the world you have created. Life is good, love is good, and so much of the created order is good. Even in the difficult moments of life, we know we are incredibly blessed. We have been told that when our life in this world is completed, our life will begin anew with you. That is great news—worth sharing with anyone who will listen. Lord, allow your Spirit to encourage me to share that news boldly and without hesitation. In your name, I pray. AMEN.

April 17

ACCEPTING RESPONSIBILITY

Read: Isaiah 64:1–11

> *O that you would tear open the heavens and come down. . . .Yet, O*
> *Lord, you are our Father; we are the clay, and you are our potter.*
> ISAIAH *64:1 & 8*

AS PEOPLE OF faith, we have to come to terms with God's deafening silence. What does it mean that the Creator of our universe—the molder of our lives—appears reluctant to speak? How can God witness the plight of our world and not intervene? Does God not hear our pleas for assistance? We have this nagging suspicion that God may have abandoned us to make our own way in the world. Or worse, we fear that God's absence and silence is evidence enough that God does not really exist. Like Isaiah, serious people of faith need to grapple with these serious questions of faith. Why is God silent? Does God not care? *"O that God would tear open the heavens and come down!"*

And yet, as the work of God's hands, perhaps we are endowed with all the wisdom, insight, and internal resources we need to meet the demands of life. Perhaps God's silence is more like that of a father who has done all he can to prepare his children for the challenges of life and thus lets them go. Perhaps God's silence is the sacred absence of one who entrusts to us the responsibility of tending to creation, knowing we can do it if we try. Perhaps our job is to take the responsibility offered to us and make the most of it.

Is there something you want from God that you are fully able to accomplish for yourself?

Lord, I cry to you in my distress, and you are quiet. Are you not speaking to me, or in the midst of all the noises and busyness of my life, am I simply unable to hear your voice? Or have you spoken deeply to me from before the moment when I was being knit together in my mother's womb, and now you trust that I am fully equipped to make it on my own? Lord, help me to accept the responsibility you have offered me. Help me to understand that your distance might be offered because you believe I am fully capable of making my way in the world. Help me to come to terms with the possibility that your silence is what allows me the opportunity to attempt to stand up for myself. In Jesus' name, I pray. AMEN.

April 18

KNOWN

Read: Jeremiah 1:4–10

Now the word of the Lord came to me saying, "Before I formed
you in the womb I knew you, and before you were born I conse-
crated you; I appointed you a prophet to the nations."
Jeremiah 1:4–5

JEREMIAH BELIEVED HE was too young and inexperienced to do the work God had assigned to him. God had commissioned Jeremiah to speak on God's behalf, but Jeremiah wasn't convinced he had what it took to undertake the task. Jeremiah didn't feel eloquent. He didn't know what he would have to say. Jeremiah also doubted the Hebrew people would listen and take direction from a child. But God knew what Jeremiah was capable of, even if Jeremiah did not. Before Jeremiah had even been born, God envisioned utilizing Jeremiah as spokesman for God among the nations. Jeremiah's life and ministry wound up being the basis for the most expansive prophetic book in the Bible. The boy who doubted his abilities became God's most prolific prophet.

God believes that we can accomplish more than we can often imagine for ourselves. That is because God knows us better than we know ourselves. God has endowed us with gifts and abilities that we may not even know we have. What we need to do is trust in God's ability to make use of us in extraordinary ways. When it comes to the work God assigns us, we are never left to accomplish it on our own. God is our co-worker, calling us forward, encouraging us to believe in our inherent abilities, and helping us to become all that we can be in this life.

Do you believe in God's ability to help you accomplish extraordinary work?

Lord, I tend to think of myself as having limited ability. While I might like to por-
tray myself as confident and self-assured, more often than not I feel a bit inadequate and

unqualified for the work before me. Yet, if the work that I am given is work you want me to do, then I must trust that you believe in my ability to do it. I also long to trust that you will not allow me to tackle your kingdom work alone. You know me. You are with me. And you will not allow me to toil alone. In Jesus' name, I hope and pray. AMEN.

April 19

REVEALED!

Read: Jeremiah 18:1–11

"Go down to the potter's house, and there I will let you hear my words."
JEREMIAH 18:2

GOD TOLD JEREMIAH to go to the local potter, and there, watching the potter at work, Jeremiah would learn something about God. Jeremiah was man of faith steeped in the faith practices of his people. However, when God was ready to reveal an important truth to Jeremiah, God didn't tell Jeremiah to pray more or read more scripture or go up to Jerusalem to hear the divine word spoken aloud by the priests in the temple. Instead, God said he would be revealed through the created order and the creative process itself.

If like Jeremiah you are a person of prayer, if you take time each morning to read scripture, if you engage regularly in Christian community, something extraordinary happens—you start seeing God, and seeing God at work all around you. Creation becomes the mouthpiece of God. For people of faith who do the daily work of faith, simply watching a potter's hands at work should reveal something about how God shapes and reshapes our lives and our world.

Can you learn something about God by observing the created order and the creative process?

Lord, open my eyes that I might see. Open my ears that I might hear. Awaken my senses so that I am able to witness your divine hand in the world around me. In Jesus' name, I pray. AMEN.

April 20

WORK IN PROGRESS

Read: Jeremiah 18:1–11

> *I went down to the potter's house, and there he was working at his wheel.*
> *The vessel he was making of clay was spoiled in the potter's hand,*
> *and he reworked it into another vessel, as seemed good to him.*
> *JEREMIAH 18:3–4*

A POTTER WILL moisten, spin, push, pull, stretch, and compress clay until it begins to take the shape the potter has in mind. Even if the clay is spoiled, the potter will work it and rework it until it is shaped into a vessel that is pleasing to its maker.

Before you were even born, God had an image of what you could become. In fact, right now God sees you—even if you don't see yourself—as strong, capable, and beautiful. But you are not there yet. God is still working on you—applying pressure, stretching you, softening you, shaping you until you conform to the image God has in mind for you. You are a work in progress.

Are you feeling pushed and pulled and pressured right now?

Lord, the pressure of my life can get depressing at times. I begin to wonder if I will ever get to a place in life where I won't constantly be weighed down by challenges and frustration. Help me to see the difficult situations I face as opportunities for you to further craft me into the person you want me to become. In your name, I pray. AMEN.

April 21

GOOD TO GOD

Read: Jeremiah 18:1–11

He reworked it into another vessel, as seemed good to him.
JEREMIAH 18:4

WHAT IS SUCCESS? You likely have an image in your mind. Our culture has come up with ways of measuring success. It can be measured by how much money you make. Success is calculated by how many material possessions you have—and by how big your material possessions are. How big is your house? How big is your car? Who has the best and biggest toys? What title is on your office door? How many friends do you have? Are you a person of influence?

Yet, who are we to judge success? We are successful when we become what God had in mind for us! You are successful when you finally give in to the hand of the potter and become what God has in mind for you. Success is God holding you in hand, looking at you, admiring the work done on you, and saying, *"It is good." "You are good."* If, in the end, you are good to God, that's all that matters.

Is your life shaping into what God has in mind for you?

Lord, I confess that I make judgments about success every day—my success and the success of those around me. Who am I to judge? In the end, only your opinion matters. In the end, you are the only one I have to please. Lord, help me to shed the measuring sticks of success that our world endorses, and help me to be content to strive to be what you created me to be . . . nothing more, nothing less. In Jesus' name, I pray. AMEN.

April 22

WE WILL BE BACK

Read: Jeremiah 32:6–15

Jeremiah said, The word of the Lord came to me: Hanamel son of your
uncle Shallum is going to come to you and say, "Buy my field that is
at Anathoth, for the right of redemption by purchase is yours."
JEREMIAH 32:6–7

AS JERUSALEM WAS being besieged by the Babylonians, Jeremiah engaged in a
real estate transaction. King Nebuchadnezzar had already taken possession of
the land of Judah, but Jeremiah drew up papers for the acquisition of a field.
Jerusalem was about to be burned to the ground, the temple was on the verge of
destruction, and the Jewish people were on the eve of exile, and Jeremiah—who
had prophesied the impending doom—made a powerful statement. By purchas-
ing his cousin's field, Jeremiah let the Jewish people know that while decades of
exile lay before them, God intended that they would be back! *"For thus says the*
Lord of hosts, the God of Israel: Houses and fields and vineyards shall again be bought in
this land."

We all have moments when we feel downtrodden, demoralized, and on the
verge of disaster. While we may not have to fear an impending exile; an impending
divorce, a job loss, or bankruptcy can feel like the end of our world. There are
situations we find ourselves in when it can feel as if all is lost. But God promises
people of faith that our end is not destruction, displacement, or death. The words
of the prophet Jeremiah remind us that God's plan for us includes joyous reunions
and rebuilt lives and even resurrection from death. While there are moments we
are cast down and out, God promises that we will one day come back!

What investment do you need to make in your future?

Lord, I am stunned by Jeremiah's act. What a foolish investment—to buy a piece of land
that had been taken into the possession of a foreign military force! And yet, what a moving

witness to the fact that the powers and principalities that oppose your plans for me will not be victorious in the end. I may experience moments when I get carried away by misfortune, but you promise that I will be back. Thank you for Jeremiah's hopeful act. And help me to invest in a similarly hopeful future—even if I can't see it or imagine it yet. In Jesus' name, I pray. AMEN.

April 23

Sweet as Honey

Read: Ezekiel 2:1—3:3

> *He said to me, Mortal, eat this scroll that I give you and fill your stomach with it. Then I ate it; and in my mouth it was as sweet as honey.*
> EZEKIEL 3:3

WE ONLY HAVE to offer to others what we have received. Whether we are offering advice or giving direction or trying to teach others, we can only share what we ourselves have learned. Therefore, if we are not in the habit of taking sound advice or listening to wise council or reading and absorbing important ideas, we will have very little if anything worthwhile to pass on to those around us.

The call of the prophet Ezekiel is filled with wonderful imagery. In jaw-dropping splendor and majesty, the Lord appeared to Ezekiel with instructions to go and speak words of condemnation and hope to the Hebrew people. But what would Ezekiel say? What did he have to offer? What words would he speak? The Lord held out a scroll with the words of God on it, and Ezekiel was told to ingest it. He was told to eat the scroll, be nourished by it, and let the word of God fill his stomach. Ezekiel found that the taste of scripture was as sweet as honey. And once the word of God got into Ezekiel, he found he had something to say to the Hebrew people. If you are filled with good words and wisdom and knowledge, you will have something of great value to share with others. Scripture was Ezekiel's diet, so he was able to powerfully share the word of God with others.

What words have nourished you, filled you, and offered you direction in life?

Lord, it is tempting to feed my mind and my soul with junk food—tabloid-like news, quasi-reality entertainment, and neighborhood gossip. No wonder I have precious little substance to share with others. Fill me with your wisdom. Allow me to be nourished by your presence. Let me taste how good it is to feast on your word. In Jesus' name, I pray. AMEN.

April 24

LIFE-GIVER

Read: Ezekiel 37:1–14

> *He said to me, "Mortal, can these bones live?" I answered, "O Lord God,*
> *you know." Then he said to me, "Prophesy to these bones, and say to*
> *them: O dry bones, hear the word of the Lord. Thus says the Lord God to*
> *these bones: I will cause breath to enter you, and you shall live."*
> *EZEKIEL 37:3–5*

GOD IS A life-giver. God took the unformed matter of the cosmos and created a living and expanding universe. God called each and every creature into being. God walked with Ezekiel through a valley of death filled with dry bones and, with a single command, proclaimed that the dead could be raised to new life. Ezekiel didn't know how such a thing could be possible. How could dry, marrowless bones be knit together again? How could the dispersed and disheartened Hebrew people ever return from exile? How could a broken nation be reborn and reunited? It seemed like an impossibility. But Ezekiel's vision was of a life-giving Lord, a God who continually creates and recreates, a Spirit that lives to fill us with life. There is no valley so deep, no despair so dark, no death so final that God cannot retrieve us and renew us!

Where in your life do you need the Lord to bring renewal?

Lord, you offer us life. Life after death, and life before death! You are always calling us forward into deeper and richer ways of living. You desire for us to have life in abundance, and you desire to share in that life with us. Thank you, and help me to claim the life you are offering me today! In Jesus' name, I pray. AMEN.

April 25

BEING DISCIPLINED

Read: Daniel 1:1–21

Please test your servants for ten days. Let us be given vegetables to eat and water to drink. You can then compare our appearance with the appearance of the young men who eat the royal rations, and deal with your servants according to what you observe.
DANIEL 1:12–13

IN CAPTIVITY IN Babylon, Daniel was chosen to be a member of the king's court. That position afforded him and a few of his friends the opportunity to feast from the king's table. That would have been a dream come true for any of the Jewish exiles in Babylon. But Daniel knew that by accepting the royal ration of food, he would be placing himself under the authority of the king, and the food itself would fatten him in unhealthy ways. Daniel believed that abstaining from excessive food would strengthen his soul and safeguard his health. Self-discipline in the face of great excess would be his way to salvation.

For many of us, the table is set, and we are invited to an all-you-can-eat buffet. We live in a day and an age when we are encouraged to consume. As a result the United States is one of the fattest nations in the world. Our waistlines widen, our debt burdens increase, and our daily schedules are overburdened with activities. We have been encouraged to saddle up to the buffet, and we don't seem to know how to stop before we are stuffed.

Somehow, like Daniel, we need to consume less, for less is often more. Eating less, buying less, doing less can be a way to salvation in an age of excess. We can consume ourselves to death, but with a little self-discipline, a little-limit setting, and a little restraint in the face of great excess, we can make our way toward spiritual and physical health.

What limits do you need to set for yourself before overindulgence strips you of your spiritual and physical health?

Lord God, I confess I am a ravenous consumer. I eat too much. I purchase too much. I am involved in too much. Help me to develop the resolve to push back from the buffet so that my health is preserved and my service to you is unimpaired. In Jesus' name, I pray. AMEN.

April 26

THE FIERY FURNACE

Read: Daniel 3

Nebuchadnezzar replied, "But I see four men unbound, walking in the middle of
the fire, and they are not hurt; and the fourth has the appearance of a god."
DANIEL 3:25

SHADRACH, MESHACH, AND Abednego got burned, figuratively, not literally. They
were required to bow down to a golden image that King Nebuchadnezzar of
Babylon had erected, and they refused. Even though they had, up until that time,
been trusted advisors and administrators of the king, they got thrown into a fiery
furnace as punishment. It was both cruel and unfair, like so much of life. They got
burned for holding on to their faith.

However, in the furnace, they were accompanied by someone who had *"the*
appearance of a god." They were not alone.

There are so many times when life seems to throw us into the fire. We get
burned—at work, at home, in relationships. It happens, and it hurts. But we are
told throughout the Bible that we are not alone in the flames. Jesus is with us, and
Jesus is well acquainted with the furnace. Jesus made it through, and he intends for
us to make it through, as well!

Do you remember a time when you were "getting burned," only to discover
that you were not alone?

Lord, there are times in my life when the heat gets turned up, when I get into hot water,
and when it feels as if I might get burned. You do not promise me that I won't get thrown in the
furnace, but you do promise to be with me whenever flames threaten to engulf my life. Thank
you for being there! In Jesus' name, I pray. AMEN.

April 27

Daniel and the Lions' Den

Read: Daniel 6

> *Daniel continued ... to get down on his knees three times a day to*
> *pray to his God and praise him, just as he had done previously.*
> Daniel 6:10

It has been said in jest that the lions could not eat Daniel because he was too big a meal for them. Daniel was too big—too full of God's Spirit—for the lions to consume him. We may not fully understand the how and why of the Daniel story, but we do know that the lions stayed away, and that Daniel was full of the Spirit of God. Daniel prayed three times a day. Daniel fasted. Daniel did not get caught up in the idolatry of his culture. Daniel is a larger than life character in the Bible, and the size and scope of his memory is directly related to his uncompromising faithfulness. The truth is, when we are full of God's Spirit and God's presence, nothing can devour us because we are already fully consumed with God.

How many times a day do you pray?

Lord, my faith is emaciated, if I am to be completely honest. I have not gotten my fill of you . . . in fact, more often than not, I skip meals entirely. As a result I am consumed by every passing worry, anxiety, and stress. Call me back to your table where I may feast on your presence. In Jesus' name, I pray. AMEN.

April 28

JONAH AND THE WHALE

Read: Jonah 1–4

> *Then the Lord said, "You are concerned about the bush, for which you did not*
> *labor and which you did not grow; it came into being in a night and per-*
> *ished in a night. And should I not be concerned about Nineveh, that great city,*
> *in which there are more than a hundred and twenty thousand persons who*
> *did not know their right hand from their left, and also many animals?"*
> JONAH 4:10–11

THE STORY OF Jonah began with God's call for Jonah to go to Nineveh, in the hope that the people of Nineveh would repent from their evil ways. God wanted to save the great city of Nineveh from itself. God's central act in this story, however, was an effort to save Jonah from himself. Jonah was a lost prophet. He had lost his way, his perspective, and his appreciation of God's mercy. The story ends with Jonah wishing he were dead and God making a case for love and mercy. While we have no final response from Jonah signaling a change in his perspective, we are drawn to recognize that God has the last word . . . and there is a lingering sense that the debate will continue until God's point is taken to heart by Jonah.

When it comes to the business of saving souls, God's ambition is boundless. God desires to save both great and small alike. God works as relentlessly to rescue an ill-tempered prophet as a thriving metropolis—in fact, even animals don't escape God's interest! It is as if God will not give up until everyone in the family is saved.

Do you need to be saved from yourself?

Lord, when I think about "being saved," images of pushy and pompously pious Christians come to mind. I am put off by the idea that there is an in-group and an out-group. But what if we are all part of the out-group: prophets, population centers, and pets alike? I may not like being told I need to be saved, but I know I need saving all the same. Save me . . . save us, I pray, in Jesus' name. AMEN.

April 29

REQUIREMENTS

Read: Micah 6:6–8

He has told you, O mortal, what is good; and what does the Lord require of you
but to do justice, and to love kindness, and to walk humbly with your God?
MICAH 6:8

WHAT DOES GOD require of us? The answer for much of Hebrew history was sacrifice—notably, animal sacrifice. Animals were sacrificed as a way to atone for the
people's sins, as a gift of gratitude for God's provision, or as a way to request God's
favor. People also offered the produce from their fields, the first fruits of their labor, as well as financial contributions to support the running of the temple. There
was even the tradition of offering, or dedicating, firstborn children to the Lord as
a way to express gratitude for all that God had done.

However, according to many passages in the Bible, God does not desire gifts
of calves or rams or rivers of oil. The best offering we can make to God is to treat
others well. We can deal justly with our neighbors. We can offer kindness to strangers. We can walk humbly in the crowd—not trying set ourselves above others. Like
so many parents of children, God essentially says, *"If you want to do something for me,*
treat each other better!" God's requirement is that we take care of each other.

How can you fulfill God's requirements?

Lord, for some reason I am more willing to give you "stuff" than I am to offer care to those
around me. But what you really want from me is improved treatment of others. You have made
this request in many different ways in the Bible. If I want to demonstrate my love for you, all
I need to do is love my neighbor. What do you require of me? Be just, kind, and humble in my
dealings with other people. You ask that I treat those around me as I would like to be treated . .
. and it will be as if that gift has been presented directly to you. In Jesus' name, I pray. AMEN.

April 30

IDENTIFICATION

Read: Zechariah 12:10—13:1

And I will pour out a spirit of compassion and supplication on the house
of David and the inhabitants of Jerusalem, so that, when they look on the
one whom they have pierced, they shall mourn for him, as one mourns for
an only child, and weep bitterly over him, as one weeps over a firstborn.
ZECHARIAH 12:10

TUCKED AWAY IN the little book of Zechariah, toward the very end of the Old Testament, is what Christians believe to be an identifying reference to Jesus. Nearly hidden in the words of a fairly obscure lesser prophet of Israel, a Messiah is spoken of who will be pierced by the Hebrew people in the city of Jerusalem, only to cleanse those people from their sins. The prophesy goes on to say, *"On that day a fountain shall be opened for the house of David and the inhabitants of Jerusalem, to cleanse them from sin and impurity."* While we know that early Christians read this text and could identify Jesus in it, it is very possible that, as a rabbi, Jesus knew of this scripture and drew strength from it. As Jesus' hands, feet, and side were being pierced at Golgotha—as Jesus forgave the soldiers who were breaking his body—he may have understood his circumstances as they had been foretold in Zechariah. Jesus may have discovered his own identity in the scriptures he had spent his life studying.

It is an astounding claim—we can find ourselves in the Bible! Our truest identity can be discovered in a book that dates back thousands of years. Scripture that revealed who Jesus was can reveal who we are. Of course, theologically speaking, this makes good sense. God spoke creation into being with a word; therefore it would stand to reason that the Word of God—the Bible—would be an identifying source for all of us who have been created. We are children of God. We are followers of Jesus Christ. We are joint heirs to a kingdom of peace, love, and justice that God is trying to bring to fruition in our world. The Bible tells us all that we need to know about ourselves and the God we have come to know through Jesus Christ.

Can you remember a time when a particular passage of scripture seemed to be speaking directly to you?

Lord, I turn to the Bible with the deep hope that your word will speak to me. I don't feel as though that happens every time I open the Bible, but there are certainly times when it seems as if a particular passage of scripture was composed specifically for me. In those precious and sacred moments, it is as if I discover who I truly am in your Word. Thank you for that gift, and help me to always open the Bible with the expectation that I can find myself and you in its pages. In Jesus' name, I pray. AMEN.

May 1

Testing God

Read: Malachi 1:2; 3:6–12

> *Bring the full tithe into the storehouse, . . . put me to the test, says*
> *the Lord of Hosts; see if I will not open the windows of heaven*
> *for you and pour down for you an overflowing blessing.*
> MALACHI 3:10

THE PRIMARY ISSUE God had with the Israelites in the book of Malachi was that they were not giving their best to God. In fact, they were giving their leftovers, and God was getting disappointed and angry. When people made their annual offering to God, they were to bring a tithe—a full tenth of their produce to the temple—and they were to sacrifice only unblemished livestock at the altar. They were supposed to offer their best to God in honor of all that God had done for them. The Israelite people and their clergy were doing quite the opposite. They were not being generous toward God. God spoke through the prophet Malachi: *Return to me, and I will return to you. Bring a full tithe into my house. Test me. I will open the windows of heaven for you and pour down for you an overflowing blessing.*

God loves you dearly, you are God's child, and God challenges you to put that love to the test with a tithe. Offer the best of what you have to the Lord. Do not hold back for fear of security. God has so much more in store for you. The blessings of heaven await you!

Are you generous?

Lord, help me to extend myself more freely to you and to those around me. Encourage me to think more deeply instead of thinking first of myself. Guide me down a path of true generosity. I want to be the person you created me to be. In Jesus' name, I pray. AMEN.

First and Last Word

Read: Matthew 1:18–23; 28:1–7

> *An angel of the Lord appeared to him in a dream and*
> *said, "Joseph, son of David, do not be afraid."*
> MATTHEW 1:20B

> *The angel said to the women, "Do not be afraid."*
> MATTHEW 28:5A

IT HAS BEEN said that there are 365 commands in the Bible that charge us not to be afraid—one for every day of the year. Whether that is entirely accurate or not, the commands *"Do not be afraid," "Do not fear," "Do not worry,"* are numerous. It is, in fact, an overarching theme in the Gospel of Matthew—*"Do not be afraid"* is the word of God at Jesus' birth and it is the word of God at Jesus' resurrection. Something new and unexpected—perhaps even troubling—had happened and the first witnesses to both events were cautioned not to fear the new thing God was doing. New birth and resurrection are not to be feared but are to be embraced.

What new event or situation in your life do you find yourself fretting about?

Lord, new is not always welcome in my life. Comfortable, familiar, predictable are the patterns I tend to gravitate toward. When the status quo in my life begins to change . . . I begin to worry. Is it not possible, however, that the change I fear is really the blessing of new life and resurrection right here and now? In Jesus' name, I pray. AMEN.

THINGS WORK OUT

Read: Matthew 1:1–17

> *So all the generations from Abraham to David are fourteen generations;*
> *and from David to the deportation to Babylon, fourteen generations; and*
> *from the deportation to Babylon to the Messiah, fourteen generations.*
> MATTHEW 1:17

GENEALOGIES ARE POSSIBLY the least appreciated texts in the Bible. They are laborious to read, with names that are difficult to pronounce and relationships that are nearly impossible to authenticate. And yet, the biblical authors felt it was important to include them. If you pay close attention to Jesus' genealogy in the Gospel of Matthew, you will notice that it includes some rather unsavory characters. Jesus' genealogy also references one of the most heartbreaking chapters in Jewish history—the Babylonian exile. This long list of names dares to suggest that there was some divine order to Jesus' rather ignominious lineage.

According to this passage of scripture, fourteen generations separated Abraham and David, and fourteen generations separated David from the Babylonia exile, and another fourteen generations passed between the exile and Jesus' birth. The message is the symmetry. It suggests things work out in the end. God brings order into the chaos of history. There is meaning and purpose in every age. Wanderers and kings and exiles play an equal role in bringing about God's will and the Messiah's reign.

What event in your life are you worried won't work out as it should?

Lord, where I see chaos, you see beauty. When I sense fear, you recognize possibility. When I feel lost, you know how to find me. To me life seems confusing and dangerous and unsettled . . . but to you everything works out just as it should. Mercy, grace, forgiveness, and love keep us winding our way toward you. In Jesus' name, I pray. AMEN.

Joseph's Dream

Read: Matthew 1:18–25

An angel of the Lord appeared to Joseph in a dream and said,
"Joseph, son of David, do not be afraid to take Mary as your wife,
for the child conceived in her is from the Holy Spirit."
MATTHEW 1:20

IT IS ONE of the most frequently offered commands in the Bible, *"Do not be afraid.""Do not worry.""Fear not!"* It as if God is continually speaking to children saying, *"Everything will be all right, just trust me."* But we are creatures prone to worry and mistrust. And yet, we have uttered the same words to our own children countless times. When a child runs to us with tears in her eyes having skinned her knee, when our teenager experiences his first relational breakup, when the first grandparent dies—without a moment of hesitation we tell our children, *"It's all right, everything will be all right, trust me."* It is as if deep down at the very core of our being we understand and believe the deep truth God speaks to us throughout the Bible. We don't know the why or how of it, but we can't shake this feeling that in the end, everything *will* be all right. God can be trusted. We have nothing to fear.

Do you trust God?

Lord, I try not to show it to others, but I am a deeply fearful person. I am scared by what I know, and by that which remains unknown to me. The world you created seems a dangerous and uncertain place. Left on my own, I do not know that everything will be all right. But you do not wish me to live alone, you desire my life to be yoked to yours so that I can rest in the trust that you are in charge when I am not . . . and I can trust that with you all things will be well. Help me, please. In Jesus' name, I pray. AMEN.

May 5

THE WISE MEN

Read: Matthew 2:1–12

> *Then Herod sent the wise men to Bethlehem, saying, "Go and*
> *search diligently for the child; and when you have found him,*
> *bring me word so that I may also go and pay him homage."*
> MATTHEW 2:8

ACCORDING TO THIS story, the wise men found Jesus, and Herod did not. Those who seek, find. Those who stand comfortably at a distance do not. The wise men left everything behind and followed a star, they held nothing back in their pursuit of a newborn king, and their investment was rewarded. Herod, who had evil intent, was interested in the Christ child, but unwilling to take the time to hunt for Jesus himself. We view this as good news, knowing that Herod's interest was fueled by a desire to kill the infant. However, if Herod, like the Magi, had searched diligently for the child, perhaps he too would have returned home by a different road . . . his course forever altered.

Are you merely curious about Jesus, or do you earnestly desire to find him?

Lord, often my faith is no more than a flirtation—a mere curiosity with you that I try to satisfy only when I feel I have the time to spare. I rarely go all-in in an attempt to reach out for you. Perhaps that is why my life of faith often feels barren and unsatisfied. Show me a star this year, and give me the resolve to follow it until I find you. In Jesus' name, I pray. AMEN.

May 6

FLIGHT TO EGYPT

Read: Matthew 2:13–23

An angel of the Lord appeared to Joseph in a dream and said, "Get up,
take the child and his mother, and flee to Egypt, and remain there until
I tell you; for Herod is about to search for the child, to destroy him."
MATTHEW 2:13

WE OFTEN THINK that faith is about courageously standing our ground. When challenged, faith should be an unshakable foundation from which we will not be moved. Jesus didn't flinch when he was tested and tried, and neither should we.

We are told, however, that all creatures, ourselves included, have within us instincts that cause us to fight, as well as instincts toward flight. We seem genetically predisposed to choose between the two—sometimes it is appropriate to stand firm and other times it is best to run away. While it may fly in the face of the image of strength so many of us covet, our faith says that there may be times when fleeing is the most faithful act we can engage in. In the Bible, Abraham, Hagar, David, Elijah, Jesus, Paul, and many other faithful people encountered situations where they had to flee for their lives—and in running away, they were following God's will for them. Our faith can be about standing up for what we believe in, but it can also be about running for the hills.

When has running away been a faithful thing for you to do?

Lord, sometimes we must run away in order to save our skin. It may strike us as cowardice in the abstract, but when we come face to face with forces that threaten to destroy us, sometimes you prompt us to run for cover. Lord, this is all very confusing. Help me to know when to stand my ground, and when to head for the hills. In Jesus' name, I pray. AMEN.

May 7

INNOCENT

Read: Matthew 2:16–18

When Herod saw that he had been tricked by the wise men, he was infuriated, and
he sent and killed all the children in and around Bethlehem who were two years
old or under, according to the time that he had learned from the wise men.
MATTHEW 2:16

THE BIBLE DOES not flinch when it comes to addressing the ugly truths of life. If the
authors of the biblical story were interested in providing us with a sanitized and
pleasing faith story, they would never have included an entry about the killing of
little children. But the Bible deals with the world as it is, and our world is one in
which the innocent are too often victimized. This is not a word of comfort—it is
simply a word of truth. We must therefore practice our faith and say our prayers
and worship our God in an environment that is hostile and callous and violent. That
is our task. There will be weeping. There will be moments when it feels as if our
innocence has been taken from us. But, if we refer to the full quote in the book of
Jeremiah (31:16–17), we find a hopeful note. *"Keep your voice from weeping, and your*
eyes from tears; for there is a reward for your work, says the Lord: they shall come back from
the land of the enemy; there is hope for your future, says the Lord: your children shall come
back to their own country." The world is a harsh place—that is truth proclaimed by the
Bible. But hostility will be overcome by hope—that is the greater truth promised
in scripture.

When did you lose your innocence?

Lord, I would like the Bible to tell me that life will be pleasant and happy and carefree.
But that is not the promise you extend to us. Life is hard, but your love overcomes all pain.
Innocence may be lost, but truth is never sacrificed. Help me to possess an honest and unflinch-
ing faith . . . Help me to embrace this world and my life as it is, and not as I would have it. In
Jesus' name, I pray. AMEN.

THE TEMPTATION OF JESUS

Read: Matthew 4:1–11

> *Jesus fasted forty days and forty nights, and afterwards he was famished. The tempter came and said to him, "If you are the Son of God, command these stones to become loaves of bread."*
> *MATTHEW 4:2–3*

THE TEMPTER APPEARED only after Jesus has fasted for forty days and forty nights, which means that the tempter might have chosen a time of particular weakness for Jesus. Can you imagine not eating for more than a month, only to be tempted by food? However, after forty days of fasting, Jesus wasn't weak . . . he was strong. Think of the alcoholic who has been sober for forty days—day forty-one is much easier than day one. The tempter should have showed up when Jesus first entered the wilderness.

When we get serious about dealing with our addictions, our bad habits, and those private sins that are known only to us, we don't get weaker as the days are added to our recovery—we get stronger. We are able to endure even more temptation that when we began. What is difficult for us on day one, is more manageable by day forty.

What temptation do you need to confront in your life in the next forty days?

Lord God, it almost sounds like an infomercial for a weight loss program—lose forty pounds in forty days. But it is true that the more committed we are, the longer we face our temptations the less tempting they become. Push me to face the temptations that rule my life so that I can turn leadership of my life over to you. In Jesus' name, I pray. AMEN.

May 9

THE BEATITUDES

Read: Matthew 5:1–12

> *Then Jesus began to speak, and taught them, saying:"Blessed are*
> *the poor in spirit, for theirs is the kingdom of heaven."*
> MATTHEW 5:2–3

THE MESSAGE OF the Beatitudes is as beautiful as it is simple. Jesus tells us that what God values and what we tend to value are often entirely different. We seek popularity, prosperity, prestige, and political power. We envy and admire people who possess such things. We want them for ourselves. Jesus lets us know that God couldn't care less about our high-profile desires. God values those who are poor and meek and hungry. God celebrates the merciful, the pure in heart, and the peacemakers. God blesses those our world hardly notices. And, God's blessing lasts a whole lot longer than the world's admiration!

What kind of people do you admire and value?

Lord, you love the least—those people who are of little interest to us—the poor, the lowly, and the unremarkable.You remind us that those we often choose last are first in line for your kingdom.The people we think of as broken, you call beloved and blessed. Help me to learn to value what you value, to love as you love, to see as you see . . . and respond accordingly. In your name, I pray. AMEN.

SHINE

Read: Matthew 5:14–16

Let your light shine before others, so that they may see your
good works and give glory to your Father in heaven.
MATTHEW 5:16

THOUGHTFUL MEN AND women find people who always talk about themselves and their exploits to be something of an annoyance. Thankfully, the adolescent desire to impress others with stories of our heroic feats tends to fade with time. With age and experience come an understanding that there is virtue in humility and discretion. We become less and less tolerant of prideful boasting in our lives and in the lives of others. We may even grow in faith to the point where we would prefer that the good we do go unnoticed and upraised. There are many people who diligently and daily labor for the glory of God who would be mortified if their efforts were recognized or celebrated by others.

There are, however, times when we need to allow the light of our good works to shine forth for all to see. This is not for our own edification, but for people to see the light of God shining through us and give glory to God for the goodness witnessed. In a speech in 1994, Nelson Mandela famously said, *"We are all meant to shine, as children do. We are born to make manifest the glory of God that is within us. It's not just in some of us, it's in everyone. And as we let our light shine, we unconsciously give others permission to do the same."*

How can you allow your light to shine this week?

Lord, without my either being or appearing overly proud or boastful, help your light to shine through me as a beacon to those around me. Not my light, but your light. Shine through me today. In Jesus' name, I pray. AMEN.

May 11

THE SERMON ON THE MOUNT

Read: Matthew 5:21–48

You have heard that it was said, "You shall love your neighbor and hate your
enemy." But I say to you, Love your enemies and pray for those who persecute you.
MATTHEW 5:43–44

IN THE SERMON on the Mount, Jesus made six different statements that began *"You*
have heard it said," followed by his own teaching that began *"But I say to you."* Jesus
took the old laws and judgments and held his followers to a much higher standard.
In this passage of scripture, Jesus commanded his followers to confront the world
and those in it with overflowing generosity, self-sacrifice, and heartfelt care. We are
called to tend to the world and our relationships as God does, sending blessings and
serving as a blessing to the good and the bad, the righteous and the unrighteous,
the faithful and the faithless alike. We are to give better than we get from others,
because we have received far better that we deserve from God. That was the way of
Jesus, and Jesus preached that it become our way too.

When will you need to turn the other cheek today?

Lord, you call us to perfection—you call us to live like you . . . and we are not sure that
is possible for us. When struck we feel empowered to fight back, when abused we get abusive,
and when hurt we quickly respond in ways that allow us to collect a lot of eyes and teeth. It's
not that we don't know any other way to live, it's just that we are fearful that if we do as you
say, we will pay a cost too heavy to bear. You tell us to be perfect like God is perfect . . . and that
bar seems far too high for us to clear. What are we to do? Help us with a first step. Help us to
set an example of generosity that we know our world needs, even if we are reluctant to offer it.
In your name, we pray. AMEN.

RADICAL SURGERY

Read: Matthew 5:27–30

If your right eye causes you to sin, tear it out and throw it away; it is better for
you to lose one of your members than for your whole body to be thrown into hell.
MATTHEW 5:29

IN THE GOSPEL of Matthew, Jesus gets serious when it comes to battling sin. If your eye causes you to sin, tear it out. If your right hand causes you to sin, cut it off. When it comes to gaining victory over sin, Jesus advocates radical surgery. Tapering off, weaning yourself off, cutting back a bit on sinful behavior is not a significant enough adjustment—when doing battle with sin, you have got to cut it out.

If you are in the habit of whiling away the hours viewing pornography on the Internet or gambling online, it's time to get rid of your connection. If you are engaging in an extramarital flirtation that threatens to turn into something more, it's time to delete the phone number and stay out of touch. If you drink too much and get crude and hurtful when you are out with the guys, it's time to get new friends. If you don't, Jesus is clear—you may find yourself in hell. When you are bound by sin, when you are being overrun by your lusts and swept away by your desires, it's time to get serious, it's time to cut it out, it's time for radical surgery.

What sin do you need to get serious about removing from your life?

Lord, you know where I falter. You know there are behaviors and vices that I need to rid
from my life. You know how I desire to be a better person than I currently am. Grant me the
courage, strength, and resolve to cut sins from my life that keep me from you, and keep me from
being the best me. In your name, I pray. AMEN.

May 13

KEEPING OUR WORD

Read: Matthew 5:33–37

"You shall not swear falsely, but carry out the vows you have made. . . . Let your word be 'Yes,Yes' or 'No, No'; anything more than this comes from the evil one."
MATTHEW 5:33 & 37

As PEOPLE OF faith, we are cautioned in the scripture to be careful about what we promise. Jesus said we should respond to requests made of us by saying *"yes"* or *"no;"* any further commitment can be hazardous. Speak plainly and clearly and don't make promises you can't keep. Do not give your word unless you are absolutely sure you can make good on it. If you do make vows and commitments, carry them out to their completion. We have all broken promises at times and failed to follow through on commitments we have made. Thankfully, scripture asserts that God forgives us for those shortcomings. However, the goal is still before us—to be people of our word.

Do you promise more than you can deliver and make commitments you can't keep?

Lord, I too often make casual promises and give my word without fully counting the costs. Help me to be more careful when I give my word, and give me resolve to make good on the commitments and vows I make. In Jesus' name, I pray. AMEN.

May 14

DOING THE UNEXPECTED

Read: Matthew 5:38–42

You have heard that it was said,"An eye for an eye and a tooth for a tooth."
But I say to you, . . . if anyone strikes you on the right cheek, turn the other
also; . . . and if anyone forces you to go one mile, go also the second mile.
MATTHEW 5:38 & 41

THE TEACHINGS OF Jesus are curious and demanding. Jesus seems to expect the impossible from us. Turn the other cheek? When someone harms us or tries to harm us, we are to offer ourselves up for more punishment? This is like the lie we told ourselves when we were young that it takes real courage to walk away from a fight. But we know better. Strong people don't let themselves get pushed around. Successful people stand their ground. Proud people don't back down from a fight. The idea that when struck we would just take it . . . is simply not the way to make it in the world. If someone forces us to go a mile, that means they are stronger than we are. The only way to regain our power is to refuse to bend to the demands of those who push us.

What Jesus knew and taught is that for relationships to change, for intractable situations to be resolved, for the cycle of anger, resentment, and violence to abate in our lives and our world, we have to be willing to do the unexpected. Meeting anger with love, meeting disappointment with hope, meeting judgment with mercy, holding back when we want to lash out, going the distance when we would rather give up—that is how the world changes. That is how we change.

What unexpected act can you perform this week that might bring about needed change?

Lord, I react so instinctively sometimes. I respond without thinking. I make gut decisions. I am more than willing to fight when challenged. I am part of a cycle of violence and careless living that keeps your world in bondage. Somehow, I need to live differently, act differently, and respond differently if that cycle is ever to be broken. Help me to do the unexpected so that unhealthy patterns of living might change. In Jesus' name, I pray. AMEN.

May 15

THAT ALL MAY GROW

Read: Matthew 5:43–47

> *God makes his sun rise on the evil and on the good, and sends*
> *rain on the righteous and on the unrighteous.*
> MATTHEW 5:45

WE MAKE JUDGMENTS and evaluate people every day; in fact, we do this every moment of our lives. We judge and evaluate the situations we find ourselves in, as well as the opportunities and challenges we encounter. We try to figure out where our time and effort is best placed. We choose to invest ourselves in the good and promising employee. We focus our attention on the attractive and captivating man or woman. We even offer a bit more of ourselves to the child of ours who behaves better. We judge the good and the bad, and we invest ourselves accordingly.

Jesus tells us that this is not the way of God. God allows sun and rain to nourish the good and the evil, the just and the unjust, the righteous and the unrighteous. Sunlight and rain are the ingredients for growth, and God makes sure everyone gets their fair share—even when God is displeased with their growth trajectory. But why? Why waste resources on unproductive and undeserving people and situations? Why should good things happen to bad people? God believes that bad people, when given the right opportunity and care, can choose to be good people. And frankly, that is good news for all of us less than perfect people.

Upon whom do we need to allow a little of our attention and care to rain?

Lord, I don't like wasting my time and effort on people and situations that appear unproductive. Why should I spend time with a troublesome employee? Why should I further commit myself to my spouse when the relationship seems to be going nowhere? Why should I work hard for a boss who does not give me the credit or the compensation I deserve? Lord, help me grasp the truth that you do more than hold out hope for those who fall short of your glory. You give everyone exactly what they need to grow and mature into good, faithful, compassionate people. Please help me to do the same. In your name, I pray. AMEN.

HOW TO PRAY

Read: Matthew 6:5–15

Pray then in this way: Our Father in heaven, hallowed be your name.
MATTHEW 6:9

JESUS TAUGHT HIS disciples to pray. His instructions were clear and direct. Pray in secret. Don't practice your piety before others. Don't offer wordy, effusive prayers. Pray simply. Trust that God knows what you need before you speak, but pray anyway. Always pray for forgiveness, and put your prayer into action by forgiving others. For Jesus, prayer should be intimate and concise, and prompt us to deal with others as we have requested that God deal with us. This might all be a way of saying to his disciples—and to us all—don't over think, just pray.

How do you pray?

Lord, let your will be done in my life and in your world. Provide for my needs. Forgive me, and help me to forgive others. Encourage me when I am tempted to falter in my faith. In Jesus' name, I pray. AMEN.

May 17

A FOLLOWING HEART

Read: Matthew 6:19–21

For where your treasure is, there your heart will be also.
MATTHEW 6:21

THIS BRIEF TEXT is often used to guilt people into giving money to the church. It is used as a way of saying, *"If you really care, if you really love Jesus, if your heart were in the right place, you would be more generous in your giving."* There is no question that Jesus cared about money. He preached and taught about it often. However, Jesus' interest in money had to do with his understanding that our love for money can get in the way of love of God and neighbor. Therefore, Jesus was always encouraging his followers to have a healthy relationship with money—use it, don't love it.

In this scripture, if you look closely at it, you will not find an admonition for greater generosity but a strategic way of investing ourselves so that we are prompted to engage in more meaningful pursuits and relationships. While it is tempting to interpret this passage of scripture as meaning that what you fund is what you care about, the ordering of the passage does not support that emphasis. This memorable text suggests that if you want your heart to be in a new place, invest your resources in that location. Place your treasure where you want your heart to wind up. When thoughtfully considered, your checkbook can help to facilitate a set of new and better priorities in your life—because your heart has a way of following your treasure!

Where do you want your heart to be?

Lord, where do you want me to invest myself in the future? Let me know. Encourage me to take a leap of faith and pour my resources in the direction you want me to go. In Jesus' name, I pray. AMEN.

May 18

DO NOT WORRY . . . *TRUST!*

Read: Matthew 6:25–34

> *Therefore, I tell you, do not worry about your life, what you will eat or what*
> *you will drink, or about your body, what you will wear. Is not life more than*
> *food, and the body more than clothing? . . . But strive first for the kingdom of*
> *God and his righteousness, and all these things will be given to you as well.*
> MATTHEW 6:25 & 33

TO FOLLOW JESUS means to dismiss anxiety. *"Do not worry"* is the way this command
is phrased, but the implicit admonition is to *trust*. Don't worry, *trust God* is the divine imperative for our earthly living. That is all well and good, but simply telling
chronically worried people to refrain from anxiety gets us only so far. How do we
banish our worries in favor of trust?

The end of this passage of scripture offers us an avenue forward: don't worry,
just do the right thing. Don't live fearfully, live righteously. Don't get anxious, just
do the work of God in the world . . . and everything else will fall into place. Jesus
says you can take your mind off your worries by fully engaging in God's work. If
you have ever tried it, you know it is true. The antidote to fretful anxiety is righteous activity!

What worries you most?

Lord, when I sit idly, I find myself overcome by worry. When I get active, and pursue the
righteousness you call me to, anxiety has a way of dissolving from my heart and mind. Help
me to occupy my mind and my life with your work so that my living doesn't get crowded out
by my worry. In your name, I pray. AMEN.

May 19

JUDGMENTALISM

Read: Matthew 7:1–5

> *First take the log out of your own eye, and then you will see*
> *clearly to take the speck out of your neighbor's eye.*
> *MATTHEW 7:5*

WE JUDGE PEOPLE all the time. We are quick to criticize. And we critique others as if we were entirely above reproach. Jesus' teaching is clear. Don't judge. How would we like the standards by which we evaluate others to be applied to our lives? Why not deal with our own issues, work on our own rough edges, and handle the glaring faults in our own lives before we try correcting someone else. Could Jesus' teaching be more direct? Work on bettering ourselves—leave the judging to God.

Whom do you judge?

Lord, who made me the judge of other people? No one! You are the judge, I am not. Keep me in my place. Help me to focus on my own issues while leaving the evaluation to you. In Jesus' name, I pray. AMEN.

May 20

SIMPLE

Read: Matthew 7:12

In everything do to others as you would have them do
to you; for this is the law and the prophets.
MATTHEW 7:12

LIFE CAN BE complicated—there is no question about that. Relational and vocational dilemmas abound. We have concerns about our health, our finances, and our children. Much of the time we feel lost and uncertain about what path to take and what direction to go in life. However, while life is complicated, our living doesn't have to be. Jesus said that to live according to the will of God, all we need to do is treat other people like we would like to be treated. In every decision and difficult circumstance in which we find ourselves, we can simply ask ourselves how we would like to be treated, and act accordingly. If we treat others with the respect, dignity, and compassion we desire, then perhaps we will find a way forward in life that is not so stressful and confusing. This is not being simplistic, because knowing what do and actually doing it can be quite a challenge. However, knowing the right way to live may just be as simple as Jesus suggests. When you find yourself in a difficult situation, ask yourself how you would like to be treated, and respond in kind.

How do you like people to treat you?

Lord, life feels complicated and challenging . . . and, in truth, there are times when I just feel downright overwhelmed. I realize, however, that I might be making too much of the difficult situations and relationships I find myself in. What if I based all my decisions and actions on how I would like to be treated? What if I fulfilled your will by simply doing as you ask? Life can be hard, but perhaps my living doesn't have to be. For this I pray, in your name. AMEN.

May 21

Good Fruit

Read: Matthew 7:15–20

> *A good tree cannot bear bad fruit, nor can a bad tree bear*
> *good fruit. . . .You will know them by their fruits.*
> MATTHEW 7:18 & 20

MOST OF US are filled with good intentions. We don't begin our day planning how we can cut corners, lie, or fill people with unreasonable expectations. Most of us start our days hopeful that we can live honestly, truthfully, and with integrity. But as the day wears on we are pressed, pushed, and pressured in a thousand different directions. By day's end we have said things we didn't mean, we have made promises we don't know how we will keep, and we have made commitments that are not in line with our best intentions.

The good news—and the bad news—is that intentions, expectations, and commitments mean nothing. Our ideas and instincts do not amount to anything until we put them into action. We are not judged by what we thought about doing or by what we intended to do or by what we planned to refrain from doing. We are known not by the promise of our lives but by the product of our lives. In the end, we are judged by what we have produced—our fruits. Did we produce good fruit or bad fruit?

What good thought can you manifest in a good act this week?

Lord, I am indeed filled with good intentions, but I find I am often hard pressed to follow through on them. It is not so much that I feel like a bad person, but I do feel like a person who thinks better than I act. Help me to produce good fruit. Help me to convert good intentions into good actions. Help me to build a legacy of good work in your world. In Jesus' name, I pray. AMEN.

May 22

THE CENTURION'S FAITH

Read: Matthew 8:5–13

When Jesus heard him, he was amazed and said to those who followed him, "Truly I tell you, in no one in Israel have I found such faith."
MATTHEW 8:10

IT TOOK A lot to impress Jesus. When we consider all that Jesus has done for us, it would be beyond presumptuous to assume that any of our actions might fill Jesus with amazement. Unless, of course, we find some new way to amaze Jesus with the depths to which we are willing to sink in our relationships with others and with God! It must be a very rare occasion when Jesus is pleasantly surprised by our actions.

However, we are told that a Roman centurion's willingness to believe, without much evidence to support his faith, filled Jesus with a degree of awe. The Gospels tell us that believing without seeing did serve to impress Jesus. Being able to trust God when you are filled with a world of doubt is an act of faith that is deeply moving to Jesus.

Are you generally inclined toward doubt or faith?

Lord, I like to have all the facts in front of me before I am willing to take a leap of faith. However, that is not faith; that is a desire for knowledge. I long for evidence while you request belief. Help me to set my needs aside so that I can pursue your desires . . . perhaps even to your amazement. In Jesus' name, I pray. AMEN.

May 23

WITH WHOM DO YOU EAT?

Read: Matthew 9:9–13

*When the Pharisees saw this, they said to Jesus' disciples, "Why
does your teacher eat with tax collectors and sinners?"*
MATTHEW 9:11

IN SCHOOL THERE was always the "cool kids' table." Maybe you sat at it, maybe you
didn't, but you remember the table. In fact, there were likely a few "cool" tables,
each varying by degrees of popularity. The cool table. The *really* cool table. The
super cool table. The rest of the tables, at which the vast majority of kids sat, were
entirely forgettable. Every kid's dream was to move up to a better table, but that
rarely happened. You sat where you sat. Your friends were your friends. And either
you were either cool or you were not. There was little comingling between cliques.

That was the remarkable thing about Jesus. Jesus broke down barriers. He sat
with people he shouldn't have. He took interest in people others had forgotten
about. And he took flack for it. Jesus was the guy who was more than willing to
move from the cool table to a less desirable table, and most people couldn't understand why. Jesus had a soft spot in his heart for those who found themselves on the
outside of the in-group . . . and so does God.

Who is in your clique, and who do you leave out?

*Lord, there are people I avoid. There are people I make fun of. There are people I can't
stand to be around. In truth, I am fairly certain there are people who feel the same way about
me. Give me the strength, courage, and resolve to sit with people who the world would like to
forget about. Help me to care about people, like you do. In your name, I pray. AMEN.*

May 24

CALLED AND PROVIDED

Read: Matthew 10:1–15

Take no gold, or silver, or copper in your belts, no bag for your journey,
or two tunics, or sandals, or a staff; for laborers deserve their food.
MATTHEW 10:9–10

JESUS CALLED THE twelve disciples to him, and then sent them out on a missionary journey to heal the sick, tend to the tormented in spirit, and preach the good news throughout Israel. They were called to certain work, and they were called away for certain worries. Jesus didn't want the disciples consumed with anxiety over making a living. All they had to do was to do the work assigned to them, and all their needs—not all their wants, but all the basic necessities of life—would be provided. Focus on the calling, let Jesus worry about your living!

If you just followed your calling, would you still worry about making a living?

Lord, what if I just did the work you assigned to me? Instead of worrying about making money and having the right wardrobe and living in the best house—what if I just did what you asked me to do? Imagine that. Do your will, and you will provide for me. Help me to understand how easy life can be if I just follow your direction. In your name, I pray. AMEN.

May 25

REJECTION

Read: Matthew 10:5–15

> *If anyone will not welcome you or listen to your words, shake off*
> *the dust from your feet as you leave that house or town.*
> MATTHEW 10:14

REJECTION IS PAINFUL. It can wound even the stoutest of spirits. Even if it is a message or a product or a service people are rejecting, it can feel downright personal if you are the one making the offer. The fishermen who became Jesus' first disciples must have been familiar with rejection—their claims of Jesus as a servant-king would have been routinely met with skepticism and indignation. Jesus' wise council was for the disciples to shake the dust from their feet when they were unwelcome or unheeded. This was to be an act of condemnation, but it is also an expression of healthy spiritual determination. Do not allow rejection to cling to you; literally shake it off like the dust of the road. Forget the failure. Continue on. Begin again.

Is there an experience of rejection that continues to cling to you?

Lord, I feel the pain of rejection so deeply and personally. I often avoid taking important risks at work, in relationships, and in my faith because I don't want to chance the embarrassment of failure. However, this may limit your call on my life, and the work you intend for me to do. Help me to share myself boldly with the world, and when I meet rejection, allow me to shake it off like the dirt I loosen from my shoes at the end of a hard day's work. For this I pray, in your name. AMEN.

May 26

Taking Criticism

Read: Matthew 11:2–15

When John heard in prison what the Messiah was doing, he sent word by his disciples and said to him, "Are you the one who is to come, or are we to wait for another?"
Matthew 11:2–3

John was confused if not downright disappointed. Jesus, one of his own disciples, the one he believed was to lead the Jewish people back to faith and back to God wasn't acting much like a Messiah. Jesus freely broke Sabbath laws, he seemed to dismiss important religious traditions, he didn't appear to be headed in a direction that would bring an end to Roman occupation and priestly abuse. So, with some exasperation, John offered a backhanded criticism of Jesus. *"Are you the Messiah or not?""And if you are, you better start acting like it."*

How did Jesus respond to that criticism? By praising John! Instead of retaliating by pointing out John's flaws and failings, Jesus regales John's faithfulness and ministry. And in doing so, we see the lights of God's kingdom begin to flicker on. Retaliation—verbal or physical—does not bring about the peace of God. Peace ushers in peace. When you are criticized, respond with praise and see what happens!

How do you respond to criticism?

Lord, I do not like being maligned. It is humiliating, and it makes me want to strike back. Help me learn not only to turn the other cheek but also to respond with graciousness and love. In Jesus' name, I pray. AMEN.

CHANGING THE RULES

Read: Matthew 12:1–14

For the Son of Man is lord of the sabbath.
MATTHEW 12:8

THERE WERE RULES that governed Sabbath in Jesus' time. You couldn't work on the Sabbath. You couldn't enjoy recreational activities. It wasn't even clear if you could help an ailing animal or human being that was suffering on the Sabbath—which appears to have made absolutely no sense to Jesus. Who was the Sabbath for anyway? Human beings or God—or both? And if the Sabbath had anything to do with glorifying God, did the Son of God not have the right to do the will of God on that particular day of the week?

Sometimes our rules get in the way of the good works God wants us to do. Rules can get in the way of mercy. Rules can restrict forgiveness. Rules have a way of nullifying grace. What if we just tried to love God and love our neighbors, as if those two rules were the only ones that really mattered? What if all things are negotiable, except for love?

What rules have you made that inhibit love, grace, and mercy?

Lord, I do have rules. I want to be respected. I want others to treat me as I have treated them. I demand that life be fair. When someone breaks any one of those rules, I dole out punishment. I speak hurtful words. I castigate people behind their back. I treat them as if I have never made a similar mistake in my life. I, I, I . . . perhaps I should be less interested in the rules I set up and administer and look to your rules instead. I should focus on loving you and loving others. Lord, your will, not mine, be done. In your name, I pray. AMEN.

May 28

FAMILY VALUES

Read: Matthew 12:46–50

> *For whoever does the will of my Father in heaven is my brother and sister and mother.*
> MATTHEW 12:50

FAMILIES ARE COMPLICATED. Family histories can be painful. And even the highest functioning families have their fair share of skeletons stuffed away in closets. Family life is messy, but family was just the kind of community Jesus tried to cultivate. Jesus' concept of family was both broad and challenging. A family member of Jesus Christ could be anyone who did the will of God. Blood relations were not nearly as important to Jesus as faith connections. For Jesus, values define God's family—not our values, but God's. If you are willing to obey your Father in heaven, then you can be assured that you have Jesus as a brother.

What are your family values?

Lord, my family of origin often disappoints me. If I am honest with myself, I know I must disappoint my family as well. Even the best families are saddled with grief, hurt feelings, and unmet expectations. Why you would want to get into the family business is beyond my ability to understand. And yet, family is what you call us to. So, help me to take my place at your side as your sibling by trying to do the will of our Father in this world. For you are all the family I ever need. In your name, I pray. AMEN.

May 29

WEEDS AND THE WHEAT

Read: Matthew 13:24–30, 36–43

The slaves said to him, "Then do you want us to go and gather them?" But he replied, "No; for in gathering the weeds you would uproot the wheat along with them."
MATTHEW 13:28B–29

MANY OF US cannot tell the difference between weeds and good plantings. When weeding, we might be able to guess correctly most of the time, but an untrained eye or an unknowledgeable gardener threatens the whole garden. An unweeded garden may not be an ideal situation for good plants to thrive, but pulling up the good with the bad is even less preferable. Jesus' admonition is clear: if you can't tell the difference between the weeds and the wheat, stay out of the field. Leave the judgment of the garden to the one who planted it in the first place, which it to say: leave the judgment of the world to God.

Who do you have no right, nor the appropriate knowledge, to judge?

Lord, if I try to separate the weeds and the wheat, I know I will make a mess of the field. I will do more damage than good. Help me to leave the judgment of the world to you, while I spend time trying to sort through the weeds and the wheat in my own life. In your name, I pray. AMEN.

May 30

THE KINGDOM OF HEAVEN . . .

Read: Matthew 13:31–32, 44–50

> *Jesus put before them another parable:"The kingdom of heaven is
> like a mustard seed that someone took and sowed in his field."*
> MATTHEW 13:31

JESUS DID NOT say what the kingdom of heaven *is*, he merely explained what the kingdom of heaven *is like*. The kingdom of heaven *is like* a mustard seed. The kingdom of God *is like* yeast. The kingdom of heaven *is like* hidden treasure and a pearl of great price and a net thrown into the sea. If Jesus didn't know exactly what the kingdom of heaven *is*, then it might be fair to say that none of us do either. But Jesus knew what it was *like*. It is more expansive than we can imagine, it is worth any price we must pay, and it is open to all who pursue it.

What do you imagine the kingdom of heaven to be?

Lord, I don't what heaven is exactly. I suspect it is eternal and loving and beautiful like you. Help me to live my life in ways that allow me to one day see that which I can now only imagine. In your name, I pray. AMEN.

May 31

A COMPANION IN THE STORM

Read: Matthew 14:22–33

Peter answered Jesus, "Lord, if it is you, command me to come to you on the water."
MATTHEW 14:28

WE ARE SURPRISINGLY fearful people. We live in the safest time and the safest place in the history of the world, and yet many of us are drowning in dread. We suffer from financial phobias, social stresses, and threats of terror. We fear being lost in an abyss where we are on our own with no one to protect us or reach down to pull us out of the pit.

On a dark and windswept night, as the waves smacked their boat, jarring loose the nailed planks of their hull, the disciples felt as though they had been left to face the terror of a sea storm on their own. Even the sight of Jesus filled them with fear—they assumed him to be a ghost! In fact, Peter tested the apparition, saying essentially, *"If it is you, Lord, you're going to have to prove it to me."* So often when we are filled with terror we see ghosts and demons and specters of darkness where there are none! In the end, the miracle of this story was not that Jesus walked on water or even that Peter treaded on the stormy seas for a few brief moments—the true miracle was that Jesus was with the disciples in the storm. The disciples didn't need to walk toward Jesus, because Jesus had already made his way toward them. Not only is Jesus with us in the storm, but he is also able to reach out and catch us when we begin to drown in fear.

When do you feel alone?

Lord, the chaos and uncertainty of life swirl about me and the fear of it all can make me feel like I am drowning. What is worse, I feel like I might be drowning alone, with no one to hear my cries. Help me to trust that you are with me—in the boat, in the water, in the wind, and even at the bottom of the sea. You are everywhere, and therefore there is nowhere I can sink apart from your sight and your presence. Thank you for that. In your name, I pray. AMEN.

June 1

GETTING OUT OF THE BOAT

Read: Matthew 14:22–33

So Peter got out of the boat, started walking on the water, and came toward Jesus.
MATTHEW 14:29

WE OFTEN THINK first about Peter's failure in this story. Peter got out on the water, and the wind and the waves so rattled his resolve that he began to sink and he needed Jesus to save him. If Peter had more faith, perhaps he wouldn't have needed a helping hand! What we often forget about are the other eleven disciples huddled in their little boat, unwilling to approach Jesus. Peter may have started to sink into the water, but the other disciples were not even willing to get out of the boat!

It has been said that if you want to walk on water, you need to be willing to get out of the boat. Peter certainly failed to make it all the way toward Jesus, but by taking a risk and stepping out onto the water he had an encounter with Jesus that affected the rest of his life. After reading this story, why would we assume that being saved by Jesus is a bad thing? It may just be the most important experience in the world! Walking on water would be a great achievement to be sure, but getting saved by Jesus is an even greater blessing.

Are you willing to step out in faith in order to step toward Jesus?

Dear Lord, I fear failure. I fear taking risks that have the potential to sink me. I prefer the safety of the boat I am in. So I never get out into the wind and the waves, I never move beyond my familiar environment, and I never throw caution to the wind in pursuit of you. Is it any wonder I don't get caught up in you? Help me to step out of the boat and into the waves so that I can find myself finally and securely in your hands. In your name, I pray. AMEN.

June 2

HEART CONDITION

Read: Matthew 15:10–20

> *It is not what goes into the mouth that defiles a per-*
> *son, but it is what comes out of the mouth that defiles.*
> *MATTHEW 15:11*

TO BE DEFILED is to be made dirty in our eyes and in the eyes of God. We tend to think that it is external influences that compromise our cleanliness, like the mud puddles we used to splash in as children. But it is not our outside that God is most interested in. God wants us clean on the inside. The gossip, slander, and foul language that comes out of our mouths are signals of a deadly heart condition within us. God is much less interested in the cholesterol, fat, and carbohydrates we ingest, and much more interested in cleaning up the language, criticism, and cynicism that proceed from our hearts. A clean mouth can be the best way to a healthy heart.

Are you careless or hurtful with your words?

Lord, I swear, I gossip, and I do not realize how hurtful my words can be to others. I am completely oblivious to how my words reflect on my own spiritual health. I have a heart condition, Lord. I need your guidance, presence, and intercession if I am to receive a clean bill of health. Help me, for I seem unable to help myself. In your name, I pray. AMEN.

June 3

THE SYROPHOENICIAN WOMAN

Read: Matthew 15:21–28

Then Jesus answered her, "Woman, great is your faith! Let it be done
for you as you wish." And her daughter was healed instantly.
MATTHEW 15:28

THIS IS POSSIBLY the most disturbing story of Jesus' entire ministry. A foreign woman approached Jesus in hope that he might heal her daughter, and Jesus refused. In fact, in a derogatory fashion he referred to the woman and her daughter as dogs. We don't like this story because Jesus doesn't present as the nice, thoughtful, and sensitive man we believe him to be. What Jesus *is* in this story, however, is *human*, and that should come as no small blessing to us. Jesus was a real person with real biases, dislikes, and cultural insensitivities—just like us.

The story ended quite differently than it began. The woman persisted in her request for her daughter's healing, and Jesus relented and granted the woman her wish. The woman was persistent, and Jesus was moved. What a gift it is to know that Jesus can be moved by us and by our desire for his healing.

If Jesus is moved by us, should we not allow ourselves to be moved by others?

Lord, too often I am immovable. I get set in my ways, in my opinions, and in my biases. I
am crude in my dealings with people who I perceive as somehow less than I am. However, Lord,
you show me the way. You show me that we can be insensitive, and yet we can change. Help me
to be moved, help me to change, and help me to be more like you. In your name, I pray. AMEN.

June 4

Praise Be to God

Read: Matthew 15:29–31

The crowd was amazed when they saw the mute speaking, the maimed whole,
the lame walking, and the blind seeing. And they praised the God of Israel.
MATTHEW 15:31

JESUS PERFORMED AMAZING signs and wonders in the world, and people gave the praise for those acts to God. Today when we see wondrous deeds accomplished in the world, we often praise the person doing them—we give them an award, we recognize them in some official way, or we put them on TV. When we accomplish something ourselves, we want the credit for it, and if we don't get the recognition we feel we deserve, we claim we have been disrespected. Jesus didn't clamor for respect and recognition. Jesus worked so that people praised God.

Do you work for your glory or for God's?

Lord, I know my priorities are skewed. I work to get ahead. I work to get noticed. I work to make a name for myself. Can it be any surprise that at the end of the day I feel empty and anxious? What if I worked for you? What if I worked so that you get noticed and your name is glorified? Would that allow me to feel more fulfilled and less stressed? I suspect so. Help me to get my priorities in line . . . in line with you. In Jesus' name, I pray. AMEN.

June 5

CHURCH FOUNDATIONS

Read: Matthew 16:13–23

And I tell you, you are Peter, and on this rock I will build my church, and the gates
of Hades will not prevail against it. . . . Get behind me, Satan! You are a stumbling
block to me; for you are setting your mind not on divine things but on human things.
MATTHEW 16:18 & 23

PETER GOT IT right and then got it very wrong. Peter announced that Jesus was
the Messiah, but then he went on to instruct Jesus on how to be a king. At one
moment Jesus heralded Peter as the foundation of the church, and in the next he
denounced Peter as Satan. How often the good and the bad coexist in people and
in institutions!

This is true for the church. There can be moments when we get things right
and something of the divine reality of the cosmos shines through our efforts, and
then a few moments later the church can display and reflect all the sin and brokenness of the world. The church can save, but it can also abuse. It can guide, and it can
mislead. It can be prophetic when it needs to be, but also silent when it shouldn't
be. Jesus proclaims that his church will be a rock as well as a stumbling block.
What a curious choice of institutions through which to be revealed to the world!
However, it is no more mystifying than God's choice to use flawed human beings to
express God's will within the cosmos.

How does it feel to be able to be both so good and so bad?

Lord, what a complex institution the church is. What complex creatures we are. We can
be loving and evil, friend and enemy, liberator and oppressor. I do not know why this is, and I
have even less of an idea why you would choose to be revealed through us. But I thank you for
making that choice. It is a gift to know that my flawed nature can at times reflect a little bit
of your divinity. In Jesus' name, I pray. AMEN.

June 6

DENYING SELF

Read: Matthew 16:24–28

> *Then Jesus told his disciples, "If any want to become my followers, let*
> *them deny themselves and take up their cross and follow me."*
> MATTHEW 16:24

SELF-DENIAL IS NOT merely giving up the things we long for and lust after. In a society and culture that places incredible emphasis on self-realization and self-actualization—and as a result, self-absorption—a call to self-denial could not be more jarring. The call to self-denial is a call to give up one's personal identity. It is a call to give up our sense of individuality and recognize that everyone and all creation are part of a whole. We are one. There is no "other." The divisions and separation and sense of alienation and fear between people are a result of misunderstanding the fact that we are one and the same, even though we appear different and disconnected from one another. When we give up our self, we can finally take on our true identity—one people, one family.

Do you focus too much on yourself?

Lord, I look out at the world and I can feel alone and disconnected, as if no one really understands me. The world itself seems consumed with division, alienation, and isolation. What if the root of all our problems is that we do not recognize our inherent interconnectedness? What if we are really One—one with you, one with each other, one with all creation? I know it is time for me to shed my sense of self for a greater sense of you . . . I am just not sure how to begin. Come to my aid . . . yet again. In Jesus' name, I pray. AMEN.

June 7

NUMBER ONE!

Read: Matthew 18:1–5

Whoever becomes humble like this child is greatest in the kingdom of heaven.
MATTHEW 18:4

THE DISCIPLES WANTED to know who was number one, who was at the head of the class, who was the greatest of them all. To make his point, Jesus took a small child and placed the child in their midst as a way of teaching them that a humble child is greater than the most impressive of kings. This instruction might be lost on those of us who believe that children are the most precious gift in the world. For many of us, our children are the greatest gifts we have every received in life. Of course children would be highly valued in heaven, because they are all ready number one in our lives here on earth!

However, in antiquity, children were of little to no value. In a subsistence existence, a child was a drain on a family's resources until they were old enough to work and make a contribution to the whole. And because the infant and child mortality rate was so high, a child could take up valuable resources and wind up dying without making the slightest contribution to the family's well-being. Children were the least important people in the world that Jesus lived and taught in. But what is weak and undervalued and unappreciated by us is beloved by God. Who is the greatest? Who is number one? Who will be first? Jesus said it time and time again: those we think of last.

Who do you overlook?

Lord, I overlook so many people in my drive to be first. I want to be a winner. I want to be great in everyone's eyes, especially my own. I suspect it is my focus on myself that often prevents me from seeing the beauty and value of others. You are number one . . . perhaps I will finally choose to live like you, to love like you, and to understand value as you do. For this I pray, in your name. AMEN.

June 8

HOW MANY TIMES?

Read: Matthew 18:21–22

Then Peter came and said to Jesus, "Lord, if another member of
the church sins against me, how often should I forgive?"
MATTHEW 18:21

DEPENDING ON THE Bible translation, the answer to Peter's question is either seventy-seven times, or seventy times seven—which is a whopping four hundred ninety times. The point is that we should forgive often and not keep too close a tally of infractions. The rationale may be more difficult to accept than it is to understand. We have been forgiven so much by God, how can we withhold an ounce of forgiveness from others? We shouldn't. And forgiveness should be quick to come, as well.

When someone offers us an unkind word or dredges up a past and painful history, when a friend or family member reacts inappropriately in the heat of a given moment, we can stew about it or forgive the offense and move on. The trouble with holding back our forgiveness is that days turn into weeks and week into months . . . and then years pass and hearts grow hard and estrangement deepens, all because no one was willing to apologize or forgive. How often should we forgive? A ton, and without delay.

Why do you withhold forgiveness?

Lord, you have forgiven me . . . I should forgive others. It is simple to understand, and yet so difficult to implement. What if someone doesn't ask for my forgiveness? Or what if the sin or offense is too great? What am I supposed to do then? I know what you have said: forgive seventy-seven times, four hundred ninety times, forgive as we would want to be forgiven, forgive often and a lot—which is exactly what you offer us. Thank you, teacher. In your name, I pray. AMEN.

June 9

MERCY

Read: Matthew 18:23–35

You wicked slave! . . . Should you not have had mercy
on your fellow slave, as I had mercy on you?
MATTHEW 18:32B–33

JESUS TOLD A story about a man who had a large debt forgiven by his master, only to ruthlessly demand the payment of a much smaller debt owed to him by another servant. This is hypocrisy at its most virulent. When someone has been forgiven an immense debt, how can they justify their own unwillingness to return that same grace and mercy to others?

Jesus told this story so that we might understand the appropriate way to respond to God's mercy. We are sinners through and through; we sin against God and one another by what we do and by what we fail to do—and yet God has forgiven us our failings and continues to forgive us still. How can we not forgive others as freely when we have been injured or wronged? For Jesus the answer was implicit—forgive the little sins others inflict upon you, because God has forgiven the immensity of your own sin.

Who do you need to forgive?

Lord, I hang on to petty grievances and grudges as if they were my lovers. When I am wronged, I fume, I rage, and I look for an opportunity for payback. I am all too often the ungrateful servant. When you have had such mercy on me and forgiven all my faults and failings, I should do the same for others . . . even when they do not ask for it. Help me and forgive me, for my reluctance to extend mercy to others is part of my own great sin. In Jesus' name, I pray. AMEN.

June 10

FAIR OR GENEROUS?

Read: Matthew 20:1–16

Am I not allowed to do what I choose with what belongs to
me? Or are you envious because I am generous?
MATTHEW 20:15

THE LABORERS DID not understand their employer's motives, and they became disgruntled. They got the compensation they had agreed to, but after working all day long, they were displeased that those who worked only an hour received the exact same paycheck. How was that fair? How can the last to be chosen receive as much as the first to get to work?

It is the great complaint of teenagers and perhaps people of every age when preferential treatment appears to be given to others, *"It's not fair!"* While we do not object to being privileged ourselves, we find it intensely objectionable when the balances seem to be titled in favor of others. But do we really want God to be fair with us? Fair means that we get exactly what we deserve. Do we really want God to give us what we deserve, or do we prefer God to be generous with us? In truth, *fair* is not all that great a deal. In the end, it is not our choice. God has chosen to give all of us better than we deserve. God is not fair, God is far better than that… our God is generous. We should be too.

Which do you prefer - fairness or generosity?

Lord, I should just be grateful. Every day I should count my blessings and realize you have given me more than I need. When I see your favor poured out abundantly on the lives of others, I shouldn't grumble—I should celebrate! You are so good to us all. Thank you. Your goodness inspires me to try to live by your example—which is yet another gift to be thankful for! In Jesus' name, I pray. AMEN.

June 11

JOCKEYING FOR POSITION

Read: Matthew 20:20–28

And Jesus said to her, "What do you want?" She said to him, "Declare that these two sons of mine will sit, one at your right hand and one at your left, in your kingdom."
MATTHEW 20:21

FOR SOME REASON, James and John's mother made an embarrassingly bold request of Jesus. She asked for her two sons to have the best seats in Jesus' kingdom. Perhaps she was the kind of parent who always advocated for her children to get ahead. Perhaps she was still annoyed that Jesus' call to her sons had left her husband alone in his fishing boat with no one to help him. Or maybe James and John had constantly shared their desire with their mother, and she was fed up with their unwillingness to act on their own impulses.

Whatever the case, she did not know what she was asking for, and Jesus told her as much. Positions in the kingdom are not Jesus' to grant. However, to choose to live like Jesus in this world was all a matter of will and passion. For all their desire, James and John did not wind up on either side of Jesus. On the cross, Jesus was flanked by two criminals—one on his right and the other on his left. Seating in the kingdom of heaven will be arranged by God, and jockeying for position next to Jesus can cost us dearly. We might want to be careful what we wish for and, instead, simply focus on doing what Jesus asks of us.

Do you want to be close to Jesus?

Lord, I want to live my life in close relationship to you. However, I do not really know what that kind of intimacy will cost. What will you ask me to do? Where will following you lead me? Does standing by your side mean hanging on a cross one day? I don't know . . . All I know is that living apart from you is not an option for me any longer. I want to be with you, on earth and in heaven. I will do my best to follow and leave the seating arrangements to you. In your name, I pray. AMEN.

June 12

WEDDING CRASHERS

Read: Matthew 22:1–14

But when the king came in to see the guests, he noticed a man there who
was not wearing a wedding robe, and he said to him, "Friend, how did you
get in here without a wedding robe?" And the man was speechless.
MATTHEW 22:11–12

THIS IS A disturbing little parable that seems to cast God in a rather unsettling light. God is portrayed as a king who gets angry when his invitations are not accepted—to the point of violence. After inviting everyone that could be found to his banquet, the king punishes a man who tried to sneak his way into the celebration. Apparently, God does not appreciate people who refuse invitations, nor does God have patience for wedding crashers who try to sneak into God's party without being announced.

There is no question that this is a rather dark portrait of God, but it may accurately reflect something of God's character. In the end, the admonition seems clear—we should come when called, and we shouldn't expect a welcome mat to be rolled out for us when we attempt to enter God's presence on our own terms, taking our own sweet time.

How do you respond to God's invitations?

Lord, I like to be discreet about my faith. I tell myself that it is because I don't want to make other people uncomfortable. I like to think of myself as thoughtful that way. But the truth is, I am a bit cowardly when it comes to faith. When you call I find something better to do with my time, and when I am finally interested in encountering you, I try to do so without being noticed. You have invited me into relationship with you, so please help me to walk in the front door to experience your embrace instead of trying to sneak in the back door for a quick peek. In Jesus' name, I pray. AMEN.

June 13

CHOSEN

Read: Matthew 22:1–14

Many are called, but few are chosen.
Matthew 22:14

IT IS EVERY child's worst fear—to be picked last for a game. Kickball, touch football, soccer—whether it be on the sandlot or the school playground—kids heed the call to line up. However, standing in that line fuels insecurity. Who will be picked first? Who will be standing alone at the end as the very last to be selected? Many are called, few are chosen. We understand that reality from a young age, and it is a reality that bears out throughout our lives. We are called here and there, and sometimes we are chosen . . . and sometimes we are not.

God calls all of us to participate with him throughout our entire lives. Unlike so many of the invitations we receive in life, there are no exclusions to this call. What is required, however, is our response. Our best work is saying *"yes"* to that call, saying *"yes"* to God's presence in our lives, and saying *"yes"* to doing the hard work of discipleship. Unlike the sandlots and playgrounds of our childhood, everyone who shows up *is* chosen by God. In fact, in the Gospels Jesus suggests the last will be chosen first and the first will be chosen last!

How is God inviting you into relationship today?

Lord, thank you for the invitation. Thank you for creating me. Thank you for my life, my family, and my friends. Thank you for inviting me to be in relationship with you for eternity. Help me to respond to your invitation every day so that, in the end, I find that I am indeed chosen. In the name of Jesus Christ, I pray. AMEN.

June 14

WARNING

Read: Matthew 24:36–44

> *Keep awake therefore, for you do not know on what day your Lord is com-*
> *ing. But understand this: if the owner of the house had known in what*
> *part of the night the thief was coming, he would have stayed awake and*
> *would not have let his house be broken into. Therefore you also must*
> *be ready, for the Son of Man is coming at an unexpected hour.*
> MATTHEW 24:42–44

JESUS WARNS US to live the life of faith even when we don't think anyone is watching. The warning is a bit alarming, but it alerts us to one of God's deepest desires.
God wants us to live as if we were in his presence even when Jesus is out of sight.
It is most pleasing when the children play nice when they aren't being watched—a
parent's truest pride . . . and God's deepest desire.

How do you act when no one is watching you?

Lord, integrity is doing what is right and pleasing to you even when no one is watching
me. I pray that I can develop that kind of integrity in all my life. In Jesus' name, I pray. AMEN.

June 15

TALENTS

Read: Matthew 25:14–30

To one he gave five talents, to another two, to another one.
MATTHEW 25:15

THE PARABLE OF the talents is as haunting as it is inspiring. Three men are said to have been given a specified number of talents—five, two, and one. A talent was worth the modern day equivalent of approximately $300,000. Therefore, the men were given $1,500,000, $600,000, and $300,000 respectively by their master. The first two men invested their talents, both doubling their master's money, while the man with one talent buried the $300,000 in the back yard for fear of losing it. The first two men were praised by their master and given a promotion, while the man who hid his talent had everything taken away from him.

God gives us talents, abilities, and natural gifts. We don't all have the same number of gifts. Some people possess an extraordinary array of abilities while others' talents are more modest in number—but everyone receives something from God. When we invest our talents in the world, God smiles on us; when we bury and hide our talents, God's countenance is filled with displeasure. Interestingly, it doesn't matter to God how much you have *increased* your talents; all God wants to see is that you are *investing* them and not putting them in a hole in the backyard where no one will ever benefit from them. God has given you talent—your job is to make the most of it!

Is there a buried talent in your life that you need to start investing and using to the glory of God?

Lord, for some reason I hold back from making the most of all that you have given me. I am tempted to play it safe rather than invest my life for all it is worth. Help me to take risks in faith daily, instead of burying the gifts you have given me until they are forgotten and lost. In your name, I pray. AMEN.

June 16

EVALUATION

Read: Matthew 25:31–46

For I was hungry and you gave me food, I was thirsty and you gave me something to drink, I was a stranger and you welcomed me, I was naked and you gave me clothing, I was sick and you took care of me, I was in prison and you visited me.
MATTHEW 25:35–36

THE BIBLE INDICATES that our lives will be evaluated. Most of us don't like the thought of having our lives judged, but according to Jesus, our reluctance will not stay the evaluative process. The good news is that the standards that we will be judged against are very manageable. We will not be judged based on what we believe or what church we go to or how often we read the Bible. Our lives will simply be evaluated on what we do to and for the people our world often chooses to disregard. Did we feed the hungry? Did we offer a drink to the thirsty? Were we welcoming to people we did not know? Did we visit the sick and the incarcerated? Did we take time to be with the people Jesus came into the world to love?

Unfortunately, the answers to these questions may be *"no."* The sick, the hungry, the lonely, the criminal element in our society are those we often choose to shy away from. However, they tend to be the people who are most readily available for relationship. Jesus sets the bar of evaluation low. All we need to do is take an interest in the people whom the world couldn't care less about . . . meaning the people most ready to accept our company. According to Jesus, the bar is low, but the stakes are high.

Do you take time to be with the poor?

Lord, homeless people are all around me when I make my way to work. The hungry and thirsty are always ready to accept assistance. Those suffering illness and incarceration want nothing more than a friendly visit. Why am I such an infrequent companion to those you call me to serve? Help me to get my priorities straight so that your desires might be mine and your evaluation of my life might be pleasing to both of us. For this I pray, in your name. AMEN.

June 17

THE PRAYER

Read: Matthew 26:36–46

And going a little farther, Jesus threw himself on the ground and prayed,"My Father,
if it is possible, let this cup pass from me; yet not what I want but what you want."
MATTHEW *26:39*

FOR MORE THAN two thousand years people have wanted to know who Jesus was and is. There have been church fights and church splits and church-sponsored violence that have accompanied the darkest moments of that questioning. Many a heart and life have been quietly troubled by the questions that surround Jesus' identity. Who was he? Was he real? Was he the Son of God, or God's own self? Was Jesus human or divine or some mixture of the two? Part of the challenge of finding an acceptable answer is that the Bible is not always clear about who Jesus was and is. Even the four Gospels seem to present slightly different perspectives on Jesus' life and ministry, as if they were looking at his life through different lens or from different angles.

What we do know is that Jesus offered perhaps the most important prayer any human being can offer—a prayer that is nothing short of divine. *"Lord, your will be done."* In the garden of Gethsemane Jesus turned his entire life over to God, even if that meant enduring hardships that he would have rather chosen to avoid. Who was Jesus? There will always be many answers. However, an answer that will always bear truth is this: one who gave his life over entirely to God.

Have you offered your life to the Lord?

Lord, with fear and trembling, and without having any idea what it might mean for
me—nor any concrete sense of how I will live it out—I offer my life to you. Your will be done.
Pass me whatever cup you see fit to offer me, and I will drink from it. In Jesus' name, I pray.
AMEN.

June 18

Selling Out

Read: Matthew 26–27

> *Then one of the twelve, who was called Judas Iscariot, went to*
> *the chief priests and said, "What will you give me if I betray*
> *Jesus to you?" They paid him thirty pieces of silver.*
> MATTHEW 26:14–15

JUDAS IS THE great villain of the Gospels. He is derided as the devilish student that handed his teacher over to the authorities who wanted him dead. Judas's name is synonymous with acts of betrayal. When someone goes behind our back and mistreats us, or hangs us out to dry, we refer to them as a "Judas." The most offensive aspect of Judas's betrayal is the kiss he bestowed upon Jesus. We struggle to reconcile an act of affection that signals an arrest. All this for thirty pieces of silver!

While Judas is forever branded the great turncoat of our Lord, the truth is, whether it was Judas's betrayal, Peter's denial, or the disciples' desertion of Jesus, those closest to Jesus were not able to stand with him in the end. Everyone failed, except Jesus. Judas got the money, and Jesus paid the price. Perhaps the ultimate and uncomfortable truth of the events that led to Jesus' crucifixion is that we fail, but Jesus does not. Therefore, it is best not to put too much faith in ourselves, and to trust in Jesus instead. Jesus can do what we cannot!

How does it feel to be weaker than Jesus?

Lord, I am told that I am supposed to be self-sufficient, self-confident, and self-satisfied. My culture tells me that my life is "all about me" and my ability to be more and do more and earn more and get more. How many times have I taken thirty pieces of silver in pursuit of my own self-interest? In ways both great and small, I have betrayed and denied and deserted you and others when I have been needed most. Judas is not some guy who two thousand years ago cut a deal to bring about your death. I am Judas. Our weaknesses are the same. I just pray your strength is enough to save me before I am completely lost. In your name, I pray. AMEN.

June 19

COMMISSIONING PROMISE

Read: Matthew 28:16–20

Go therefore and make disciples of all nations, baptizing them in
the name of the Father and of the Son and of the Holy Spirit. . . .
And remember, I am with you always, to the end of the age.
MATTHEW 28:19–20B

THE MISSION OF the Christian faith is nothing less than the transformation of the entire world. All nations and all people are supposed to be converted to a way of living and being that reflects the message of Jesus and the will of God. That is a grand and bold vision, and it must have seemed wildly unrealistic to that handful of fishermen, tax collectors, and women who stood with Jesus on a mountain in Galilee. However, the vision and mission came with a promise: *"I am with you always."* The goal is the complete transformation of the world, but that is not work we will be left to do alone. Jesus will be with us. Jesus is or co-worker. Jesus will labor by our side until all that God wills is accomplished. The mission is grand, and our Savior is present!

What would it be like to truly work with Jesus?

Lord, you have dreamed big for us. In fact, the vision and mission you lay before us is one we are unable to accomplish on our own. We cannot even begin to imagine a world that overflows with love, peace, and justice for all. But you can and you have, and you promise to work with us until what you dream is what we experience. In your name, I pray. AMEN.

June 20

AWAITING INVITATION

Read: Mark 1:16–20; 2:13–17

As Jesus was walking along, he saw Levi son of Alphaeus sitting at the tax
booth, and he said to him, "Follow me." And he got up and followed him.
MARK 2:14

LIFE WITH JESUS starts with an invitation. In our culture which values self-starters, people who take initiative, and those blessed with entrepreneurial spirit, we often forget the invitational nature of Jesus' ministry with us. Jesus called the disciples away from the lives they had always known—and perhaps felt shackled to—to a new adventure that would prove to be the time of their lives. It is very possible that Peter, Andrew, James, and John mending their fishing nets and Levi at his tax booth were dying inside—wanting a life of deeper meaning where they could make a difference. However, the pathway to a new and enlivening existence did not commence as a result of the force of their own will. All they did was accept an invitation to take a walk with Jesus. Jesus made the first move, they simply responded.

Perhaps the way to a new and more meaningful life is not to suddenly decide to do something innovative and exciting that takes us in a different direction, but to simply accept invitations when they come our way. Living invitationally—accepting requests from others—may be the means by which Jesus himself welcomes us to walk in his ways.

What invitation have you received lately?

Lord, when I feel like I want to make changes in my life, I believe I must somehow take the initiative. I must assert myself—impress my will on a certain situation—in order to effect change. But what if the life you intend us to lead is a series of invitations you invite us to accept? What if the most faithful path forward in life is saying "yes" to the next invitation that comes my way? Perhaps an invitation is your way of calling me to follow you. In your name, I pray. AMEN.

June 21

SAYING NO . . . AND YES

Read: Mark 1:35–39

> *When the disciples found Jesus, they said to him, "Everyone is search-*
> *ing for you." Jesus answered, "Let us go on to the neighboring towns."*
> MARK 1:37–38A

AS JESUS BEGAN his earthly ministry, crowds often swarmed around him, longing for him to make them well. They wanted Jesus to be a celebrity healer, but Jesus knew his primary work was to be a faithful preacher. Early one morning, as the people once again hounded him for his healing power, Jesus had to put his foot down. *"Let's go somewhere else."* Jesus said *"no"* to the demands and desires of the crowd so that he could say *"yes"* to his true calling.

Each one of us has been uniquely gifted to serve others to the glory of God. God has equipped us with talents meant to benefit the world, but there are also countless demands that invade our lives each and every day. The challenge is finding ways to say *"no"* to the diversions so that we can say *"yes"* to making the most of our God-given abilities.

What distractions are preventing you from utilizing your unique gifts?

Lord, so often I forget that you have called me into your service. I get so caught up in making a living that I forget to make a life that is pleasing to you. Help me to meet my responsibilities without getting carried away by all the distractions. Remind me of my gifted-ness, and help me to focus on making the most of the talents you have given me. In Jesus' name, I pray. AMEN.

June 22

Forgiven and Healed

Read: Mark 2:1–12

When Jesus saw their faith, he said to the paralytic, "Son, your sins are forgiven."
MARK 2:5

THIS IS AN odd story. A paralyzed man had some friends who would stop at nothing to facilitate his healing. In order to get to Jesus, they dug through the roof of someone's house to lower their friend into Jesus' presence. They did this with the hope that Jesus might grant their paralyzed friend the ability to move about on his own. They pursued healing.

What Jesus offered, however, was forgiveness. It is true that in the ancient world physical infirmities were believed to be the consequence of less than faithful living. If you were not well physically, it was an indication that you were not well spiritually. Whatever the case, Jesus judged that the man's true infirmity was spiritual in nature. The man was brought to Jesus for a physical healing, but Jesus responded first to his spiritual ailment. In truth, it is often our soul that aches more than our body. The wrongs we have committed, the harm we have done, the injuries we have inflicted on others trap us in a stasis of sin. We often find that we cannot take a single step forward in life unless we are willing to go back and deal with the infractions of our past. Soul healing is our most pressing need, and that is the need Jesus first responds to—get the soul right, and then we can get to work on the body.

Do you long to be forgiven?

Lord, I am too often paralyzed by my past. My sins of yesterday haunt my living today.
I need healing if I am to truly move forward. Please forgive me. Call me from off my mat and
send me forth into a new and more abundant life. In your name, I pray. AMEN.

June 23

DIVERSIFICATION

Read: Mark 4:1–9

A sower went out to sow. And as he sowed, some seed fell
on the path, and the birds came and ate it up.
MARK 4:3–4

JESUS TOLD A story of a farmer who scattered seed on the ground. The seed fell on the hardened path, on the rocky ground, and among the thorns. Most of the seed failed to grow, but some seed fell on "good soil," and that seed increased thirty, sixty, and a hundredfold! If we follow Jesus' example, we might choose to toss our love out into the world, and to scatter the seeds of blessing everywhere. Spread good works throughout our families, our communities, and our world—and then wait and see what takes root.

Jesus encourages this kind of diversification because you just don't know where your next good friend will come from. You don't know how a kind word to a self-centered teenager today can transform their life years from now. You just don't know how the faithful ministry of one person can unlock God's eternal blessing in the world. After all, who would have thought that an obscure Nazarene prophet who was killed after three years of ministry could change the world? Jesus teaches us that abundant blessing comes from diversification. Invest yourself everywhere you can, and you will find you win more than you lose. And when you win, you will win big—thirty, sixty, and a hundredfold!

With whom, or where, do you need to sow some love, care, and generosity this week?

Lord, I do not think of investing myself as much as I think of investing my money. As I open the stock index this week, as I do strategic planning in my workplace, as I debate what to do with my time, encourage me to think about how I can invest myself, my love, and my care broadly so that they take root and grow in the world and in the lives of those closest to me. In your name, I pray. AMEN.

June 24

How Things Grow

Read: Mark 4:26–29

Jesus also said, "The kingdom of God is as if someone would scat-
ter seed on the ground, and would sleep and rise night and day,
and the seed would sprout and grow, he does not know how."
MARK 4:26–27

THE GRASS GROWS at night. We can fertilize it and water it and work to eliminate the weeds that invade it. We can do much helpful work during daylight hours. We understand the biology of growth. We also know how to harm and inhibit growth. But in the end, much growth happens without our assistance. Seeds can germinate and mature without our helping hands and watchful eyes. As the apostle Paul reminds us in his letter to the Christians at Corinth, we can plant and water, but in the end it is God who gives the growth. There is only so much we can do: grass continues to grow at night, and much is produced when our hand is off the plow. This truth can serve as a call to humility, as well as a call to sabbath. God is in charge, we are not. God gives growth, we do not. God is at work, even when we are not . . . in fact, God may work best when we are off the clock! So, perhaps, our most faithful response at certain times is to rest and rejoice at all that God can do.

Can you rest and trust, or do you prefer to work and produce?

Lord, I am a worker. I gauge my worth in large part on my productivity. That is how so much of the world works, and I am driven by that emphasis. I know this should not be the way—it is not your way—but I do not know any other way forward. Lead me along a better path. In Jesus' name, I pray. AMEN.

June 25

ASLEEP IN THE STERN

Read: Mark 4:35–41

A great windstorm arose, and the waves beat into the boat, so that the boat was
already being swamped. But Jesus was in the stern, asleep on the cushion.
Mark 4:37–38

THE DISCIPLES MUST have thought Jesus negligent. There was a storm. The boat was being swamped. And Jesus slept. Did he not understand the danger they were in— and not just their tiny boat but also the other boats that were with them? After spending hours by the seashore teaching the people, was Jesus going to allow the day to end in a mass drowning? Didn't Jesus care?

To be asleep at the wheel is negligent, but to be asleep in the stern is trusting. That was what the disciples failed to understand. Jesus wasn't at the helm at this perilous moment. Jesus was simply along for the ride. Jesus rested in the wind and waves of God, trusting that the God of heaven and earth and sea and storm would take care of him in this life and in the next. With faith like that, what is left to fear?

Can you rest in the middle of a storm?

Lord—storms make me anxious. In fact, the mere prospect of a storm can get my heart and my mind racing. Whether it be a storm in a relationship or on the job or in my finances, the worry of it all does not allow me to sleep. I spend my nighttime hours pondering possible destruction and peril. This means that I do not trust, I do not believe, and I do not have faith that all will be well whether I make it through the storm or go down with the ship. I so desperately need your help. Speak to me so that all that rages in my heart and mind might become peaceful and still. In your name, I pray. AMEN.

The Gerasene Demoniac

Read: Mark 5:1–20

> *They came to Jesus and saw the demoniac sitting there, clothed and in his right mind, the very man who had the legion; and they were afraid. . . . Then they began to beg Jesus to leave their neighborhood.*
>
> Mark 5:15 & 17

For the Gerasenes, the man possessed with a legion of demons was fearsome. He could not be bound or contained or controlled. The demoniac was a public menace, and a fearful presence in the Gerasene countryside. When Jesus cast the man's demons into a herd of nearby swine, however, the news was greeted with an even greater fear—a fear that prompted the people of that country to demand that Jesus leave their land. A man filled with demons was scary to be sure, but a man who could radically change your life in an instant was downright terrifying. If Jesus could transform the fearsome creature who lived among the tombs into an entirely different man, what might Jesus do the rest of the people living in that lakeside community? What might Jesus be able to do with us?

How might Jesus change your life if you were to encounter him?

Dear Lord, I choose comfort over conversation. I prefer dealing with the hidden demons of my life rather than the uncertainty that change might bring. I would probably choose to live amidst the tombs of past miseries rather than to step into the new life you invite me into. Which means, like the Gerasenes, I would likely shoo you away rather than invite you into my life. Please, please, please, Lord . . . break through my fears so that I can embrace the freedom and new life you are offering me. In your name, I pray. AMEN.

Pursuing Healing

Read: Mark 5:21–43

She had heard about Jesus, and came up behind him in the crowd and touched
his cloak, for she said, "If I but touch his clothes, I will be made well."
MARK 5:27

JESUS DIDN'T HEAL everyone. In fact, we must assume that most of the people struggling with physical, emotional, or spiritual ill-health were not healed by Jesus.
There were plenty of people who never made their way to Jesus. Jesus never healed
folks indiscriminately. Jesus responded to requests. If a person didn't request healing, they didn't receive it. In this story, a little girl and an elderly woman are made
whole because healing was pursued. Wellness was sought, and Jesus responded to
both pleas.

It is as true in the Gospels as it is in our lives—we must participate in our own
wellness. If we can't request healing—or if we are unaware of the maladies of our
lives—we will not experience restored health. We must step forward, we must
seek healing, we must strive to be whole if we want to become well. Jesus can heal
us, but we must make our way to him first.

Do you need to be made well?

Lord, sometimes it is difficult to step forward and request healing. I am not always sure
of the healing I need. My lack of self-awareness and my reticence to step out of the crowd in
pursuit of you prohibits me from living in healthy and whole ways. Lord, grant me the courage
and the resolve to reach out for the hem of your garment, and as I reach toward you, please
bring healing to me. In your name, I pray. AMEN.

June 28

REJECTION

Read: Mark 6:1–6a

"Is not this the carpenter, the son of Mary and brother of James and Joses and Judah and Simon, and are not his sisters here with us?"And they took offense at him.
MARK 6:3

IF YOU LOOK closely at Jesus' life and ministry, you will see a pattern of rejection. Herod tried to eliminate the baby Jesus by force, the scribes and Pharisees tried to denounce Jesus by utilizing Jewish law and tradition, the people of Jesus' hometown who knew him best seemed to doubt him most, and, of course, in the end, Jesus was tortured and killed like a criminal by the Roman and Jewish authorities in Jerusalem. Jesus seemed to encounter rejection at every turn.

What the world and worldly authorities reject, however, God often uses to inspire and transform. As Jesus himself quoted, the stone the builders reject can wind up being the cornerstone that anchors an entire structure. The world may have rejected Jesus, but Jesus still saved the world. Maybe the next time we encounter rejection we should not become demoralized by it but assume it is but a prelude to an even greater work of God.

When have you been rejected?

Lord, no one likes rejection, but it is part of life. Jesus experienced it, so why would we assume we would be able to avoid it? We can't, but we can refuse to be deterred by it. Moments of rejection were not the end for Jesus but the beginning of something new and enlivening— resurrection occurred only after rejection! Help me to persevere when I experience obstacles and objections, trusting that what the world rejects you just might rejoice in. In Jesus' name, I pray. AMEN.

JESUS WALKS ON WATER

Read: Mark 6:45–52

But immediately Jesus spoke to the disciples and said,
"Take heart, it is I; do not be afraid."
MARK 6:50

THE DISCIPLES SAW Jesus walking on the water and they thought he was a ghost. Whether or not we believe in ghosts, seeing a man walking on the water past our boat in the dark of the night would be enough to scare most of us to death. However, Jesus moved quickly to address the disciples' growing anxiety. *"Take heart, it is I."* Jesus changed his course, got in their boat, and extinguished the disciples' fear. Which is to say that Jesus' trip across the lake was interrupted by his compassion for his friends. He responded to their needs. Jesus calmed the storm on the sea as well as the storm in their souls.

What fear or storm do you need Jesus to quiet in your life?

Lord, I often have more fear in my life than faith. See me as I am straining to make my way forward, come out to visit me, hear my fearful cries, and climb into my boat and calm my heart. In your name, I pray. AMEN.

June 30

LEARNING TO LOVE DOGS

Read: Mark 7:24–30

> *Jesus said to her, "Let the children be fed first, for it is not fair*
> *to take the children's food and throw it to the dogs."*
> MARK 7:27

A WOMAN PURSUED Jesus in the hope that he will heal her daughter, and Jesus responded by calling the woman and her child dogs. For those of us who like to think of Jesus as unconditionally loving, this story appears to be an unfortunate stain on that image. While scholars and pastors have tried to explain away this story, there is no denying that Jesus had little interest in tending to the needs of this foreign woman. If you were not a Jew, you did not have access to Jesus.

After being rebuffed by Jesus, however, the woman pressed further. *"Sir, even the dogs under the table eat the children's crumbs."* There was something about that response that softened Jesus' heart. Jesus changed. Jesus gave to the woman what he had formerly withheld. The woman and child Jesus called *dogs* were revealed as beloved children of *God*. In that moment Jesus' heart expanded, and so did the scope of his ministry. He learned that every dog, every sinner, and every fallen child is beloved by God and deserving of healing.

Who do you consider a dog?

Lord, there are so many people I look down upon. There are family members, colleagues, and members of my community that I choose not to associate with. While I might not call them dogs to their faces, I know I treat my own pets better than I treat some of them. I pray that if you can change perhaps I can too. Help me to expand my heart so that I too can enlarge my mission in this world. In your name, I pray. AMEN.

July 1

LISTEN

Read: Mark 9:2–8

This is my Son, the Beloved; listen to him!
MARK 9:7B

LISTENING TENDS NOT to be a relational strength for most of us. Action, problem solving, and hard work may come naturally to us, while being silent, listening, and paying attention during conversation can be our Achilles' heel. Yet listening is the key to developing healthy, meaningful, and intimate relationships. We can't learn unless we listen. We can't really love another unless we listen. We can't effectively lead others unless we listen.

If we want strong relationships with our spouses and enduring relationships with our children, we must listen to them. Likewise, if we want a meaningful relationship with God, we must listen to Jesus. How are we to listen to Jesus? Talk less. Read the Gospels more. Pray often. Worship. If we make listening our best work, all our relationships will grow and thrive.

Whom do you need to set aside some time to listen to this week?

Lord, I like to talk. I like to speak my mind. I like to hear my voice above others. Can it really surprise me that my relationships seem hollow at times? Help me to listen. Help me to be attentive to those around me. Help me to be silent so that I can hear your voice speaking to me. Teach me to truly listen to those around me so that my relationships grow in depth and meaning. In your name, I pray. AMEN.

THE RICH MAN

Read: Mark 10:17–31

> *As Jesus was setting out on a journey, a man ran up*
> *and knelt before him, and asked him,*
> *"Good Teacher, what must I do to inherit eternal life?"*
> MARK 10:17

THE EXCHANGE BETWEEN Jesus and the rich man is both heartwarming and heartbreaking. Jesus told the man to obey the commandments of God. The man said he had done that since his youth. Then the text reads, *"Jesus, looking at him, loved him and said, 'You lack one thing; go, sell what you own, and give the money to the poor, and you will have treasure in heaven; then come, follow me.'"* The story ends with the man leaving disappointed because he had a lot of stuff he didn't want to part with.

What we often miss in this story is that Jesus' answer to the request for eternal life was for the man to obey the commandments. If the man had not pressed Jesus for more, Jesus might not have suggested he sell all his possessions. We can only assume that living a good and faithful life still didn't seem like enough for the man. He wanted an even more intimate and committed relationship with God. That kind of relationship, according to Jesus, requires even greater sacrifice. We don't have to give everything away to be inheritors of eternity, but if we long for a closer walk with Jesus, we might have to do just that.

Do you long for a deeper relationship with God?

Lord, all I need to do in order to lead a faithful life is obey your rules. But sometimes being a person who simply does the right thing is not enough. There are times when I long for something more—a deeper connection, a more passionate relationship, and a more intimate conversation with you. That might cost me more than I am willing to pay . . . but I know it would be worth it. Don't allow me to leave your presence disappointed. Please. In your name, I pray. AMEN.

July 3

HEALING BLINDNESS

Read: Mark 10:46–52

> *The blind man said to him, "My teacher, let me see again." Jesus*
> *said to him, "Go; your faith has made you well." Immediately*
> *he regained his sight and followed him on the way.*
> MARK 10:51B–52

JESUS HEALS BLINDNESS—PHYSICAL blindness and spiritual blindness. When familiarity blinds us to the goodness and beauty of the friends and family who are closest to us, when we are blind to our own giftedness and value, when we can no longer see a way out of seemingly intractable situations, Jesus offers us both sight and insight. Obedience to the commands and counsel of Jesus can illuminate our living. When we stop stumbling around in the dark and start clinging to Jesus, we are led into the light. How does this happen? Why does this happen? What is the theology behind Jesus' ability to heal us? We don't know—he just does. Somehow, through Jesus, faith and faithfulness makes us well.

Where do you need regain sight in your life?

Lord, I confess that there is much I don't understand about you and your ways. I do not understand how you heal, how you give sight, and how you cure blindness. But you do. I am blind in so many ways. I want to follow you out of the darkness of my life into your radiant light. I am blind . . . but I want to see. In Jesus' name, I pray. AMEN.

July 4

Jesus' Triumphant Entry

Read: Mark 11:1–11

Many people spread their cloaks on the road, and others spread leafy branches that they had cut in the fields. Then those who went ahead and those who followed were shouting, "Hosanna! Blessed is the one who comes in the name of the Lord! Blessed is the coming kingdom of our ancestor David! Hosanna in the highest heaven!"

MARK 11:8–10

THIS STORY SEEMS to be a most imprudent display of celebration. This is the ticker-tape parade before the championship has been won, it is the victory lap before victory has been had, it is the celebratory headline printed in the paper in anticipation of an accomplishment that has not yet been achieved. The people along the road were celebrating Jesus as if he were a conquering hero, even though he had neither conquered anyone nor done anything particularly heroic. This is the kind of display of enthusiasm that most prudent people would never dare getting sucked into.

Those who followed Jesus, however, were anything but prudent. They were grateful. They were hopeful. They were excited. They had an unquenchable sense that Jesus represented something new and different and wonderful entering the world. They felt that they were in the presence of a Lord, a Savior, a God who would change the course of history and establish heaven on earth. Right or wrong, they decided to celebrate the presence of Jesus in their midst.

When was the last time you got really excited about Jesus' presence in your life?

Dear Lord, I can't remember the last time I got excited about our relationship. I am sure there was a time, but it eludes my memory. I think about the people jammed along the roadside hoping to catch a glimpse of you, or hoping that you would catch a glimpse of them, and I can't help being a bit envious. I long for that kind of enthusiastic faith, but I have chosen a more placid spirituality. And, truthfully, I am bored . . . and I am not growing. I want to catch a glimpse of you that prompts me to throw my coat on the ground, wave palm branches in the air, and shout "Hosanna!" at the top of my lungs. Please, hear my prayer. In your name, I pray. AMEN.

July 5

POP QUIZ

Read: Mark 12:18–27

Jesus said to the Sadducees, "Is not this the reason you are wrong,
that you know neither the scriptures nor the power of God?"
MARK 12:24

THE SADDUCEES WANTED to trick Jesus by asking him a foolish question crafted to demonstrate Jesus' lack of religious training and insight. It was a *"how many angels can you fit on the tip of a pin?"* kind of question. Jesus didn't tolerate that type of superfluous religious debate and examination. Instead, Jesus went right to the heart of the issue—the Sadducees were willing to dabble in little religious tricks and tests, because they didn't know their scripture and they didn't know God. Theological gymnastics is not what faith is about; knowing God's will and doing it are the hallmarks of religious belief. Stop giving religious quizzes and start putting faith into action. Don't waste time playing catechetical games, get to work on building God's kingdom today. Trying to trip Jesus up turns out to be far less rewarding than following in his footsteps.

Do you spend more time thinking about faith or putting your faith into action?

Lord, I might not be as deliberate as the Sadducees, but I know I am more inclined to play games than to get serious about my faith. I would rather keep my religion in my head than to have to activate it in my life. Faith costs less if I compartmentalize it. But you call me out of my safe religious ruminations and into a daring life where I can actually walk as you walked, act as you acted, and try to live as you lived. Theological quizzes can be intriguing and fun, but putting our faith to the test by putting it into action is what you desire. Help me to do just that. In your name, I pray. AMEN.

July 6

THE GREAT COMMANDMENT

Read: Mark 12:28–34

One of the scribes came near. . . . He asked Jesus,
"Which commandment is the first of all?"
MARK 12:28

LOVE. WHEN ALL the rules and regulations of this life—as well as the rules of the Bible—are scrutinized, Jesus' message rings true. Love fulfills the law. Love God and love your neighbor and you will never find yourself breaking any rules. While it can seem impossibly difficult to love at certain times and to love certain people, love is the simple answer to living well and righteously before God. If we loved, we would not abuse. If we loved, we would not cheat or steal. If we loved, we would not horde for ourselves. If we loved . . . God's will would reign on earth as it is in heaven.

Why do you find it difficult to love?

Lord, help me to love others as I hope you love me. When I confront all kinds of evil and abuse and misfortune, let me respond in love. When I am grieved, or feel injured, or disappointed by others, let me respond in love. When I have the choice to lash out and retaliate and press my own rights, let me respond in love. Train me to make love my default setting. I so desperately want to love better and more completely. In Jesus' name, I pray. AMEN.

July 7

NEW TRADITIONS

Read: Mark 14:12–25

On the first day of Unleavened Bread, when the Passover lamb is sacri-
ficed, . . . while they were eating, Jesus took a loaf of bread, and after bless-
ing it he broke it, gave it to them, and said, "Take; this is my body."
MARK 14:12A & 22B

NEW TRADITIONS ARE often difficult to accept. Tradition, by definition, is about a ritual that remains constant. In an ever-changing world that increases in complexity, and does so with alarming haste, traditions can seem as important as ever. We want things we can count on. Like turkey at Thanksgiving, fireworks on the Fourth of July, and the national anthem sung before a ballgame. When new traditions are suggested, there is often something deep within our spirit that resists them. New traditions, however, recognize that time and people and relationships do change, and those changes need to be acknowledged and affirmed. So, even though for generations unleavened bread had symbolized the food eaten by the Hebrew slaves in Egypt on the night they fled captivity, breaking the bread in front of the disciples as an expression of Jesus' broken body bespoke a new and important reality. Bread can be a reminder of freedom from slavery as well as a way to remember Jesus' promise of freedom from death. Keeping old traditions faithfully should not mean that new traditions aren't embraced.

What new tradition are you reluctant to embrace?

Lord, for all the change in my life—or because of how swiftly life itself changes—I am
reluctant to change or expand my traditions. I have enough "new" in my life; I want something
old, reliable, and grounding. And yet, I must recognize your promise that you will continue to
do new things in my life and the world. Lord, help me not to resist change for change's sake . .
. Help me to be open to that which is old and familiar while embracing that which is new and
enlivening . . . for both are gifts from you. In Jesus' name, I pray. AMEN.

July 8

NO SMALL ROLES

Read: Mark 15:21–47

They compelled a passer-by, who was coming in from the country, to carry Jesus' cross;
it was Simon of Cyrene.... Joseph of Arimathea, a respected member of the council, ...
went boldly to Pilate and asked for the body of Jesus.
MARK 15:21 & 43

SIMON OF CYRENE and Joseph of Arimathea are both mentioned toward the end of the story of Jesus' life and death. Simon was the man the Roman authorities compelled to help Jesus carry his cross to Golgotha, and Joseph was the man who went to Pilate to ask for Jesus' body after his crucifixion. We know nothing of these two men other than their individual acts of faith—carrying a cross and burying a body. Simon and Joseph are named in the scriptures, so we know they are people of significance, but their acts of faith are fairly ordinary and unremarkable in comparison to many of the miraculous stories of the Bible.

God does not call all of us to great and expansive world-changing life work. Men like Jesus, Gandhi, and Martin Luther King Jr., for example, are a rare breed. Few if any of us will be called upon to play a leading role in God's epic human drama. But we can take on our small roles with great passion and conviction. We can choose to be a faithful spouse, a present and participatory parent or grandparent, or a fair and honest employer. We can step forward when called upon. Stepping up and giving our best, carrying crosses when that is called for, and taking modest but important risks of faith is exactly what God asks of us.

Is there a task, job, or responsibility for which you have given less than your best effort because you felt it was of little importance or value?

Lord, help me to reenvision my life so that I am able to see significance and meaning in all that I do. Allow me to give my best effort at work, at home, and in all my relationships so that I might experience the joy of doing all things to your glory. Help me avoid the trap of being a small-minded actor; instead, inspire me take on my small role in life with great passion. In Jesus' name, I pray. AMEN.

July 9

ZECHARIAH'S VISION

Read: Luke 1:5–25

> *Zechariah said to the angel, "How will I know that this is so? For*
> *I am an old man, and my wife is getting on in years."*
> LUKE 1:18

AN ANGEL OF the Lord appeared to Zechariah with the news that his wife, Elizabeth, would conceive and give birth to a son who was to be named John. In their old age, Zechariah and Elizabeth were going to be parents. Zechariah responded to this news by asking for some proof of this unbelievably wonderful promise. *"How will I know this is true?"* he asked the angel.

First of all, Elizabeth will tell Zechariah that "she's late." And then her belly will begin to grow round. Finally, she'll demand that Zechariah go out in the middle of the night to get her some ice cream and pickles. How will he know?! Zechariah's impatience and doubt got the best of him, as they do us. We want to *know*, when God simply wants us to have *faith*. With most matters of faith in life, we don't need to *know*, we just need to *trust*.

What knowledge do you wish God would provide for you?

Lord, I want to know, I don't want to have to trust. I long for that which is concrete, and become frustrated when it feels as if I have fistfuls of air. I cry out "How will I know?" and you respond, "Don't be afraid, have faith, trust." Help me not only to accept that response but also to embrace it. In Jesus' name, I pray. AMEN.

July 10

THE ANNUNCIATION

Read: Luke 1:26–38

> *Then Mary said, "Here am I, the servant of the Lord; let it be with me*
> *according to your word." Then the angel departed from her.*
> LUKE 1:38

MARY SAID, *"I accept."* An angel of the Lord told Mary she would become an unwed pregnant woman in a culture that often condemned such women to death. The angel didn't say she had a choice in the matter, but Mary's willingness to play whatever role was assigned to her is impressive all the same.

When we are given assignments, we often accept them grudgingly, and perhaps even approach them halfheartedly. Mary was given a heavy burden to carry— a daunting chore—and the hymn of praise she sings in the following chapter lets us know she embraced her role with enthusiasm and even joy.

Can you approach the chores and work you are assigned with joy—as if the work itself was a gift from God?

Lord, the work you set before me often seems like a burden. And yet, I have this feeling that if I approach my duties with the right mindset, the work itself might be a blessing and a joy. Thank you for the productive work you will set before me today. Keep me ever mindful of those people who long for work—who long for a sense of meaning, purpose, and worth, only to find that it eludes them. In Jesus' name, I pray. AMEN.

July 11

JOURNEY TO BETHLEHEM

Read: Luke 2:1–7

And Mary gave birth to her firstborn son and wrapped him in bands of cloth,
and laid him in a manger, because there was no place for them in the inn.
Luke 2:7

THERE WAS NO room for them in the inn. We know that part of the story. The baby Jesus was placed in a cattle trough as if it were a bassinet that first night, because there was no one willing to open heart or home to the little family from Nazareth. Even as paying customers, the innkeeper refused to put the pregnant couple up for the night . . . what a mess to have a guest give birth in your hotel!

What we also know is that this initial exclusion foreshadows the end of Jesus' earthly ministry. In the beginning there was no room for Jesus at the inn, and by the end, there was no room for Jesus in the world. The powers and principalities of the world conspired to snuff Jesus out, because the world has little room for one who speaks truth and offers God's love to all. There was no room in the inn for Jesus, there was no room in the world for Jesus . . . the only question that remains is whether there is room for Jesus in our lives.

Will you open your heart and life to Jesus?

Lord, I want to say "yes" to that question, but I don't know what I am in for if I do. Will life get messy for me? Will I get into trouble with the powers that be? Will I have to finally be honest with others and offer my love unreservedly? It would be so much easier to shut the door to all that uncomfortable uncertainty. But I desperately want to keep that door open. I want you in my life. I want to risk living in prophetic ways. In your name, I pray. AMEN.

July 12

SHEPHERDS AND ANGELS

Read: Luke 2:8–20

In that region there were shepherds living in the fields, keep-
ing watch over their flock by night. Then an angel of the Lord stood
before them, and the glory of the Lord shone around them.
LUKE 2:8–9A

THE SHEPHERDS WERE always the last to know everything. They picked up pieces of gossip and rumor now and then that they readily shared among themselves while leading their flocks across the countryside. When it came to official notifications, they were the ones last and least informed. Shepherds occupied, and occupy to this day, the lowest rung on the economic ladder. They have a job, but that job allows them no social clout whatsoever.

Therefore, angels appearing first to the shepherds to announce the birth of a king was something very unusual indeed. It was a birth announcement that put the world on notice. This new king would proclaim to the entire world that in the kingdom of God the first might be last and the last might find themselves first. Angels will appear to shepherds, and the wisest of men will bow to infants.

Who are the overlooked shepherds in your life?

Lord, you came to turn the world on its head. From the moment of your birth, it was clear
that your values were going to be quite different from our own. To this day, we still have so
much to learn. If we want to be attended by your angels, we might just have to take our place
in line with your shepherds. In your name, I pray. AMEN.

July 13

SPECIAL

Read: Luke 2:22–38

> *Simeon took him in his arms and praised God, saying, "Master, now you are dismissing your servant in peace, according to your word; for my eyes have seen your salvation, which you have prepared in the presence of all peoples, a light for revelation to the Gentiles and for glory to your people Israel."*
>
> LUKE 2:28–32

SIMEON TOOK THE infant Jesus in his arms and proclaimed for everyone in the temple to hear that Jesus was special—destined for greatness. In Jesus, Simeon saw glory and light and salvation. How could Simeon have known all that the moment Jesus and his family entered the temple? Unless, somehow, that is the divine hope God has for every child born into the world. We were created to be light. We were born to glorify God. And we have within us the power to be a saving presence in the world. We cannot know the exact details for certain, and the text indicates that only Jesus received this particular acknowledgment, but what if every child brought to the temple was taken up in Simeon's arms and hailed as special? What a gift that would be . . . It would be the kind of gift God would choose to give to all children and their parents.

Do you feel special?

Lord, I worry about feeling special. When people feel uniquely gifted or blessed, that is often followed by a sense of superiority and arrogance. I do not want to be like that, so I often downplay my importance in the world. However, while you may encourage humility within us, you still love us and call us to great and important work that sheds light and glory and salvation throughout your world. Special or not, I want to be a part of that. In Jesus' name, I pray. AMEN.

GROWING UP JESUS

Read: Luke 2:41–52

*Jesus said to them, "Why were you searching for me? Did you
not know that I must be in my Father's house?"*
LUKE 2:49

THE STORY OF Jesus in the temple as a boy is fascinating, because at one moment the account conveys an image of a child far wiser than his years, while in the next it demonstrates a youth's careless disregard for his parents. As a boy Jesus was wise, but he was still very much a boy. From a young age we are told that Jesus appeared both human and divine. He understood that there were more expansive definitions of family than the ones traditionally held, while at the same time he callously worried his immediate family of origin.

This brief story ends with a hint of repentance. It says that after disappearing from the family caravan and causing his mother and father to frantically search Jerusalem for him, Jesus become obedient. He chose to follow the instruction of his earthly parents, and he grew in age and wisdom as well as divine and human favor. Jesus made a mistake, he needlessly frightened his parents, and he chose never to be that careless toward his family again. Jesus grew up.

When did you grow up?

Lord, I have this image of a perfect Jesus—a Jesus who was divine from conception. Is it not possible that divinity is something he grew into . . . as you encourage us all to grow up and grow closer to you? So many aspects of faith confuse me, but imagining Jesus dealing with some of the same flaws I recognize in my own life encourages me to believe that I can learn to be more faithful too. In Jesus' name, I pray. AMEN.

Heaven's Opening

Read: Luke 3:21–22

Now when all the people were baptized, and when Jesus also had
been baptized and was praying, the heaven was opened.
Luke 3:21

In the Gospel of Luke, Jesus' baptism and heaven's pronouncement are more gradual than in the other Gospels. Matthew and Mark seem to indicate that just as Jesus was coming up out of the water the heavens were immediately torn open for all to see, and the voice of God bellowed forth for all to hear. Luke's account is quieter and more personal. Jesus had been baptized. He was off praying. Then, for a moment, it was as if the heavens opened, a dove seemed to descend, and Jesus sensed God's affirmation of his life.

There are some people for whom coming to faith is an unmistakable thunderclap experience. But for many, many others, the experience of the divine is more subtle, mistakable, and something that requires continued faith. If Jesus was entirely certain about his connection with God, if he did not have moments of doubt, if he had conclusive proof of who he was, then he is entirely unlike most human beings. If Jesus' own religious epiphany was a bit more nuanced, however, then he is fully prepared to be the Lord and Savior of those of us who are less than certain about most issues in heaven and on earth.

Do you want Jesus to be a superhero who is impervious to doubts, or do you want Jesus to be your Savior, who struggled through the trials of life on his way to faith?

Lord, the great promise of our Christian faith is that you have walked the paths we walk, you have suffered the same fear and doubt and affliction that we endure, and you have grappled with the same questions and concerns that plague our own lives. Because you made your way through a life similar to ours, you have the power to lead us to a life that is similar to yours. Thank you for that gift and for your ever-present guidance. In your name, I pray. AMEN.

July 16

DEFENDED BY THE WORD

Read: Luke 4:1–11

Jesus answered him, "It is written, 'One does not live by bread alone.'"
LUKE 4:4

WE ARE TOLD that Jesus was led by the Spirit of God into the wilderness to pray and to fast and to be tested. Forty days without food and without companionship would likely drive most of us mad. Throbbing hunger and aching loneliness are mighty tests in and of themselves. However, it was toward the end of his wilderness experience that the real challenges came. If Jesus could sustain himself in the desert for more than a month, what else might be possible for him? Turn stones into bread? Impress people with high profile acts of faith? Rule the world?

We aren't told what the tempter looked like. Was there a tail and a pitchfork, or just a gnawing desire within Jesus to lead an impressive and impactful life of his own choosing? We do not know. We do know, however, that it was the word of God that sustained Jesus in the wilderness. Jesus confronted every temptation with scripture. In the face of hunger, loneliness, and temptation, scripture was Jesus' sustenance. When you have filled your mind and life with the words of God, it gives you the strength to endure just about anything, and it affords you the ability to do the right thing.

Is your life filled with the words of God?

Lord, turn my mind to your word. Help me to take advantage of opportunities to study scripture. Renew my desire for Bible study. Fill me with your words . . . for my own words, for the words I see and hear all around me are not enough to sustain my life and give me direction. In your name, I pray. AMEN.

Temptation

Read: Luke 4:1–12

*Then the devil led Jesus up and showed him in an instant all the kingdoms of
the world. And then the devil said to him, "To you I will give their glory and
all this authority. . . . If you, then, will worship me, it will all be yours."*
LUKE 4:5–7

THE DEVIL OFFERED Jesus the same things God offered him. The kingdom. Authority.
Glory. There was one significant difference. The devil offered Jesus an easy way to
achieve his goals. With the devil there is no cross. The devil offers all the gain without
any of the pain. This is the devil's "get rich quick" scheme. All Jesus had to be willing
to do was cut a few corners, make a few compromises, and then he could sidestep
the cross on his way to greatness. However, while he may have achieved his ends
more expeditiously, if Jesus had accepted the devil's offer, he would have likely lost
his soul in the transaction. Jesus was destined to turn over tables, transform hearts,
and bring healing to all people . . . and he would have to pay the price for doing it.

In truth, crosses build character. Hard work builds endurance. Overcoming
obstacles builds resilience and resolve. Salvation comes through sacrifice. For God,
there are no shortcuts. God is trying to build a kingdom in this world. God is trying to build us into people of integrity, wisdom, and compassion. That is hard and
demanding work—for us, and for God. And God wants it done right.

Are you trying to sidestep any of the necessary demands of your life right now?

*Lord, there are no shortcuts toward my growth into a person of integrity, wisdom, and
compassion. You know how I am tempted to cut corners, pursue the course of least resistance,
and take the easy way out. The devil's deal is indeed tempting. I am tempted daily. I long to
avoid the cross . . . but in doing so I realize that I may miss out on becoming the person you
are shaping me to be. Do not let my fear of the cross scare me away from who you have created
me to be. In Jesus' name, I pray. AMEN.*

July 18

INTERRUPTIONS

Read: Luke 5:1–11

Jesus got into one of the boats, the one belonging to Simon,
and asked him to put out a little way from the shore.
LUKE 5:3

SIMON PETER AND Andrew had been out fishing all night long and had caught nothing. They were tired, frustrated, and concerned they wouldn't be able to feed their families. What they were doing wasn't working for them, and then, into their boat stepped Jesus. Jesus asked to take a boat ride—likely the last thing Peter wanted to do after a long and disappointing night of work—a most unwelcome interruption! By the end of the boat trip Peter had a huge catch of fish and a new vocation—he became a disciple of Jesus Christ, and he would go on to be one of the most important Christian leaders of all time.

What do you do when things are not working out as you had hoped? What do you do when the dream job turns out to be a nightmare? What do you do when you start feeling that your Mr. or Mrs. Right has, over the years, devolved into Mr. or Mrs. Wrong? What do you do when the retirement you worked your whole life to get to has you bitter and bored? Like Peter, you need to welcome interruptions. An interruption may be Jesus trying to get into your boat. You need to be willing to do the unconventional in order to break out of unproductive routines. And, finally, you've got to be willing to trust that God knows what you need better than you do.

Do you think of interruptions as inconveniences or as opportunities for God to get your attention and redirect your life?

Lord, help me to welcome you when you are trying to get into my boat and redirect my course. The next time I am interrupted, the next time my routine is disturbed, the next time someone inconveniences me, help me to recognize that it might be you trying to get my attention . . . in order to change my direction. In Jesus' name, I pray. AMEN.

July 19

Do You Choose?

Read: Luke 5:12–16

> *There was a man covered with leprosy. . . . Jesus stretched out his hand, touched*
> *him, and said, "I do choose. Be made clean." Immediately the leprosy left him.*
> LUKE *5:12, 13*

ALL KINDS OF healing can occur when we are willing to reach out and make connections
with others. A boy's faintheartedness can be healed when a father places his hand on
his son and says, *"I know you can do this."* The estrangement within a family begins to
heal when someone finally stretches beyond the old grudges and places a long overdue
phone call. Marriages are healed when couples are willing to venture beyond their
comfort zones and sit down with a counselor who can help them work on better communication skills. When we are willing to reach out, when we are willing to stretch a
bit, when we are willing to risk associations with people who are hurting, that is when
healing happens. And it begins with a choice. *"Lord, if you choose, you can make me clean."*

For us all, there is someone in our life—a family member, a forgotten friend,
a classmate, a colleague, the homeless person we walk past on our way to work—
who other people choose to avoid. The good news is that each of us has the power
to bring healing to that person. We have the ability to reach out and make a difference. It is not as difficult as we might believe; we just need to stretch ourselves a
bit. So, the question for us is the same as it was for Jesus—will we choose?

This week, will you choose to reach out to someone you know who is lonely,
hurting, or maligned by others?

Lord, I tend to step over, past, or on top of a lot of people. There are people I choose to
avoid. There are people I make fun of with my friends. And, of course, there are plenty of people
I simply don't take notice of. Help me to stop. Help me to reach out. Help me to take notice
of the needs of those around me. Encourage me to care more than I often do. And help me to
bring healing where I can. In Jesus' name, I pray. AMEN.

July 20

WHAT IF?

Read: Luke 6:27–36

> *But I say to you that listen, Love your enemies, do good to*
> *those who hate you, . . . pray for those who abuse you.*
> LUKE 6:27–28

THIS MUST BE the most difficult of all Jesus' teachings. Love your enemies. Turn the other cheek. Be merciful to the wicked. Why? The text says that we will be rewarded. But what is the reward for letting people walk all over you? What could be worth that indignity and injustice? We have serious questions and grave misgivings about this line of teaching! And yet, what if the reward is a world where people give better than they get? What if the reward is a peace born out of unbridled generosity? What if the reward is being called children of God, who respond to the trials and triumphs of life as the Lord would? What if the reward for godly living was to become divine ourselves? Would that be compensation enough?

Whom do you need to love, pray for, and give to?

Lord, I don't like this lesson. It is too demanding. It is more than I can bear. But what if that is the cost of a different kind of world where love, peace, and mercy abound? I do not know if I have the courage to allow it to start with me, but it really did start with you. You forgave those who nailed you to the cross, and you loved those who denied and abandoned you. You have even offered eternal life to those of us who spend most of our time forgetting about you. You have led, let me follow. In your name, I pray. AMEN.

July 21

ASSURANCE OF PARDON

Read: Luke 7:36–50

> *"Therefore, I tell you, her sins, which were many, have been forgiven; hence she*
> *has shown great love. . . ."Then Jesus said to her, "Your sins are forgiven."*
> LUKE 7:47A & 48

WHEN DOES FORGIVENESS take place? When does healing take place? It is a question not easily answered when looking at the Gospels and the ministry of Jesus. Numerous times in the Gospels the text says that a person was healed or forgiven only for Jesus to say, after the fact, *"You are healed,"* or *"You are forgiven."* In this story, Jesus indicated that the sinful woman's love and outward affection were the result of her extensive sins being forgiven. Therefore, it would seem to indicate that the woman had been forgiven before Jesus pronounced forgiveness.

Perhaps we are forgiven by God the moment our hearts turn back in God's direction. Perhaps forgiveness is offered upon our very first corrective step. Before we have even made a concrete offering of love, perhaps our change of heart is enough to elicit God's mercy. If this is so, then Jesus' words are simply an assurance of pardon. The woman had been forgiven; hence she showed Jesus' great love. However, Jesus still speaks words of forgiveness to seal her transformation. We are forgiven when we begin to return our lives to God, and Jesus offers the assurance that such a gift has indeed been extended to us.

What does "assurance of pardon" mean to you?

Lord God, you are generous and merciful and forgiving. Thank you. Thank you for the forgiveness, and thank you for the assurance and the confirmation that such forgiveness has been offered to me. In Jesus' name, I pray. AMEN.

July 22

QUESTIONING THE CROWDS

Read: Luke 8:4–8, 11–15

When a great crowd gathered and people from town after town came to him,
he said in a parable:"A sower went out to sow his seed; and as he sowed, some
fell on the path and was trampled on, and the birds of the air ate it up."
LUKE 8:4–5

JESUS TOLD THE parable of the sower and the seeds to a large gathering of people who had made their way to Jesus. We often view a gathered crowd as evidence of success. There are plenty of preachers who would feel wildly successful if they were standing in front of a congregation of thousands. This does not appear to be the case with Jesus. We know that Jesus was accustomed to speaking to enormous crowds, but when looking out at them, Jesus knew that numbers could be deceiving. In fact, Jesus suggested in this parable that he expected that as many as seventy-five percent of the people who made their way to him to fall from the faith. Most folks who flocked to Jesus would drift away from his teachings one way or another. There was a remnant in the crowd, however—maybe only a quarter of the people—who would fully embrace Jesus' message and allow that message to change their lives. And Jesus believed that those changed lives would produce more than anyone could imagine. What a remarkable thing for a leader of thousands to say! Don't trust the crowds, don't be overly impressed with numbers, and don't be entirely disheartened when many of the people you thought were engaged disappear. Our efforts in this life do not have to do with producing numbers but with transforming people. There will be disappointments along the way, the crowds will dwindle at times, but in the end, we will be surprised by how much difference we have made in the lives that truly receive our message.

Are crowds a sign of success for you?

Lord, if a crowd gathers, we believe something good must be going on.We believe numbers
denote success. If people flock, maybe we should too. But you encourage us to look beyond the
numbers to lives changed and relationships transformed. Crowds can be fun, but seeing even a
single life transformed is a true joy. In Jesus' name, I pray. AMEN.

July 23

PACKING LIGHT

Read: Luke 9:1–6

> *He said to them, "Take nothing for your journey, no staff, nor*
> *bag, nor bread, nor money—not even an extra tunic."*
> *LUKE 9:3*

WHAT DO YOU pack when preparing for a trip? Clothes? Food? A wallet full of cash and credit cards? When we travel, we want to be as prepared as we can be for any and every eventuality. We pack all we can fit into our suitcases and stuff as many bags as we can in the car. We don't want to forget anything!

Jesus had an entirely different desire for his disciples as he sent them out to travel and teach in the region of Galilee. Jesus didn't want his disciples to pack for every eventuality; he wanted them to be prepared to depend on God. Jesus wanted his disciples to travel light. He wanted his disciples to be unencumbered by excess "stuff." When in need, Jesus didn't want his disciples to first look in their suitcases, or their wallets, or in the pocket of their tunics. When in need, Jesus wanted his disciples to first turn to God.

When traveling, do you pack more than you need?

Lord, I want to be prepared. When I travel, I want to make sure I have everything I need. I would rather have too much than too little. However, in my packing, I wind up leaving very little room for you. Help me to pack less into my life, so that there is more space for you. In Jesus' name, I pray. AMEN.

CHANGING PRAYER

Read: Luke 9:28–35

And while Jesus was praying, the appearance of his face
changed, and his clothes became dazzling white.
LUKE 9:29

IT HAS BEEN said that our prayers don't change God but that our times of prayer have a way of changing us. That appears to have been the case in the story of Jesus' transfiguration as it is told in the Gospel of Luke. Jesus went up a mountain to pray, as was his custom. Jesus took Peter, James, and John with him. It was an act he had undertaken countless times before. But this time when Jesus prayed, something happened to him—he changed—he appeared to be in the company of the great luminaries of the Hebrew faith. For a moment Jesus appeared divine . . . Godlike. It was as if his true character was on display for anyone who happened to be around to see.

Who knows how many times Jesus went off to pray and nothing happened. There must have been plenty of times when God seemed silent, Jesus felt unmoved, and there were no dazzling visions to be seen. But Jesus persisted, and in time prayer changed him so much that he didn't even look like the same person to those who knew him best. That's what prayer can do—it can change us, it can illuminate us, and it can make our lives dazzling!

How do times of prayer affect you?

Lord, I actually pray a fair bit, and I often wonder if it is working. By working, I tend to mean, are you working on my behalf? But what if the efficacy of prayer has less to do with you and more to do with me? What if the benefit of prayer is not that you change my life circumstances in favorable ways but that times of prayer have a way of changing me favorably? That would be a gift. I will pray for that today, in your name. AMEN.

THE GOOD SAMARITAN

Read: Luke 10:25–37

> *But a Samaritan while traveling came near him; and*
> *when he saw him, he was moved with pity.*
> LUKE 10:33

THE HERO OF this story is a traveling Samaritan. Samaritans were not people held in high regard by Jesus' listening audience. Hebrew priests and Levites were the people who were granted honor and respect. However, in this familiar story, we are told that the professionally religious people could not be bothered to help someone in need.

Even today most ministry is done not by professional clergy but by lay people as they engage in their daily living. A traveling businessman offers to buy lunch for someone he meets who is in need of food. A doctor takes a few extra minutes to hear about the relational heartache one of her patients is experiencing. A teacher decides to mentor a student who is struggling with challenges at home. Ministry requires a whole host of good Samaritans.

What is your ministry?

Lord, we fail so often in life. We fail in compassion. We fail in recognition of need. We fail in our commitment to serve others. Create in us a Samaritan spirit so that no matter where we are or when we see a need, we can be moved by pity and offer assistance. In your name, I pray. AMEN.

July 26

MARY AND MARTHA

Read: Luke 10:38–42

But Martha was distracted by her many tasks; so she came to him and asked,
"Lord, do you not care that my sister has left me to do all the work by myself?
Tell her then to help me."
LUKE 10:40

MARTHA FELT NEGLECTED. She had been the one who had opened her house to Jesus and his friends, she had been the one who was serving as the hostess of this event, and it looked like she would be the one to clean up the mess when the evening drew to an end. This might not have been quite so irksome if her sister Mary were helping her out, instead of doing what Martha would have preferred to do—sitting with and listening to Jesus as he taught. Martha fumed as she began to do the dishes, and she wondered if anyone noticed, let alone cared about all she was doing. She let her work and her disappointment get the best of her. In the end, we learn Jesus would have preferred to have Martha do less and enjoy the company of her guests more.

When have you missed out on the joy of company because you were embittered by what other people were not doing to help out?

Dear Lord, if you were to come to my home, like Martha, I would have done all I could to prepare and provide for your visit. I'd clean the house, set the table, make the meal, serve the guests, . . . and when I saw my company enjoying themselves while I slaved away, I might get annoyed. Help me to enjoy providing for others, and if I can't, grant me the resolve to let the dishes sit for a moment while I enjoy the party I chose to host. In your name, I pray. AMEN.

July 27

"You Devil!"

Read: Luke 11:14–23

But some of them said, "He casts out demons by Beelzebul, the ruler of demons."
Luke 11:15

Jesus was healing people, teaching them about God, and casting out demons . . . and he was essentially called the devil—or at the very least—he was accused of being in league with the devil. It may seem to be a ridiculous claim, until we recognize that many Jews and Jewish religious leaders of Jesus' day took offense when Jesus broke commonly accepted Sabbath laws and ritual observances. At first glance, Jesus could have easily been viewed as an enemy of the faith. Jesus was doing something new, and even if that new thing was good, the changes in cultural and religious practices Jesus was suggesting were greeted with fear and anger by many. Only a devil could inspire such a response in people of faith! Well, not exactly. Sometimes we fear a cure as much as an illness. Good medicine can be hard to swallow. A Savior can be more unwelcome than a serpent!

How would you respond to Jesus if he confronted you and told you that you had to change your ways?

Lord, we like to think we would welcome you with open arms if you were to walk into our lives. We believe we would be your faithful followers cheering you on as you challenged the world. But it is very possible that we would deride you for trying to make a mess of our comfortable lives. We might even be tempted to call you names. Thank you for being a Lord and Savior who has a love big enough to include even those of us who might think of you as an enemy. In your name, I pray. AMEN.

THE RICH FOOL

Read: Luke 12:13–21

But God said to him, "You fool! This very night your life is being demanded
of you. And the things you have prepared, whose will they be?"
LUKE 12:20

THERE IS A danger in obsessive saving and storing up. That is the point of the parable
of the rich fool. Those who spend a lifetime in efforts of accumulation find that
when they die, they have lost both their treasure and their soul. True wealth in life
has something to do with a richness of relationship with God. That relationship
is most richly textured when we take what God gives us and share it with others
instead of hording it for ourselves.

Do you build larger barns instead of sharing more of what you have been given?

Lord, we are savers. We store up for ourselves. We have rainy day funds. We believe that
prudent financial planning is our way to salvation. We take out expensive life insurance poli-
cies as a way to protect us from all unfortunate eventualities. But you call us to a different
way of living—a way of life that is generous and daring and care-full of others. We resist your
way, Lord . . . Convert us . . . we need to be living instead of dying inside. In Jesus' name, we
pray. AMEN.

July 29

LOVE AND LAMENT

Read: Luke 13:31–35; 19:41–44

> *"Jerusalem, Jerusalem, the city that kills the prophets and stones those who*
> *are sent to it! How often have I desired to gather your children together as*
> *a hen gathers her brood under her wings, and you were not willing!"*
> LUKE 13:34

JESUS WEPT OVER Jerusalem as he warned about its destruction. He talked of future tribulation through tears. He lamented the city he loved . . . a city that would never love him back. How often our great disappointments align with our greatest loves! The ones we love are the very ones we have the highest hopes for, and when those hopes are not realized our hearts can break. This was as true for Jesus as it is for us. Great lament might be the outcome of great love, but in the end, love is worth any price we must pay. Jerusalem might have disappointed Jesus, but Jesus never deserted Jerusalem.

What is your greatest love and your greatest lament?

Lord, I know what it feels like to have a broken heart. It is the pain born of dreams dashed and love lost. It is a feeling a person believes they will never recover from. It is as much a physical pain as an emotional one. Heartbreak can be so hurtful that we might even be tempted to believe it is not worth it in the end. But love is worth it, even though lament is so often love's bedfellow. Lament always passes . . . Love endures. Thank you for that gift, Lord. In Jesus' name, I pray. AMEN.

July 30

DINNER WITH JESUS

Read: Luke 14:1–24

> *On one occasion when Jesus was going to the house of a leader of the*
> *Pharisees to eat a meal on the sabbath, they were watching him closely.*
> LUKE 14:1

CAN'T WE JUST have a nice, quiet dinner without getting into any arguments? Apparently the answer from Jesus was always a resounding, *No!* If you invited Jesus over for dinner, if you invited Jesus into your life, if you engaged Jesus in conversation—you best be prepared to be challenged! A leading Pharisee had invited Jesus over for the holy Shabbat meal and found himself and his guests embroiled in controversial conversations about Sabbath observance, appropriate seating arrangements, and who will be welcomed at God's banquet table. Jesus did not waste time with pleasantries and polite conversation. When we welcome Jesus into our homes or our lives, Jesus confronts our faults and failings so that we might turn our lives toward God and start living more fully and faithfully.

What issues would Jesus confront you with, if you invited him over to dinner?

Lord, I like to think that inviting you into my life would be a pleasant and affirming experience. I envision you and I having a leisurely conversation about all the joys and sorrows of the world and what we might do to address them. However, if I look at your life in the Bible, I know our dinner conversation would be anything but innocuous. You would confront me. You would convict me. And you would attempt to convert me to a more faithful way of living. That may be reason enough to keep you out of my home and out of my life. But, deep down, in that place I don't like to admit exists, I know I need to change. So, please, join me for dinner— enter my house, enter my life . . . and tell me how I should live. In your name, I pray. AMEN.

July 31

Table Manners

Read: Luke 14:1–14

When he noticed how the guests chose the places of honor, he told them a parable.
Luke 14:7

WHEN JESUS GAVE a lesson on table manners, he wasn't concerned with people putting their elbows on the table or about which fork to use for the second course or chewing with your mouth open. Jesus was concerned with humility and generosity. First, don't think too much of yourself, otherwise you will be embarrassed. Second, be generous in your invitations to the table so that no one is left out. Simple table manners are the keys to honor in this life and to glory in the next!

How do you choose your seats, and whom do you invite to sit with you?

Lord, I need to learn better manners. I am too concerned with etiquette, and too little concerned with the fellowship around the table. Help me. In Jesus' name, I pray. AMEN.

August 1

AS YOU ARE

Read: Luke 15:11–24

> *But while he was still far off, his father saw him and was filled with com-*
> *passion; he ran and put his arms around him and kissed him.*
> *LUKE 15:20*

IN THIS MOST beloved of parables, Jesus expressed the way God loves us and recon-
ciles us to him. Even when we have taken all God has given us and run off, even
when we have wasted all that we have received, even when the mud of the pigpen
and the stink of our sins cover us . . . God is waiting. God is loving. God is hoping.
God doesn't even need us to clean ourselves off; all God looks for is our turning
toward home, and that return fills God with joy. In fact, even when we are *"still far*
off," even when we haven't made it back yet, even before we have tried to explain
ourselves, even before we have the opportunity to offer our confession . . . God
runs to reunite with us. How amazing is that?! God welcomes us as we are, and
immediately celebrates our return.

It is time to return to God?

Lord, I have gone off and lived in a far-off land. I have set a great distance between you
and me. I have lived as if you were dead, taking my inheritance and spending it like a drunken
sailor. And yet you anxiously wait for me to return. You love me even when I am unlovable to
myself. You run to greet me the moment I turn in your direction. How great is your love! I will
be forever thankful. In Jesus' name, I pray. AMEN.

August 2

The Prodigal Son

Read: Luke 15:11–32

> *Then the father said to him, "Son, you are always with me, and all that is*
> *mine is yours. But we had to celebrate and rejoice, because this brother of*
> *yours was dead and has come to life; he was lost and has been found."*
> *Luke 15:31–32*

IT CAN BE very difficult to be the good child. You can feel forgotten, as attention and concern is lavished on wayward siblings. When the will is read and the estate is divided evenly between the white and black sheep of the family, being the good child doesn't appear to have any benefits. In fact, when the family gathers and begins to reminisce about the past, it is the bad deeds that everyone survived that are remembered and laughed about. Whereas the good deeds that were done day in and day out seem to be forgotten entirely.

It must have irritated the Pharisees that Jesus focused so much of his attention on sinners, tax collectors, and people of ill repute. Why didn't Jesus take note of their good deeds? Why didn't they receive applause and recognition for their efforts? Why did the wayward siblings of the house of Israel capture so much of Jesus' interest and devotion? Is there no benefit in doing what is right and good and trying to live in ways that please God? Yes. Good sons and daughters never have to endure separation from their parent. They never find themselves groveling in a pigsty. They don't die with unresolved relational issues plaguing their heart. They may not get the big homecoming party thrown in their honor, but they do get to enjoy the love and embrace of family each and every day of their lives.

Whose homecoming do you begrudge?

Lord, I try to do what is good and right, and it irks me when I see undeserving people celebrated as if they are favorite sons and daughters. It just doesn't seem fair—somehow the more faithful the person, the bigger the party should be, in my opinion. But in my bitterness,

I often forget that I am blessed to know your goodness every day of my life. I have not had to endure being lost, and I have not had to live separated from your love. As I begrudge your generosity toward others, I also forget that if anyone deserves a party thrown in their honor, it is you. Please forgive me for my hardness of heart. And thank you for allowing me to live by your side. In Jesus' name, I pray. AMEN.

August 3

ETERNAL CONSEQUENCES

Read: Luke 16:19–31

> *But Abraham said, "Child, remember that during your life-*
> *time you received good things, and Lazarus in like manner evil*
> *things; but now he is comforted here, and you are in agony."*
> LUKE 16:25

OUR LIVES CARRY the weight of eternal significance. How we choose to live on earth makes a difference in heaven. The choices we make in our daily lives leave an impression that is remembered for all eternity. The point of the story of the rich man and Lazarus was as a rebuke of the Pharisees who challenged Jesus at every turn and who refused to receive his teaching. But the story also reveals Jesus' understanding of the significance of our lives and our choices.

We often think of ourselves as small, insignificant, and unable to make a lasting impression on the world. Jesus, however, challenges that notion time and time again, asserting that every choice we make, every action we engage in, every relationship we enter into matters to God. Our lives and our living will not be forgotten. The good that we do and the injury we cause will be remembered. This is an awesome and a fearsome reality. This may make us feel uncomfortable, but it is exactly how Jesus said God works. God does not forget . . . God remembers—*forever.*

How do you want to be remembered?

Lord, I recoil at the prospect of judgment, particularly when it has to do with eternity. I don't like thinking of you as a punishing deity. However, you must not like thinking of me as a sinner who regularly overlooks the needs of people in desperate need—especially those who are right in front of me. The flipside of this, Lord, is that my own suffering, my own loss, and my own acts of generosity are not forgotten by you. You remember and you love. Those characteristics are recounted throughout the Bible. So, thank you for being mindful of my life, and help me to live up to the responsibility that comes with eternally significant living. In Jesus' name, I pray. AMEN.

August 4

ONE IN TEN

Read: Luke 17:11–19

Were not ten made clean? But the other nine, where are they?
LUKE 17:17

ON A ROAD in Galilee Jesus was approached by ten lepers with their skin peeling off their bodies in the most disfiguring of ways. They were people we would likely cross to the other side of the street to avoid coming in contact with. But Jesus not only received them, he also healed them. After being healed, however, only one of the lepers returned to thank Jesus and to praise him for what he had done. Jesus asked the man, *"Were not ten made clean? But the other nine, where are they?"*

We bow head, heart, and knee when we are in need, but do we remember God when we are brought through our difficulties? We would like to picture ourselves as the one faithful leper returning to thank Jesus, but more often than not, we find ourselves among the other nine. Why is that? Why do only one in ten people respond gratefully to the blessings of God in their lives?

What do you need to do to appropriately respond to God's goodness in your life?

Lord, I think of me more than I think of you. I turn to you when I am in desperate need, but when all is well and good I turn away like a spoiled and ungrateful child. Help me to remember to return each week to give you thanks. In your name, I pray. AMEN.

August 5

BEING A GOOD PERSON

Read: Luke 18:9–14

The Pharisee, standing by himself, was praying thus, "God, I thank you that I am
not like other people: thieves, rogues, adulterers, or even like this tax collector."
LUKE 18:11

I AM A good person. I don't cheat on my taxes. I don't sleep around. I am not purposefully cruel to people. I do my part. When I look at the world and all the bad actors out there, I feel fairly justified in indulging in a little self-righteous indignation.

When we feel this way, we find we are the Pharisee in this story. It's not that
we are completely prideful, but there is more than a little condescension in the
way we look at others. We overstate our own goodness as we look with disproval
on the lives and decisions of others. But being a good person is not just about being
the least offensive creature on the planet. Jesus said no one but God alone is good.
Therefore, we should be honest with ourselves and confess our sins to God. We are
all sinners in need of God's grace and forgiveness. That is the truth. And it is *good*
to admit it to ourselves, and to God.

What do you think of yourself?

Lord, I am a sinner. There may be certain sins that I have been able to avoid, but I have
not been able to steer clear of a fair amount of pride, self-importance, and condescension. I
look down on others. I do not know if I do so in an attempt to feel better about myself, or
because I am naturally inclined to submit others to a judgmentalism that I would never want
to have to endure myself. Whatever the case, Lord, I am flawed. I am as broken and as sinful as
the next person. Have mercy on me. Forgive me. Love me. In your name, I pray. AMEN.

August 6

Everyone's Welcome

Read: Luke 18:15–17

But Jesus called for the children and said, "Let the little children come to me, and do not stop them; for it is to such as these that the kingdom of God belongs."
LUKE 18:16

THERE ARE SO many debates about who is acceptable to God. Attempts at religious exclusion have been ongoing throughout human history. In-groups and out-groups litter the religious landscape of our world. Even Jesus' first disciples had their own sense of who was worthy and unworthy to enter into Jesus' presence. For those disciples, children were unwelcome. Children had no status in first century Palestine. Children were not to be heard, and preferably, not seen either!

The Bible tells us that Jesus was indignant, and he instructed his disciples to allow the little children into his presence. Everyone was welcomed by Jesus. The only thing a person needed to approach Jesus was the will to do so. With Jesus, there are no outsiders, there are no untouchables – there are no exclusions whatsoever. If you want to meet Jesus, you are more than welcome!

Do you exclude people?

Lord, I wouldn't want to be told I wasn't allowed to approach you, even though I am more than willing to erect and maintain barriers that keep people I dislike at a distance. Somehow, I really do think I am empowered to decide who is and who is not worthy of my time and attention. In fact, given the opportunity, I would certainly voice my opinions about who is worthy and unworthy of your time and attention. Please remind me that those are not judgments I am called to make. Everyone is welcome. Everyone is worthy of time and attention. Everyone is a recipient of your love and grace – even me. In thanksgiving I pray, in your name. AMEN.

DEATH AND LIFE

Read: Luke 18:31–34

But the disciples understood nothing about all these things; in fact, what
Jesus said was hidden from them, and they did not grasp what was said.
LUKE 18:34

OFTEN TIMES WE don't hear what we don't want to hear. We can be deaf to news that would be too troubling for us to bear. This is likely what happened to Jesus' disciples. This scripture represents the third time in the Gospel of Luke in which Jesus spoke of his impending death and resurrection. And yet, the disciples were entirely unable to grasp what he was saying. The only explanation for this is that they did not want to hear it, they did not want to believe it, and so they conveniently chose to ignore it.

Jesus' message was, of course, that he was going to have to die to live. And that is so much of the message he tried to impart to the world. We might have to die to truly live. Our lust and longings, our dreams and desires, our initiative and identity might need to die before we can live more fully as the people God intends us to be. That is a scary proposition for many of us. It is a message most of us might choose to ignore. But our ignorance does not make the teaching less true or less relevant today. If you want to live, you just might have to die.

Do we listen to what Jesus has to say, or do we tune him out so that we can keep doing things are own way?

Lord, I do my best to ignore you. In fact, I am so used to tuning you out, it doesn't take much effort to accomplish any more. You tell me time and time again what is necessary for a meaningful life, and I plug my fingers in my ears and start humming as loud as I can to cover your speech. I don't want to hear you tell me that death might have to precede real life. I don't want to hear it, but, oddly, my soul longs for it. Help me to listen more closely to my soul and to my Savior. In your name, I pray. AMEN.

August 8

ZACCHAEUS

Read: Luke 19:1–10

> *Zacchaeus stood there and said to the Lord, "Look, half of my pos-*
> *sessions, Lord, I will give to the poor; and if I have defrauded any-*
> *one of anything, I will pay back four times as much."*
> *LUKE 19:8*

WHEN WE HEAR the word *repent* we might cringe. The word conjures up images of holier-than-thou preachers who seem to be saying, *"You better change, or else.""You better become like us, or else."* The story of Zacchaeus is the story of one of the most disliked men in Jericho being recognized and befriended by Jesus. Thus, in that moment, Zacchaeus became the most popular man in Jericho. Jesus said, *"I must stay at your house today,"* and everything began to change for Zacchaeus—one gracious act of acceptance and the little tax collector's life began to turn around. Zacchaeus repented.

However we might choose to respond to the idea of repentance, Zacchaeus responded to the invitation to turn his life around with unbridled generosity and joy. You can sense Zacchaeus's exuberance. *"Look! Half my possessions, Lord. I will give to the poor!"* Zacchaeus's life had begun anew, and he leapt into it with generosity and enthusiasm. When we are lost, it is a joy to be found. When we are headed in the wrong direction, it is a blessing to have our course corrected. When we are not living as we should, it is a gift to repent.

Will you welcome the opportunity Jesus affords to turn your life around?

Lord God, I know I am lost. I may not like someone telling me how I am headed in the wrong direction, but perhaps that is a form of defensiveness born of truth. I am not living as I should. I want to turn around. I imagine what a profound joy it would be to turn toward you. Please call me down from my perch. Invite yourself into my life so that I might be found in you. In Jesus' name, I pray. AMEN.

August 9

FORGIVING CRUCIFIXION

Read: Luke 23:26–49

Then Jesus said, "Father, forgive them, for they do not know what they are doing."
LUKE 23:34

HOW DO YOU forgive someone as they are hanging you on a cross? How do you express empathy to someone who is in the process of abusing you? How do you embrace a colleague or a friend or a family member who makes a habit of maligning you behind your back? This moment of crucifixion and forgiveness is when it becomes abundantly clear that Jesus is Lord and we are not. Jesus is able to do something that most of us—perhaps all of us—would be unable to do. But perhaps the point of the story is not about what we should or shouldn't be able to do. This story is about Jesus and his capacity to forgive. If he can forgive Roman centurions pounding nails through his flesh and bone, then he can forgive us. What a gift. We crucify Christ anew every time we injure or malign or disregard other people . . . and Jesus is prepared to forgive us before we even ask for pardon. Jesus looks at us and understands how ignorant we are . . . but loves us still, even when our sins are so painfully evident. Jesus' forgiveness must be a sign that there is hope. Hope that we can turn from our sinful ways. Hope that one day love and compassion will prevail. Hope for the world!

Can you forgive and accept forgiveness?

Lord, I cannot comprehend the kind of forgiveness Jesus extended to his torturers and executioners. How is such an act possible? Like so many things, what is impossible for us is possible for you. You are our hope. Thank you. Help me to be a bit more forgiving the next time I am injured. In Jesus' name, I pray. AMEN.

August 10

THE ROAD TO EMMAUS

Read: Luke 24:13–35

While they were talking and discussing, Jesus himself came near and went
with them, but their eyes were kept from recognizing him. . . .When he was
at table with them, he took bread, blessed and broke it, and gave it to them.
Then their eyes were opened . . . ; and he vanished from their sight.
LUKE *24:15–16 & 30–31*

IT IS AN audacious claim: a country preacher, who died in the big city, appeared
after his death on a lonely road that led to the town of Emmaus. What makes the
story all the more remarkable—or questionable—is that the two disciples did not
recognize Jesus at first. When they finally saw Jesus for who he was, he vanished
from their sight.

This would be an easy story to refute, if it were not for the fact that many
people have caught glimpses of Jesus over the centuries. Most of the time we don't
recognize him because he comes in a form that is unexpected. A nurse speaking
tenderly to a patient, a teacher offering encouragement to a struggling student, a
friend consoling another friend after a loss. Jesus is just as real and just as alive as
the care and connection we share with others.

Where have you seen Jesus at work?

Dear Lord, I want to see you at work in the world. But sometimes the image of who I
think you should be obscures my view of who you really are and where you are. Open my eyes
that I can see you, and open my heart so that I can serve you in those I meet on the road. In
your name, I pray. AMEN.

August 11

Ascension and Blessing

Read: Luke 24:50–52

Then he led them out as far as Bethany, and, lifting up his hands, he blessed them.
LUKE 24:50

TO BE BLESSED is to experience God's favor. That was Jesus' desire for his disciples and for us. Jesus' last act according to the Gospel of Luke was to confer God's blessing on his students. This act must have meant much more than just *"I wish you well, go in peace."* This wasn't just a pleasant good-bye until their next meeting. Jesus' hope was that the disciples would experience the favor and presence and possibility of God as he had experienced it in his own life. At this moment when Jesus' physical presence would leave the world, his desire for those who followed him was to know and love God, and to derive deep satisfaction and purpose from that relationship. He raised his hands and spoke words of blessing to his friends so that all that had been his would be theirs.

What would it be like to receive Jesus' blessing?

Lord, I wish I could go through the day with an image of your hands raised in my direction offering me encouragement, resolve, and faith. What could I do if I felt your support and blessing daily in my life? Please speak words of encouragement to me today. In your name, I pray. AMEN.

August 12

THE WEDDING AT CANA

Read: John 2:1–12

When the steward tasted the water that had become wine, and did not
know where it came from . . . Jesus did this, the first of his signs, in Cana
of Galilee, and revealed his glory; and his disciples believed in him.
JOHN 2:9A & 11

DURING A WEDDING in Cana, Jesus turned water into wine. It was his first miracle as recorded in the Gospel of John. It is a curious initial miracle, because it seems something akin to a first century beer run. The keg was kicked and Jesus was called upon to make sure that the party rolled on uninterrupted.

Odd or not, this first miracle suggested that Jesus' ministry was going to take place among ordinary people in ordinary circumstances. Jesus was not only a Lord and Savior but he was also a friend, a brother, and even a wedding guest. His ministry was also going to be a ministry of celebration. Jesus' ministry was about bringing good news, and, on occasion, it was about bringing good cheer. Jesus would challenge the world, but he could also be the life of the party.

Can you imagine being at a party with Jesus?

Dear Lord, you dwelled with us, as one of us. You experienced joy and sorrow, celebration
and solemnity. You broke up some parties while encouraging others. Just like us, there are times
when you seemed—and still seem—a confusing mix of contradictions. However, you do not
ask us to understand you, simply to follow you . . . and that invitation is reason enough to
celebrate. In your name, I pray. AMEN.

August 13

CLEANING OUT THE CLUTTER

Read: John 2:13–22

In the temple Jesus found people selling cattle, sheep, and
doves, and the money changers seated at their tables.
JOHN 2:14

WHEN JESUS WENT up to the temple in Jerusalem, he was angered by what he saw. Merchants were selling doves, sheep, and cattle in the portico of the temple. Money changers were changing currency. The temple, the most holy place in all Judaism, the earthly home of God, had become cluttered. The entrenched buying and selling, the commerce and commercialism, and the corruption and the disorder of the temple had made it nearly impossible for the people to the divine presence. Jesus decided it was time to take action. He made a whip of cords and began driving the merchants, the livestock, and the money changers out of the temple.

Like the temple in Jesus' day, our lives get so cluttered that we cannot feel the Spirit of the living God moving within us. The concerns, frustrations, and anxieties within us obscure our view of God. The hustle and bustle of our busy lives drowns out the still small voice of God, who is trying to get our attention. We assume God has gone silent or that God is dead or that God has gone on vacation when the truth is that we are the ones who are lost. There comes a time when we have to whip our lives back into shape. There comes a time when we need to clean out the clutter in our lives because it is getting in the way of God's purpose for us. There is a time when we finally have to get serious about our faith. Jesus took bold action in the temple—our actions need to be equally bold if we are to reclaim a sense of God's sacred presence in our lives.

What are some things that clutter your life and prevent you from being moved by the Spirit of God?

Lord, my life is cluttered with so many things. Anger, frustration, resentment, pride, envy—all these things choke out your Spirit within me. Help me to cleanse the temple within. Bring order to my life. Help me to clean out some of the clutter so that I am able to see and hear and feel your holy guidance in my life. In Jesus' name, I pray. AMEN.

August 14

CLEANSING THE TEMPLE

Read: John 2:13–25

> *Making a whip of cords, Jesus drove all of them out of the tem-*
> *ple, both the sheep and the cattle. He also poured out the coins*
> *of the money changers and overturned their tables.*
> JOHN 2:15

WE MIGHT BE inclined to call it *holy* anger, but it was anger to be sure. Jesus got furious. Jesus threw a fit. Jesus got a bit hostile. This act of aggression might not fit with our image of Jesus—and the God he called *"Father"*—as unwaveringly loving. However, to be a person of love, to love others as yourself, to have your character defined by love does not mean you can't get upset. In fact, when you love deeply, and when that emotion is challenged or threatened, a fit of rage is often our most human response.

The fact that Jesus got up riled up indicates that for all his transcendent characteristics, he was still very much one of us. He lived where we live, he understood our struggles, and he was even vulnerable to the same emotions we wrestle with. Our Lord and Savior was one of us, and that is what makes him so special. He was one of us, but he was not overcome by the things that tend to overwhelm us. Jesus might have gotten angry—perhaps he gets angry still—but his anger never overcomes his love for us.

How do you feel about Jesus' angry outburst?

Lord God, how could you not get angry with us—with me? Sometimes, we get most upset with those we love ...Why would the same not hold true for you? There must be days when you want to make another whip of cords and turn over tables and shout that the way we are living should not be so! It is tempting to be alarmed at such a response to our living ...And yet, for us to be in full communion with one another, we must share all things together ... our loves, our hurts, our angers, and our joys. Thank you for not standing at a distance from us but get-ting close enough to get riled up by our actions and our inaction. In your name, I pray. AMEN.

August 15

CHALLENGING

Read: John 3:1–10

> *Jesus answered Nicodemus, "Are you a teacher of Israel,*
> *and yet you do not understand these things?"*
> *JOHN 3:10*

JESUS WAS NOT a pastoral caregiver or a counselor. Jesus was not in the business of carefully listening and gently responding to the needs and questions of those who approached him. Jesus could be harsh, unflinching, and challenging. When old Nicodemus approached Jesus under the cover of darkness in order to find out more about the fiery Galilean prophet, Jesus berated him. *"You need to be reborn. You need to be moved by the Spirit. You don't understand anything!"*

One thing we need to understand about Jesus is that he does not intend to help us on our way to a more comfortable and successful life. Jesus isn't interested in incremental steps toward holiness and blessing. Jesus entered the world intent on radical change. People needed to repent of their sins. People needed to start aiming their lives in the right direction no matter the cost. People needed to face up to their flaws and failed understandings and make major changes to their lives. Jesus challenged people, because Jesus wanted to change people.

What challenging words do you think Jesus would speak to your life?

Lord, I would like you to deal gently and lovingly with me. I do not want your harsh criticism anymore than I want anyone else's. Perhaps that is why my life always seems the same. Day in and day out, I make the same mistakes, travel the same sinful paths, and settle for the same kind of unremarkable living I always do. Challenge me, change me, and grant me the courage to welcome your correction. In your name, I pray. AMEN.

August 16

CROSSING THE LINE

Read: John 4:1–42

Jesus left Judea and started back to Galilee. But he had to go through Samaria.
JOHN 4:3–4

THERE WERE TWO routes by which an individual could make passage between Judea and Galilee, and only one required traveling through Samaria. In fact, the Samarian highway was notoriously dangerous, and people avoided traveling that route if at all possible. The assertion the Jesus *"had to"* go through Samaria on his way to Galilee is not geographically accurate, which suggests that it may have been theologically essential. Jesus was drawn by God to go to the land of the Samaritans, those people long despised by the Judean Jews, to demonstrate God's all-inclusive love for people. To do the will of God, Jesus *"had to"* cross a line most Jews we unwilling to even approach.

Sitting by Jacob's well in Samaria, Jesus broke through shocking barriers. He entered a region of Palestine viewed as ritually unclean; he spoke alone with a woman, which was socially unacceptable; and the woman with whom he spoke was of questionable moral standing. Jesus made a habit of going where others refused to go, speaking with people others walked past without taking notice, and keeping company with people with whom Jews refused to associate. To follow in Jesus' example means to cross lines that separate people from one another so that God's family might be united in friendship, fellowship, and love.

What line do you need to cross today?

Lord, I spend far too much time trying to do what is perceived as socially appropriate and acceptable. I live within the lines, I live within cultural norms, I live within social structures that are comfortable to me. When I read of your life and ministry, however, I see you continually crossing lines to engage in relationship. What would my life be if you had not crossed over into it? What imaginary lines should I cross? In your name, I pray. AMEN.

August 17

Stand Up!

Read: John 5:1–9

When Jesus saw him lying there and knew that he had been there a
long time, he said to him, "Do you want to be made well?"
John 5:6

For thirty-eight years a man had been lying by the pool at the Sheep Gate in Jerusalem hoping, dreaming, wishing he could get to a better place in life—but doing nothing to change his circumstances. Thirty-eight years! Looking at the stagnation and illness of this man's life, Jesus asked, *"Do you want to be made well?"* *"Do you desire health?"* *"Do you really want to be free to live as God created you to live?"* The root of these questions was Jesus' desire for the man to take responsibility for his life and wellness.

Thirty-eight years is too long to wait for a miracle. It was thirty-eight years of daydreams and pipe dreams. Thirty-eight years of wasting away by the pool hoping and wishing for things to be different. Thirty-eight years of inaction. Most of us don't have another thirty-eight years to wait to find the person God created us to be. We don't have another twenty years to waste. In fact, we shouldn't waste another day! No matter what ails us, it is time to heed Jesus' command, *"Stand up, take your mat and walk."* When we start walking, that's when we start healing!

What issue, situation, or relationship has been keeping you down?

Lord, I am tired of waiting. Call me out of my illness, help to surround me with the right
people, allow me to break out of the dysfunctional systems that grip my life, encourage me to
stop making excuses for myself . . . and then command me to start walking toward healing. In
your name, I pray. AMEN.

Quiz Time

Read: John 6:1–15

When he looked up and saw a large crowd coming toward him, Jesus said
to Philip, "Where are we to buy bread for all these people to eat?" He
said this to test him, for he himself knew what he was going to do.
John 6:5–6

Jesus asked a trick question as a teaching technique. How do you feed thousands of people? Philip and the disciples had no idea. How can we blame them? If we found ourselves in need of feeding five thousand people, we would be at a loss to know how to do it. Where do you find all that money? How do you provide for people out of your own meager resources? Five loaves of bread and two fish cannot possibly be enough!

Jesus' test was a method of teaching. He wasn't expecting Philip or the other disciples to have the answer. No. Jesus wanted to teach something new. Where can you buy bread for five thousand people on the shores of the Sea of Galilee? The answer is, you can't! You can't provide for all these people. You don't have enough to get the job done. Your resources are not sufficient. To feed the crowd, to accomplish the goal, to take care of everyone is beyond your ability. A task like that requires something more, *someone more*—God . . . and God will not disappoint. The answer to Jesus' quiz is that to meet the demand, God will need to supply the resources. Once the disciples and Jesus began dividing up what they had, that is exactly what happened—God provided!

What question might Jesus ask you?

Lord, you are always teaching us, instructing us, desiring to show us the way. You do not seem to be interested in our grades but in our learning. Thank you for that grace, and please continue our education. In Jesus' name, I pray. AMEN.

STILL WORKING

Read: John 8:1–11

> *When they kept questioning Jesus, he straightened up and said to them, "Let anyone among you who is without sin be the first to throw a stone at her."*
> *JOHN 8:7*

THIS IS ONE of the most moving and beloved stories of Jesus found in all the Gospel accounts of his life and ministry. It is a story infused with grace and wisdom, which calls us and causes us to reflect on our own brokenness before we take others to task for their shortcomings. It is a brilliant teaching moment that is attributed to Jesus. However, most scholars agree that this story is not part of the original Gospel account but rather a later addition that attempts to capture the prophetic message and profound love Jesus had for all God's people in the world. It is unclear whether this interaction between Jesus and a woman caught in adultery ever occurred.

Some Christians might find this belief unnerving at best and heretical at worst; however, it may be a most important testament of Jesus' continued presence with us. Long after his ministry on earth, Jesus' guiding Spirit continued to inspire stories of his life. We don't know if this story actually happened as it was written, but we know without a doubt that it is exactly what Jesus would do. The Gospel story might be set in stone, but Jesus' Spirit keeps working in our midst.

What is a true story?

Lord, I don't know about so many of the stories in the Bible. Honestly, I have plenty of questions. Did you really walk on water? How did a couple of fish and a few loaves of bread feed thousands of people? Who was standing next to you taking copious notes at all your lectures? And yet the portrait I get of you through the Gospels helps to give direction and purpose to my life. You worked faithfully in the world before your crucifixion, and your Spirit helped to shape the New Testament long after your resurrection, . . . and I dare to believe you are still working in my life and in the world this very day. For all this I give thanks and praise, in your name. AMEN.

ALL I KNOW

Read: John 9:1–41

> *I do not know whether he is a sinner. One thing I do*
> *know, that though I was blind, now I see.*
> *JOHN 9:25*

FAITH CANNOT BE fully explained. There are some beliefs that defy logic—and yet you just know them to be true! This does not impress people who place priority on reason and concrete knowledge. Either you have a rational explanation or you don't, in their opinion. The man born blind said he didn't know who Jesus was, but he knew that Jesus had healed him. The *how* of the event didn't seem to matter to the formerly blind man. What was the reason or the operative methodology behind the healing? What was Jesus' title? By what authority did the miracle take place? In the end, who cares! The man didn't know how he had gotten healed, he just knew Jesus had done it. When it comes to the most important things we believe in, our best witness may not be a rational response but rather that basic affirmation of our experience. We may not be able to answer how God works in our lives and our world—we just know God does . . . And for some of us, that is answer enough.

What do you believe?

Lord, I do not understand . . . but I believe. I believe in you. I believe that you love me. I believe you can do what the Bible says you can do. I believe you care. How do you do this? Why do you do this? I can't explain it for the life of me . . . but I am a believer—I believe in you. In Jesus' name, I pray. AMEN.

August 21

THE RAISING OF LAZARUS

Read: John 11:1–44

*Accordingly, though Jesus loved Martha and her sister and Lazarus, after having
heard that Lazarus was ill, he stayed two days longer in the place where he was.*
JOHN 11:5–6

JESUS LOVED MARTHA, Mary, and Lazarus, but, according to this story, Jesus intentionally refrained from going to Lazarus's bedside when he was gravely ill. Jesus told
the disciples that Lazarus's condition was to be used for God's glory. Apparently,
Lazarus's death was intended as a staged display of God's power. Lazarus would die,
Jesus would raise him from the dead, and God would be glorified—all according
to plan!

Whatever we make of this story, there is a terrible truth we need to grapple
with. Our timetables and God's timetable are different. What we want and how
God responds to those desires can be wildly divergent. We don't control Jesus;
Jesus—and God—do as they please. However, the result of divine action is always
good. We cannot know when God's Spirit will move in our lives, but we can trust
that when that Spirit does move we will experience blessing beyond our wildest
dreams. Martha, Mary, and Lazarus had to endure delay and death, but in the end,
all three experienced resurrection.

Where in your life does it seem as if God is delayed in meeting your needs?

*Lord God, you will do what you will do, when you want to do it. You are in charge, I am
not. My job is to try to be patient, trusting that when you do move, the dead will be raised,
hope will be restored, and my sadness will be replaced with joy. In Jesus' name, I pray. AMEN.*

August 22

JESUS WASHING THE DISCIPLES' FEET

Read: John 13:1–20

So if I, your Lord and Teacher, have washed your feet, you also
ought to wash one another's feet. For I have set you an exam-
ple, that you also should do as I have done to you.
JOHN 13:14–15

WE ARE REPULSED at the thought of someone having to wash us. It might be the single greatest fear of aging—that we would not be able to care for or clean ourselves! It is through this most intimate and personal act of washing that Jesus chooses to demonstrate how we are to care for one another. We are to get down on our hands and knees to help people get clean. This means that as followers of Jesus no task is beneath us when it comes to tending to others. We wouldn't have believed it unless we had seen it for ourselves—Jesus, Lord and Savior, washing the dirt off of sweaty, smelly, and misshapen feet. Leading by example, Jesus tells us to take care of people according to his example. Get down on our hands and knees, get up close and intimate with others, and do whatever we can to help people out.

Have you ever washed someone's feet?

Dear Lord, truthfully, the only feet I willingly wash are my own. The thought of washing someone's feet is uncomfortable to me because it is such a personal, intimate, and culturally foreign act. But you, Lord, want me to get that close to people. You want me never to flinch at an opportunity to care for others. You want me to follow your example. You have served us all, and you call us to do the same. Help me to humble myself so that kneeling before others is a natural act for me. In your name, I pray. AMEN.

August 23

ONE GOOD MISTAKE

Read: John 18:15–18, 25–27; 21:1–19

Now Simon Peter was standing [by the fire] and warming himself. They asked him,
"You are not also one of Jesus' disciples, are you?" Peter denied it and said, "I am not."
JOHN 18:25

YOU MAY BE one good mistake away from being truly useful to God. This is a difficult concept for competent people to grasp. Our own competence may be the most significant barrier to accomplishing great work for God. Peter, the most self-confident of all the disciples, did not become truly useful to Jesus until he had utterly failed Jesus.

We are often so confident in our own abilities, in our own insights, and in our own sense of direction that God is unable to lead us toward true greatness. We believe we have proved our worth on more than one occasion, so we are disinclined to feel a need to wait for God's advice and direction. We charge ahead, pressing our own agenda, seeking to make our own way in the world, bent on achieving the goals we set for ourselves. As a result, we are often useless to God. God needs people who will listen. God needs people who can be led. God needs people who can learn.

The good news is that, like Peter, we may be only one good mistake away from being useful to God. One good mistake may be all it takes for us to regain perspective. One good mistake might be all it takes to start trusting God more than we trust ourselves.

How have the mistakes in your life made room for God?

Lord, as I stumble, help me to realize that the mistakes I make are not the end of me but rather the beginning of my true usefulness to you. In your name, I pray. AMEN.

August 24

MARY AT THE EMPTY TOMB

Read: John 20:11–18

Mary turned around and saw Jesus standing there,
but she did not know that it was Jesus.
JOHN 20:14B & C

WE ARE IN the hunt to know and understand how the world was created. We want to know upon what foundation the world is built. We want to know how the world works and how it runs. We look deep into the created order—into the cosmic and subatomic universe. We look into a world of neutrinos that move faster than light and unwitnessed matter that we call "dark." We desperately want to unravel the mystery of life in this world, never fully wanting to consider that the mystery has already been revealed to us.

The veil of mystery momentarily parted when Mary encountered—or was encountered by—Jesus at the tomb on Easter morning. Mary didn't recognize all that had taken place at first. She thought Jesus was the gardener, and she thought a body had gone missing, because up until that point she had no evidence on which to base a belief in the resurrection of the dead. However, the veil of this life was parted for a moment in time, and what was revealed was *eternity*—eternal love, eternal life, and eternal relationships.

Are you comfortable with mystery?

Dear Lord, I want to believe in you. I want to believe that life and love and relationships are eternal. I want to believe that when I come to my end, life is just beginning for me. But I don't really know. And I want to know. We all want to know. We don't like mysteries where our lives and our future hang in the balance. However, mystery is what you offer us. You offer us a glimpse of a gardener, who underneath it all, turns out to be a Savior. In your name, I pray. AMEN.

August 25

DEMANDING PROOF

Read: John 20:19–29

But Thomas said to them, "Unless I see the mark of the nails in his hands, and put
my finger in the mark of the nails and my hand in his side, I will not believe."
JOHN 20:25B & C

WE UNDERSTAND THOMAS'S doubt. He needed proof like we need proof. For us, "seeing is believing," and that was all Thomas was asking for—a little evidence. Resurrection is a wildly outlandish claim, and it strains even the most robust imaginations. This incident, however, branded Thomas forever as the doubter, an unflattering title we all could be shouldered with. *Doubter* can sound a little harsh, so we refer to ourselves instead as critical or practical or rational thinkers. But Jesus wants us to be called *believers*, so he returns. Jesus didn't desert Thomas because of his lack of faith, and he won't desert us in the midst of our skepticism either. And Jesus doesn't rest until we come to believe and exclaim as Thomas did, *"My Lord and my God!"*

What kind of proof do you need to believe?

Lord, if I demand proof, then what I am really looking for is knowledge, not belief.
You desire us to have faith in you. You want us to trust, even when every fiber of our being is
prepared to doubt. My Lord and my God, return to me, until I fully believe in you. In Jesus'
name, I pray. AMEN.

PETER, DO YOU LOVE ME?

Read: John 21

> *"Very truly, I tell you, when you were younger, you used to fasten your own*
> *belt and go wherever you wished. But when you grow old, you will stretch*
> *out your hands, and someone else will fasten a belt around you and take you*
> *where you do not wish to go."...After this he said to him, "Follow me."*
> JOHN 21:18–19

PETER'S STORY ENDS much like it began. Peter had been a fisherman, an outspoken disciple of Jesus Christ, and an absolute failure when he denied ever knowing his teacher. The specter of the cross seemed to bring out the worst in all the disciples as they abandoned Jesus, leaving him to face his adversaries on his own. However, Peter stands alone as the disciple who boastfully promised never to leave Jesus' side, only to entirely disown Jesus when the going got too rough.

Most people are familiar with this story of profound forgiveness. Jesus allowed Peter the opportunity to profess his love for Jesus, thus undoing the guilt and shame of Peter's threefold denial. What we might fail to notice is that this was also a moment of new beginning. The very last command Jesus issued to Peter in this Gospel was also the very first command extended to Jesus' disciples: *"Follow me."* The end of this Gospel points back to the very beginning. Not only does Jesus forgive Peter, he also says, *"Okay Peter, let's try this all over again . . . Start by following me."* What a joy it is to know that our Lord doesn't only allow us to retake the tests we have failed, but Jesus is willing to review the entire course of study—from the very first lesson!

Do you have to go back to the beginning and start following Jesus all over again?

Dear Lord, thank you for your willingness to forgive us when we fail, and for allowing us to start all over again with the reassurance that you are still in the lead. In your name, I pray. AMEN.

August 27

Waiting for the Promise

Read: Acts 1:1–5

> *While staying with them, Jesus ordered them not to leave*
> *Jerusalem, but to wait there for the promise of the Father.*
> *Acts 1:4*

"What do we do now?" must have been the most pressing question on the disciples' hearts and minds. Jesus was resurrected. The witness needed to be shared. There was work to be done. A church needed to be built! I suspect the disciples, so used to Jesus handing them their marching orders, assumed that Jesus would assign them tasks and send them on their way. Jesus' command, however, was not for the disciples to *go*, but rather to *wait*. Wait for the promise of the Father. Wait to see what God was up to. Wait and see what direction God offered. Isn't it curious that the book called *Acts* begins with a command to *wait*?

It is a great discipline to withstand the temptation to assert our own will so that we can discern what God is already doing in the world and join in those holy pursuits. Waiting is often the first step toward engaging in the *acts* of faith God wants us participating in. Don't be in a rush to assert yourself—wait on God.

Where in your life are you *acting* when you would be better served *waiting*?

Lord, you know me. You know my proclivity for charging off in whatever direction suits my fancy. My life is so much more about me than it is about you—which means I am not living a properly oriented life. And if my life is not oriented in the right direction, then my efforts will be misguided, and I may overlook the important work you intend for me. Grant me the courage to wait for you. Grant me the patience to wait to see what you are already doing in my life and in the world. Help me to trust that pausing is every bit as essential as acting. In Jesus' name, I pray. AMEN.

August 28

WITNESS

Read: Acts 1:6–11

It is not for you to know the times or periods that the Father has set
by his own authority. But . . . you will be my witnesses in Jerusalem,
in all Judea and Samaria, and to the ends of the earth.
ACTS 1:7–8

THERE IS A limit to what we can know about God. The disciples wanted Jesus to tell them about God's eternal plans, but Jesus said those plans were known only to God. The cosmos is too vast, time too expansive, and the workings of creation far too mysterious for us to grasp. Our call is not to *know* but to *witness* to our experiences of God. You can stand in awe of creation even if you can't fully understand it. Our lives can't always revolve around what we *know*; oftentimes we have to set our course based on what we *believe*. While ignorance may be one of the great evils at work in the world, dismissing the holy mysteries of creation might be equally unwise. Life without reverence for the unknown is careless and foolish. Jesus tempered our insatiable thirst for knowledge, encouraging us instead toward a holy awe for the divine mysteries of God. You don't have to be able to explain the beauty of the world; you just have to be able to appreciate it and celebrate it by sharing your experiences with others.

How have you experienced the awesome nature of God?

Lord God, absolute knowledge of you and your creation is beyond our grasp. Every new scientific discovery seems to saddle us with a slew of additional unanswered questions. There is so much we do not know. Perhaps knowledge is too much for us to expect in this life. Maybe serving as witnesses to your presence in the world is our true calling. In Jesus' name, I pray. AMEN.

August 29

Casting Lots

Read: Acts 1:15–26

And they cast lots, . . . and the lot fell on Matthias;
and he was added to the eleven apostles.
Acts 1:26

THE ELEVEN APOSTLES were making plans—casting dice and flipping coins—trying to decide among themselves who should be the twelfth apostle. They selected two men, Joseph and Matthias, as potential candidates. They prayed to God to show them which man was worthy of the position, and Matthias was chosen. On the other side of Jerusalem, a Roman Jew named Saul was at work persecuting Christ's church. The apostles didn't know it—and Saul didn't know it—but God was already at work selecting *Saul* as the next apostle. Saul ultimately became the apostle Paul, the man most responsible for spreading the gospel throughout the Mediterranean world. Matthias, on the other hand, is never again mentioned in the Bible.

Woody Allen is quoted as saying, *"If you want to make God laugh, tell him your plans."* The eleven apostles had made plans, they'd cast lots, and they'd tried to forecast the future. All the time God was working ahead of them to produce the most miraculous results. That is the extraordinary thing about God. While we make plans, God makes progress. We cast lots, God changes lives. We envision the future, God creates the future. Sometimes it is best to hold off making plans long enough to see where God is already at work.

As you make your plans, have you considered what God might be planning for you?

Lord, thank you for working ahead of me. Help me to remember that you are always at work preparing situations, changing lives, and transforming communities. Continue to work in my life and in the world . . . and allow me to be attentive to it all. In Jesus' name, I pray. AMEN.

August 30

PENTECOST

Read: Acts 2

And at this sound the crowd gathered and was bewildered, because
each one heard them speaking in the native language of each.
ACTS 2:6

WHEN THE SPIRIT of God breaks into the world, people become confused. When a successful businessperson chooses to leave their lucrative job to teach at an underperforming high school, the world doesn't understand. When a gifted doctor decides to leave a prestigious hospital to start a practice in a developing country, the world doesn't understand. When someone decides to cross a line of division to enter into community with a former adversary, the world does not understand. The ways of God are bewildering to those who are steeped in the ways of the world.

When God's Spirit is at work, disparate people come together in unity, people are prompted to learn and appreciate other languages and cultures, and old divisions give way to a new and wonderfully confusing world.

Where is God's Spirit bewildering you?

Dear Lord, allow your Spirit to break into my life like the rush of a violent wind. Set me on fire. Blessedly bewilder me. Shake me up so that new possibilities and opportunities might unsettle and then resettle my life according to your will. In Jesus' name, I pray. AMEN.

August 31

COMING TOGETHER

Read: Acts 2:1–13

In our own languages we hear them speaking about God's deeds of power.
ACTS 2:11

THERE ARE A lot of people and plenty of churches that claim to have unique access to God's will, God's Spirit, and God's agenda. There continues to be a *"we're in, and you're out"* mentality in so many communities of faith. But how do we know whose side God is on? How can so many different groups of people claim special knowledge of God? Who is *right*?

On Pentecost, God's Spirit was revealed in the unification of a diverse gathering of people. While the people were said to be *"devout Jews,"* they were from all over the world, and likely held diverse perspectives on faith. And yet somehow—miraculously—this group came together in the Spirit of God. They literally heard a group of Galileans speaking to them in their native languages. For a brief and holy moment, these disparate people found themselves on the same page. They were knit together by God's Spirit.

When we want to see God at work, we need to look for people or organizations that bring people together in unity. If you claim special knowledge about God, then you should possess a particular gift for drawing diverse people together for a common and loving purpose. God's Spirit is a Spirit of unity, not division. Therefore, where unity is found, you can be fairly certain God's Spirit is there at work. Where division exists . . . God's Spirit and presence is sorely needed.

Where do you witness the unifying power of God?

Lord, we live in a divisive age. Therefore, I must assume that somehow your Spirit is absent in the hateful and hurtful exchanges that shape much of our world. Help me to look for and participate in communities of unity. Help me to serve as a witness to your desire for your family to come together in loving embrace. Help me to usher your Spirit into the divisive places that exist in my life and in the world. Help us all to speak in tongues that are respectful of and intelligible to others. In Jesus' name, I pray. AMEN.

September 1

LORD AND SAVIOR

Read: Acts 2:14–36

Everyone who calls on the name of the Lord shall be saved. . . . God has
made him both Lord and Messiah, this Jesus whom you crucified.
ACTS 2:21, 36

JESUS IS SPECIAL. Unique. He is different from you and me and Peter. Jesus is Lord
and Savior even of those who abandoned, betrayed, denied, and crucified him. Can
you imagine unjustly killing someone only to have the individual you murdered
pardon you for your offense? Who could do that? How could that happen? Could
we be so generous and forgiving? No. Only Jesus.

Peter, the man who denied his relationship with Jesus, had found himself
embraced and forgiven by his resurrected Lord. Peter had firsthand experience
of a previously unimaginable grace, and he wanted to share his experiences with
anyone and everyone who would listen. Peter's Pentecost sermon was simple and
direct: Jesus is Lord. Jesus is Savior. Jesus forgives sinners just like us. Believe it!
Accept it! Live it!

What does Lord and Savior mean to you?

Lord, I am a sinner—you know it and I know it. If you could forgive Peter, the disciples,
and those who killed you, if you were willing to offer them the grace of a second chance,
perhaps you can pardon me too. You are my Lord; be my Savior as well. In your name, I pray.
AMEN.

September 2

BY THE NUMBERS

Read: Acts 2:37–42

Those who welcomed Peter's message were baptized, and that
day about three thousand persons were added.
ACTS 2:41

WHEN THE DAY of Pentecost had dawned, there were only one hundred twenty committed followers of Jesus Christ. However, by sunset of that same day, after the rush of the Spirit and after Peter's inaugural sermon, three thousand people committed themselves to Jesus Christ and his community. Even by today's mega-church standards, those numbers are impressive. What is even more notable is that the conversion took place after Peter's first sermon. Peter, who was known for his faltering and failing, delivered his first sermon and the results were staggering. The author's intent is clear: something far greater than Peter was at work on the day of Pentecost. The Holy Spirit of God was at work! In an instant, thousands of lives were redirected toward God. It may be as much a promise as it is a threat: when God's Spirit enters a room, people should brace themselves for extraordinary signs and wonders!

Do you expect incredible results when you allow God's Spirit to lead you?

Lord, I do not experience exponential—Pentecostal—growth in my life or in my work. I want to believe it is possible, but I can't even imagine experiencing it. Perhaps that is why such dynamic growth is foreign to me—I don't believe it is even possible. Or perhaps I am not truly and fully opening my life up to the power and presence of your Spirit. Lord, help me to unfurl the sails of my life so that I might catch the wind of your Spirit and be propelled by your will to places and experiences that lie beyond my imagination. In Jesus' name, I pray. AMEN.

September 3

SOCIALISM

Read: Acts 2:43–47

> *All who believed were together and had all things in common; they would sell*
> *their possessions and goods and distribute the proceeds to all, as any had need.*
> Acts 2:44–45

HISTORICALLY, ONE OF the great political flashpoints in our country centers around the accusation of "socialism." The way some speak heatedly of it, you would think that the prospect of redistributing wealth and power were akin to a financial and political holocaust. It is amazing to witness the vitriol that is stirred up when people contemplate sharing their goods and assets for the welfare of all.

And yet, sharing wealth for the benefit of all was a hallmark of the early church. Concern for the commonwealth of all people was a cornerstone of Christian faith. The earliest Christians understood that their lives and their resources were gifts from God—gifts they believed they did not deserve. For those first Christians, nothing was *earned*, all was *given*. Therefore, reciprocal generosity seemed the only faithful way to live.

Why do so many Christians become angry and fearful when it comes to sharing their wealth for the benefit of others?

Lord, I cling to what I believe is mine with singular tenacity. The idea that I would share what I have earned with people too lazy to fend for themselves appalls me. Why is that? Do I not trust in your provision? Do I not care about people in need? What is my objection to the Christian and biblical discipline of sharing wealth? I do not have the answer, but I know I need the help. In Jesus' name, I pray. AMEN.

September 4

GIVING WHAT WE HAVE

Read: Acts 3:1–10

Peter said, "I have no silver or gold, but what I have I give you; in
the name of Jesus Christ of Nazareth, stand up and walk."
ACTS 3:6

WHAT IS MOST precious to you? Your stock portfolio? Your checking account? Your home? Your family? Your life? Can you imagine having a relationship with Jesus that is so intimate and real that you consider it the most valuable asset in your life? Questions like these can remind us how far we have to go before we can live a life of true faithfulness and devotion to Jesus. However, it may be important to remember that Peter, who willingly shared Jesus with the crippled beggar in this text, is the same Peter who left Jesus for dead in the Garden of Gethsemane. Peter is proof that while our priorities and values may be jarringly out of order, there is still hope that through Jesus our lives can be refocused in ways so meaningful that even our passing shadows can bring healing to others.

What is the most precious thing in your life?

Lord, I am more like Peter before he experienced your resurrection and your forgiveness.
I am fearful. I am weak-willed. I am less than generous. Surround me with your expansive
love so that my life might freely exude your hope, help, and healing. Become the most precious
possession of my life . . . and make me your possession, now and forever. In Jesus' name, I pray.
AMEN.

September 5

GOD'S PLAN

Read: Acts 3:11–26

> *. . . Universal restoration that God announced long ago through his holy proph-*
> *ets. . . . "in your descendants all the families of the earth shall be blessed."*
> *ACTS 3:21 & 25*

JESUS DIDN'T COME to save Christians. Jesus is part of an ancient prophesy, an ancient covenant that God made with Abraham. This promise revealed that God's plan for creation is nothing less than *"universal restoration,"* a restoration that will take the form of a blessing for *"all the families of the earth."* God is not exclusive. God wants the entire human family to gather together in joyous reunion. No one is to be left out of the celebration.

It may be interesting to note that this promise of universal salvation was offered to Abraham, who is regarded as the father of Judaism, Christianity, and Islam. Perhaps if we could stop fighting with each other, we could find ways to bridge the estrangement that exists between different faiths. It would appear that God's family is as dysfunctional as any family, but thankfully God hasn't given up on us yet! God has a plan.

Is God's plan universal?

Lord, we are a mess. We are a family. Your family. Please keep working with us until we come together as you have long desired. In Jesus' name, I pray. AMEN.

September 6

RESISTANCE

Read: Acts 4:1–22

Whether it is right in God's sight to listen to you rather than to God, you must judge; for we cannot keep from speaking about what we have seen and heard.
ACTS 4:20

IT WASN'T LONG before Peter and John were hauled before the Jewish council for preaching and teaching that *"in Jesus there is the resurrection of the dead."* When something is new, people often resist it, even if what is new is better than what is old. It is part of our human nature that we gravitate toward that which is familiar, comfortable, and safe. God, however, calls us to lives that are daring, bold, and a little risky. For when we push out into the new world and the new life God extends before us, that is when we grow into new people. Peter and John were experiencing the blessing of the new thing God was doing in their lives, and there was no way in the world they were going to keep quiet about it.

What new thing are you resisting in life?

Lord, grant me the courage to break out of the well-worn patterns of my life so that I can branch out in new directions. You call us to shed our old habits and vices, to claim a renewed and redeemed life. Push me, pull me, prod me—do whatever you have to do to get me to move into new experiences without reservation. In Jesus' name, I pray. AMEN.

September 7

Prayer for Boldness

Read: Acts 4:23–31

> *Lord, look at their threats, and grant to your ser-*
> *vants to speak your word with all boldness.*
> *Acts 4:29*

It is scary to feel threatened. When we feel as though we are in danger, we often back off and look for a safe haven. After Peter and John's first altercation with the religious authorities in Jerusalem, they must have been tempted to tone down the rhetoric. While the story doesn't directly indicate a willingness to retreat, the fact that the church was praying for holy boldness in the midst of the threatening circumstances suggests that Peter and John were in need of encouragement.

Every human being grows faint of heart from time to time, but when God is with us, when the Holy Spirit empowers boldness, when Jesus promises to be with us until the end of the age, we can be more courageous than we might have imagined ourselves to be. The text also indicates that the early church knew to pray for what they needed. If you grow faint of heart, pray for courage. If you face powerful adversaries, pray for protection. If there is a story that must be shared against all odds, pray for boldness.

What do you need to pray for today?

Lord, my faith is timid at times. I am reluctant to speak of you or your presence in my life for fear that the people around me will think me odd. I do not want to be perceived as a religious kook. I would rather remain silent than be outed as a person of faith. Yet my quiet and private faith does not adequately mirror your generosity and blessings to me. I need to pray for many things, but one request that I am reluctant to make needs to be voiced—give me the resolve to speak boldly to others about my relationship with you. In Jesus' name, I pray. AMEN.

September 8

PRIVATE VERSUS PUBLIC

Read: Acts 4:32–37

No one claimed private ownership of any possessions, but every-
thing they owned was held in common.
ACTS 4:32

IT MAY BE a uniquely American or capitalist belief that when people have an ownership stake in something, they are more attentive to its care and upkeep. Private
property is better maintained than public land. Homeowners respect their property more than those who rent. Therefore, private wealth is preferable to public
welfare.

However, when you see some of the great public parks in New York, Boston,
Paris, London, and other dynamic and diverse cities, you find that people treasure
and maintain public space with great zeal. There is a sense that deep down we
understand that things we hold in common are the things that are most valuable to
us. And when we recognize that we should have a stake in what is common to us all,
our obsession with that which is private is revealed for what is truly is: idolatrous,
selfish, and evil.

Do you place more value in what is privately held or what is publically shared?

Lord, you do not invite us to indulge in private living but in extravagant sharing. You
call us to a way of living that is generous and communal. You encourage us to be more like you,
offering what we have to others so that no one is ever in need. What a remarkable way of life
you call us to! In Jesus' name, I pray. AMEN.

September 9

WITHHOLDING

Read: Acts 5:1–11

> *"Ananias,"Peter asked,"why has Satan filled your heart to lie .*
> *. . and to keep back part of the proceeds of the land?". . .When*
> *Ananias heard these words, he fell down and died.*
> Acts 5:3 & 5

THE STORY OF Ananias and Sapphira is direct and jarring. The message is stark—people who horde goods and resources for themselves die; those who share with one another live. The consequences of greed and gluttony may not be immediate death, but there is a very real spiritual death that comes from not sharing with others. Ananias and Sapphira began to die the moment they began to commiserate about what they would withhold for themselves, and withhold from God.

Our world is imperiled not by a lack of resources but by a lack of generosity. There is a personal consequence to our lack of generosity: the spirit within us shrivels and our lives begin to shrink from the grand design God has for them. Greed brings death; generosity produces life.

What are you holding back from God?

Lord, I am not nearly as generous as I could or should be. I do not think expansively of my giving, therefore there are limits to my living. I withhold so much for myself that my spiritual growth is stunted and my faith falters. Help to unleash my generosity—and the generosity of all your people—so that everyone will have what they need. In Jesus' name, I pray. AMEN.

September 10

CHURCH GROWTH

Read: Acts 5:12–16

Yet more than ever believers were added to the Lord. . . . A great number of
people would also gather from the towns around Jerusalem, bringing the
sick and those tormented by unclean spirits, and they were all cured.
ACTS 5:14 & 16

ACTS IS A story about the church, for the church. It tells of the first days of Jesus'
community and how that community grew. There appear to be three catalysts for
the remarkable growth that the early church experienced. The community witnessed to and taught people about Jesus. The community shared their goods and
resources with people in need. The community healed the sick. Teaching, sharing,
and healing were the primary "business" of the church, and that "business" was so
attractive that converts were made by the thousands. The building maintenance issues, budgetary matters, and coffee service that so consume our churches do not
seem to be a central focus of the church in Acts. Perhaps that is why the community
in Acts seems so much more vital than many of our churches. If we focused on the
ministries our earliest Christian brothers and sisters believed were essential, we
would likely feel as vital and spirit-filled as they did.

Are teaching, sharing, and healing the primary ministries of your community
of faith?

Lord, your church has been imperfect from its inception, because it is filled with sinners
and malcontents just like me. But when we get out of ourselves and focus on our primary mis-
sions and ministries, it is amazing the growth we can experience—in the church and in our
individual lives. In Jesus' name, I pray. AMEN.

September 11

GAMALIEL

Read: Acts 5:17–42

But a Pharisee in the council named Gamaliel, a teacher of the law, respected by
all the people, stood up and . . . said . . . "If this plan or this undertaking is of
human origin, it will fail; but if it is of God, you will not be able to overthrow
them—in that case you may even be found to be fighting against God!"
ACTS 5:34 & 38–39

WE OFTEN FORGET that God is at work in *all* our lives, and God is at work in *all*
situations. Even in the most intractable of situations and in the most hardened of
lives, God's Spirit is seeking an "in." God's ability to influence the course of history
is in direct proportion to how open and available we are to the movement of God's
Spirit. We can never know whose heart is being opened by the power and presence
of God. God often works behind the scenes, and out of our view, to effect change.

The apostles assumed the council that was deciding their fate was corrupt,
immovable, and dead set against them. They believed that the spiteful and hateful
religious authorities who had killed Jesus would never change! But God was moving in the heart of a priest named Gamaliel, and through Gamaliel the council's
vengeful motives were thwarted. Who could have imagined that God was working behind the scenes of that gathering of religious leaders, changing hearts and
motives in ways that would protect the people the council was set on destroying?
God imagined, and the situation changed!

Where might God be working behind the scenes in your life right now?

Lord, on so many occasions I assume that I have come to a dead end. I feel as though I have
encountered an obstacle that cannot be overcome. Or I find myself in a difficult situation or relation-
ship that seems to have no resolution. I long to believe that you are working in my life, but I often
forget that you are also working beyond my view in the other lives affected in a particular moment.
If you are working all the angles of a situation, perhaps I should trust in your ability to move moun-
tains, and simply expect to be surprised by your creative imagination. In Jesus' name, I pray. AMEN.

— 293 —

September 12

Focus

Read: Acts 6:1–7

Select from among yourselves seven men of good standing, full of the
Spirit and of wisdom, whom we may appoint to this task, while we, for
our part, will devote ourselves to prayer and to serving the word.
ACTS 6:3–4

GOD DOESN'T ASK us individuals to do everything. In fact, when we attempt to do it all ourselves, we injure Christ's community and overlook the endowed giftedness of others.

The apostles were in charge of all aspects of church life, from preaching and teaching to dispute resolution and food distribution. As a result, important community duties were falling through the cracks and conflict began to simmer. The answer to this untenable situation was for the apostles to hand over some of their leadership responsibilities to others, while focusing their efforts on what Jesus had specifically called them to do. That focus, combined with an emphasis on shared leadership, allowed the community to continue to flourish.

What work do you need to let others tend to so that you can focus on your primary calling?

Lord, when I try to do it all myself, I find I am actually trying to replace your position in my life. You are Lord. You are Savior. You assign work to us as you desire. Why don't I just do my part and entrust the rest to you and to other people you are working through? In the end, as it was in the beginning, this is your work—I am just a laborer. In Jesus' name, I pray. AMEN.

September 13

HOLY GLOW

Read: Acts 6:8–15

And all who sat in the council looked intently at Stephen, and
they saw that his face was like the face of an angel.
ACTS 6:15

STEPHEN HAD BEEN dragged before the religious leaders in Jerusalem, and he had been charged with blasphemy and leading people astray from traditional Jewish faith and teachings. Within moments, and after a stirring personal defense, Stephen was stoned to death. The end of Stephen's life was imminent, and yet, we are told his countenance was angelic in the face of persecution. The holy glow about Stephen was reminiscent of Moses' face shining like the sun when he descended from Mount Sinai after an encounter with God.

When we open our lives up to God's presence, when God's love flows through us, when we are willing to be moved by God's Holy Spirit no matter where it takes us, we reflect divine light and truth to others. Even in the face of persecution, we radiate that divine presence in ways that are visible to those around us.

Do you glow with God's presence?

Lord, draw me close to you so that your presence shines through me. When I am chal-
lenged, when I am bullied, when I am unjustly accused, allow my countenance to demonstrate
something other than defensiveness. Allow my life to exude the generosity and love that I have
received from you. In Jesus' name, I pray. AMEN.

September 14

HISTORY

Read: Acts 7:1–53

Stephen replied:"Brothers and fathers, listen to me. The God of glory appeared to our ancestor Abraham when he was in Mesopotamia, before he lived in Haran, and said to him, 'Leave your country and your relatives and go to the land that I will show you.'"
ACTS 7:2–3

WE OFTEN FAIL to remember all that God has done in our lives. We forget God's history with us. When we are confronted with a new challenge or when the course of our life suddenly changes, we often forget that God is right there with us, shepherding us through unknown territory.

As Stephen stood in front of members of a hostile religious council who were angered by his proclamations about Jesus Christ, Stephen looked back over the history of Israel and witnessed to the activity of God in and through it all. Stephen reflected on God's past actions in an attempt to explain God's present movement. This happens so often in the Bible; memories of God's faithful history are retold to encourage people's faith in God's continued and present activity in the world.

It doesn't take much examination of our own personal histories to see God's activity and presence. If God has been faithful to us in the past, why wouldn't we assume God's faithful presence in future? It is important to remember God's history with us.

Can you look back over your life—the many twists and turns—and witness God's guiding hand at work?

Lord, thank you for never leaving me forsaken. Thank you for faithfully tending to my life even when I was unaware of it. When I look back, I see your hand at work. With such history between us, how could I ever fear for our future together? In Jesus' name, I pray. AMEN.

September 15

PRESENT IN PERSECUTION

Read: Acts 7:54–60

I see the heavens opened and the Son of Man standing at the right hand of God!
ACTS 7:56

AS THE CROWD picked up stones and began to throw them at Stephen, we are told that Stephen looked toward the heavens and saw Jesus. Jesus was there in the midst of persecution. Stephen fell to the ground and died while uttering words of pardon similar to those that Jesus extended to his executioners at Golgotha: *"Lord, do not hold this against them."*

Even if we were to doubt the reality of Stephen's vision, I suspect we know that if Jesus is anywhere in the world, he is present in places of suffering. Jesus, the Suffering Servant, who did not avoid the cross, makes his home in broken places and broken lives. Therefore, we can have confidence that Jesus will not avoid attending to us in our moments of trial and tribulation. When Jesus is with us in moments of persecution, as he was with Stephen, we can even die with grace and love.

The next time you feel persecuted, remember Jesus is there with you.

Lord, we would prefer to avoid suffering, but we are grateful that you are with us in whatever trials and troubles we face. If you are with us in the most difficult moments of life—if you are there as we pass from life to death—what do we have to fear? We might even find, in the end, that we can forgive those who assail us when we possess such faith. In your name, I pray. AMEN.

September 16

SCATTERED?

Read: Acts 8:1–3

That day a severe persecution began against the church in Jerusalem, and all except
the apostles were scattered throughout the countryside of Judea and Samaria.
ACTS 8:1

THE DEATH AND resurrection of Jesus may not have changed human nature, but it surely transformed the lives of the apostles. When Jesus was arrested in Gethsemane, the disciples ran for their lives, leaving Jesus to face the consequences of his ministry alone. However, in this passage, as the apostles took up the mantle of leadership themselves, they were no longer easily shaken from their mission. Whereas they scattered in fear of persecution in Gethsemane, in this story they were the only ones to stand firm as the church faced persecution in Jerusalem. They were no longer chaff driven by the wind, but rather rocks upon which a community of faith could be built—a community against which the gates of hell will not prevail.

The real and unfolding grace of this story is that God uses the church members who fled Jerusalem to found new Christian communities throughout the Roman Empire. The church scatters, and yet God used the dispersed fragments of that community to seed faith in regions the church had not even considered entering. God can use us for blessing whether we are gathered or scattered, whether we are faithful or fainthearted, whether we are rock solid or windblown.

Are you scattered, or are your feet planted in the bedrock of faith?

Lord, I know that my faith and my commitment to you are shaky at times. I would likely scatter in the face of persecution. I would flee from your side like the disciples and the members of the Jerusalem church. And yet, I rejoice in the fact that you can use me to your glory, even when I am running for my life in the opposite direction. How glorious—you are faithful even when I am not! In your name, I pray. AMEN.

INTENTION

Read: Acts 8:4–25

Simon [the magician] . . . offered them money, saying, "Give me also this power so that anyone on whom I lay my hands may receive the Holy Spirit."
ACTS 8:18–19

SIMON WAS A local magician in Samaria. He was popular, he was important, and he had wealth. When Philip came to town preaching about Jesus, casting out demons and healing the sick, Simon was shown for the pretender he was. Simon saw real power and he bowed to it, being baptized in the name of Jesus and following Philip wherever he went.

However, once Simon saw how Peter and John conferred the power of the Holy Spirit upon people, he wanted that power for himself, and he was more than willing to pay for it. Not only was his request refused but he also was told his life would be cursed if he did not repent of his evil intentions. Simon shows us that bad intentions can corrupt even the most holy of powers.

Is there a power or ability you desire with less than faithful intentions?

Lord, my motives are rarely better than Simon's. The ambition within me is far less than pure. Without you to redirect my course—without you to rebuke me at times—I would be lost. I pray that you forgive me my failings and instruct me on the way of righteousness. In Jesus' name, I pray. AMEN.

September 18

LED

Read: Acts 8:26–40

> *Then an angel of the Lord said to Philip, "Get up and go toward the*
> *south to the road that goes down from Jerusalem to Gaza."...Then the*
> *Spirit said to Philip, "Go over to the chariot and join it."...The Spirit of*
> *the Lord snatched Philip away; ... Philip found himself at Azotus.*
> *Acts 8:26, 29, 39–40*

THE SPIRIT OF God leads us and guides us if we are open to its movement. The Holy Spirit of God will set us on the course God wants us to be on, if we are receptive to its leading. As a man who steeped himself in prayer, in the study of scripture, and in the discipline of listening for God in his life, Philip was able to be moved by the Spirit of God. God took Philip and placed him where God wanted him to be.

We spend a lot of time envisioning the life we want to lead. What job will we do? What career path will we take? What community will we live in? These are important, and frankly, exciting questions to both ask and answer. But we often engage these questions without asking for God's input. It is as if we do not trust in the Lord's ability to lead us. And yet, when we defer to God's direction, our lives are richer, more meaningful, and can have a greater impact than we could ever have imagined. When in the lead, God also has a way of taking us to very interesting and wonderfully unlikely destinations!

Where could God take you if you yielded to God's direction?

Lord, I want to trust that if I follow, you will lead me. In fact, I suspect that my life would be more meaningful and more interesting if I yielded to your guidance. Why do I assume I need to make my own way in the world? Why do I insist on always taking the initiative? Scripture attests that if I wait on you, you will open the doors you want me to walk through and close the doors that would take me down paths that are unwise for me to travel. Lord, I so dearly want you to take a leading role in my life. Help me to follow. In your name, I pray. AMEN.

September 19

BREAKTHROUGH

Read: Acts 9:1–19

Saul fell to the ground and heard a voice saying to him, "Saul, Saul, why do you perse-cute me?" Saul got up from the ground, and though his eyes were open, he could see nothing; so they led him by the hand and brought him to Damascus.

ACTS 9:4, 8

OFTENTIMES IT TAKES a breakdown before we can experience a breakthrough. Saul was a confident religious zealot, persecuting the early church with righteous indig-nation. Saul was successful, respected by his peers, and feared by those he opposed. His attack on the followers of Jesus ensured that he would continue to climb in the esteem of his colleagues. It wasn't until his conversion on the road to Damascus, however, that his life mission and legacy were revealed. For Saul to be converted from a relentless Jewish zealot to a passionate Christian missionary, he had to be broken.

When Jesus encountered Saul on the road to Damascus, Saul fell to the ground, he was struck blind, and, because he could not navigate on his own, he had to be led by the hand to his destination. After being broken, Saul experienced a breakthrough that would not only reorient his life but would also transform the world. Having been struck blind, Saul finally began to see. Saul became Paul, and the world has never been the same.

Could your present brokenness be a prelude to a powerful breakthrough?

Lord, I don't want to be broken any more than I want to discover that the way I am living my life is set against your will and purposes. However, I need the truth. I need you to stop me in my tracks if I am headed in the wrong direction, and I need to be broken if that will be the way I experience a breakthrough in my life. In Jesus' name, I pray. AMEN.

September 20

IMPOSSIBLE

Read: Acts 9:19–22

> *Immediately Saul began to proclaim Jesus in the synagogues, saying, "He is the*
> *Son of God." All who heard him were amazed and said, "Is not this the man*
> *who made havoc in Jerusalem among those who invoked Jesus' name?"*
> Acts 9:20–21

SCRIPTURE PROMISES THAT with God anything is possible, but we seldom believe that claim to be true. With the story of Saul's conversion, we have undeniable evidence that God can take a vile enemy and transform him into a powerful advocate. Saul, who was intent on exterminating the early followers of Jesus Christ, turned out to be the one who brought the gospel to the gentile world! Without Saul the church as we know it, perhaps Christianity as we know it, would not exist. In the conversion of Saul to the apostle Paul, we are reminded that nothing—*nothing*—is impossible for our God.

What impossible situation or relationship do you need God to transform today?

Lord, you can do everything—infinitely more than we can ever ask or imagine! How can we doubt you and say, "Impossible!?" That word does not exist for you. In Jesus' name, I pray. AMEN.

September 21

ESCAPE

Read: Acts 9:23–25

> *The Jews plotted to kill him, but their plot became known to*
> *Saul. . . . His disciples took him by night and let him down*
> *through an opening in a wall, lowering him in a basket.*
> ACTS 9:23 & 25

EARLIER IN THE story of Acts we found out that God would use Saul for mighty purposes, but Saul would also suffer as a result of his new calling. It wasn't long before the people Saul had once stood beside in condemnation of Jesus' followers began taking aim at him. The Jews waited by the gates of Damascus to seize Saul, but God provided Saul a way out. The plot was made known, a breach in the city wall was identified, and friends lowered Saul to safety in a basket in a daring escape.

When we are cornered in life, when powerful forces are arrayed against us, when all hope seems to be lost, that is when God seems to find a way out for us. It is as if God waits for the very moment when we say *"Only God can save me now"* to do just that.

Do you have a "lowered in a basket" story of God's saving grace in your life?

Lord, there have been times when I have been absolutely convinced that you saved me. You swept me out of harm's way and safely delivered me to another day. I remember promising you I would never forget. But I did. I became silent about the miracles you have bestowed on my life, and in time I not only stopped thinking about them but I also lost the ability to trust in them. Thank you for the many times you have saved me. Help me to remember and trust in your ability to deliver me, even when all hope appears lost. In your name, I pray. AMEN.

September 22

BARNABAS

Read: Acts 9:26–31

*Barnabas took Saul, brought him to the apostles, and described
to them how on the road Saul had seen the Lord.*
ACTS 9:27

THE APOSTLES HAD known Saul to be an enemy and persecutor of the church. Therefore, they were reluctant to believe in Saul's conversion and hesitated to welcome him into their community. Enter Barnabas, a respected member of the church. Barnabas was a man of standing who had been financially generous to the fledgling church. Barnabas, who'd had his own conversion experience, came to Saul's defense. Eventually, on Barnabas's word, Saul was accepted.

When you live in right relationship with God, when you follow God's lead, when you allow conversion to take hold of you, God will take care of you. God will find a way to advocate for you. God may even provide a Barnabas to speak on your behalf.

Who has been a Barnabas for you?

Lord, if Barnabas had not stood in Saul's defense, who knows if your church would have succeeded in traveling around the globe! Thankfully, Barnabas was there speaking your truth to powerful and prophetic men. I thank you for Barnabas and for the many people who have come to my defense. Help me to stand up for others when support is needed and deserved. In your name, I pray. AMEN.

September 23

BIT PARTS

Read: Acts 9:32–43

Meanwhile Peter stayed in Joppa for some time with a certain Simon, a tanner.
ACTS 9:43

AENEAS WAS AN invalid. Tabitha was a seamstress. Simon was a tanner. We know little more than this about these three people of faith. They are very small players in the story of Acts—they had only bit parts to play in early church history. But the little roles they played are important in the grand scheme of God's redemptive work. The healing of Aeneas, the raising of Tabitha, and the hospitality of Simon each serve as a catalyst for people turning their lives toward Jesus Christ. These bit players are what make up the salvation drama that God is performing throughout the world, and throughout history.

What role does God want you to play?

Lord, when I hear the great names and great stories of the Bible, I struggle to believe that my story fits in. I cannot part seas, I cannot feed thousands, I cannot preach people to faith. Perhaps that is why your Word is filled with people playing small but essential roles of faith that allow for the advancement of your Spirit in the world. I may never be a Peter or Mary or Paul, but I might just be an Aeneas, a Tabitha, or a Simon. Give me a role, Lord, and I will attempt to play it. In Jesus' name, I pray. AMEN.

NO PARTIALITY

Read: Acts 10:1–33

The voice said to Peter again, a second time, "What God
has made clean, you must not call profane."
ACTS 10:15

THE STORY OF Peter and Cornelius is a testament to the fact that God loves what God creates. Going back to Genesis, we remember that after God created, God looked at all that had been made and called it *good*. What therefore God has created and deemed good we must not call profane or unclean or repulsive.

The revelation to Peter in this passage was that Gentiles, just like the Roman Centurion Cornelius, were as beloved by God as the Jews. Gentiles had been viewed by Jews as dirty and unholy. Suddenly Peter had undeniable proof that God loved everyone . . . Therefore we should too. Barriers to love are a human construction, not a God-erected reality. For God shows no partiality—God loves us all and asks us to do the same.

Who do you view as unworthy of your love?

Lord, we live and participate in a world that spends a lot of time and effort demeaning people. We try to tell different groups of people they are less than we are. Gay and lesbian people, people of color, women, Muslims, indigenous peoples—the powerful often malign those who seem different. But you, O Lord, demonstrate love for all you have created. Please help me to do the same. In Jesus' name, I pray. AMEN.

September 25

Primary Actor

Read: Acts 10:44–48

> *While Peter was still speaking, the Holy Spirit fell upon all who heard the word.*
> *Acts 10:44*

So much preaching and teaching in the Christian faith is anthropocentric—it's all about *us*. However, the Bible, and all the stories therein, are decidedly theocentric—all about *God*. God is the primary actor in the Bible. Our job is simply to respond to what God has done in scripture and to what God is doing in our lives and in our world.

In this passage, Peter's sermon was interrupted by God's Holy Spirit falling upon the people listening to his message. God appropriately upstaged Peter. Even when it seemed Peter was in complete control, mesmerizing the crowd before him with his preaching, an interruption reminded him that God was the primary actor, the primary mover, the primary teacher. God was in charge, Peter was not—we are not.

Has God ever interrupted your life?

Lord, much of the time I like to be in control—I like to think of myself as the primary actor. I can, at least for a while, take comfort in my ability to act and initiate. But then there are moments—moments of powerful clarity—when I grow weary of having everything in my life centered on my whims and fancies. I grow weary of everything being about me. Deep down I long for my life to be about you. Help make it so, Lord . . . for I am getting tired of myself. I need you. In Jesus' name, I pray. AMEN.

September 26

CONFLICT

Read: Acts 11:1–18

Now the apostles and the believers who were in Judea heard that the Gentiles had also accepted the word of God. So when Peter went up to Jerusalem, the circumcised believers criticized him saying, "Why did you go to uncircumcised men and eat with them?"
ACTS 11:1–3

A GOOD ARGUMENT can be a great achievement. An argument can be truly productive when it is seen as a holy opportunity. Conflict can be life-giving if we don't avoid it. We often assume that healthy and wholesome churches, organizations, and families are those that don't experience tension and disagreement. The truth is, however, those seemingly conflict-free entities are just sweeping issues under the carpet. For we know that whenever two or three are gathered—whether Jesus is there or not—there will be conflict.

When real and important conflicts arise, if they are addressed directly and carefully, new life and opportunity for growth can be experienced. The apostles in Jerusalem were initially upset that Peter had spent time ministering to Gentiles, thus breaking centuries-old religious laws. With the issues on the table, however, the apostles were able to have a thorough and thoughtful conversation that wound up expanding the understanding of who God calls into relationship. The conflict ended with a hopeful resolution: *When the apostles heard this, "they were silenced. And they praised God, saying, 'Then God has given even to the Gentiles the repentance that leads to life.'"*

Are you avoiding conflict and thus missing an opportunity for growth and new life?

Lord, I would prefer to avoid conflict—to simply pretend it is not there. I want life to go smoothly, and I don't want to be embroiled in uncomfortable and personal squabbles. "Live and let live" is what I often say. However, I know that I can't fully live with issues piling up under the carpet. They always lie in wait, prepared to trip me up. Help me to lay aside my aversion to conflict and instead deal with issues that arise, trusting that you are at work even in the most difficult situations. In Jesus' name, I pray. AMEN.

September 27

NO OUTSIDERS

Read: Acts 11:1–18

> *What God has made clean, you must not call profane.*
> *ACTS 11:9B*

IN THIS PASSAGE, Peter tells the believers in Jerusalem that no one is outside God's love. God had made it clear to Peter that both Jew and Gentile—clean and unclean—were part of the family of God, and joint heirs to the blessings of that lineage. God doesn't make clean and unclean people—God only makes *children*. In this passage, it becomes clear that God's love is all-inclusive. *"What God has made clean, you must not call profane!"* No one is outside God's care. That became a founding principle of the Christian church. There are to be no outsiders, only family members!

When we come to grips with the reality that God's love and blessing extend to the entire world, we are forced to recognize that things have to change in our lives. First, God's all-embracing love *convicts us* because it reveals to us the failure of our own exclusive nature. Second, it should create in us a renewed sense of *compassion* for the people we struggle to be around; if God loves and cares for the people we can't stand, then we should find ways to offer our love and care to them as well. And finally, if God's love allows God to see the best in us, then we should make the *changes* necessary in our lives to live up to that love and belief.

What conviction, compassion, or change needs to take root in your life?

Lord, I cannot thank you enough for the love you have for me. I know I do not deserve your love and care. And yet you offer it freely to me and to all humanity. Help me to take hold of your love in ways that convict me, build compassion in my life, and prompt me to make the changes that reflect your belief in me. In Jesus, name I pray. AMEN.

September 28

CHEERLEADERS

Read: Acts 11:19–26

When Barnabas came and saw the grace of God [in Antioch], he rejoiced,
and he exhorted them all to remain faithful to the Lord with steady devo-
tion; for he was a good man, full of the Holy Spirit and of faith.
ACTS 11:23–24

GOD CALLS ALL kinds of people with a variety of gifts into ministry. Barnabas was not known for his great preaching, he was not known for his administrative abilities, nor he was he known for his intellect. Barnabas was recognized in the story of Acts for his generosity and his encouragement. He sold a field to support the early ministry of the apostles. He stood up for Paul in Jerusalem when the other apostles doubted Paul's conversion. And in this story, Barnabas cheered on the newly formed Christian community in Antioch. Barnabas was an enthusiastic cheerleader—and God knows we all need that kind of encouragement from time to time. We need cheerleaders!

Who are you cheering on and encouraging today?

Lord, thank you for the many people you set in my path to encourage me on my way. Their applause, their cheering, and their support have been nothing short of divine. Thank you. Guide me to places and relationships where I can return the blessing. It is my turn to cheer. In Jesus' name, I pray. AMEN.

September 29

ANGELS

Read: Acts 12:1–19

Suddenly an angel of the Lord appeared and a light shone in the cell.
He tapped Peter on the side and woke him, saying, "Get up quickly."
ACTS 12:7

WE HAVE AN image of angels that include wings, halos, and perhaps even playful bows and arrows. We hang angels on Christmas trees, place ceramic angels on our mantels, and we have plenty of children's story books—and even more adult versions—that feature white-winged creatures. The way we buy and sell angels would give even the most committed believer doubts about their reality.

There are no wings or cherubs or ceramic angels in this scripture. Just a man quietly entering a prison cell, with a light, and the ability to unlock chains and unbar doors. The truth is, the angel in this story could have been anyone with courage enough to act on the will of God. For in the end, that is exactly who angels are—individuals that work on behalf of God.

Can you remember a time when a flesh and blood angel came to your rescue?

Lord, I do not believe in the angels on Hallmark greeting cards. But I do believe that you send real angels to tend to us in those difficult and dark moments of our lives. I thank you for the angels that have visited my life. And I pray that you continue to send angels to those who find themselves imprisoned in one way or another in this life. In Jesus, name I pray. AMEN.

September 30

GIVING CREDIT

Read: Acts 12:20–25

The people kept shouting, "The voice of a god, and not of a mortal!" And
immediately, because Herod had not given the glory to God, an angel of
the Lord struck him down, and he was eaten by worms and died.
ACTS 12:22–23

WHEN WE DO not give credit to God for all God has done for us, we die. Little
by little, day by day, consumed by our own self-importance we grow smaller. We
shrivel. We become short sighted and tightfisted people whose lives do not reflect
the grandeur of God. We live entirely forgettable lives that are fit only for worms
to feed on when we expire.

God calls us to grand living—expansive and appreciative living. The kind of
living that prompts an athlete to point to the heavens after making a great play,
publicly acknowledging that all good things—all talent and ability and good for-
tune—originate in God.

Have you given thanks to God today?

Lord, if I were to give you adequate thanks and praise for all you have done and for all
you are doing in my life, there would little time for any other activities in the course of my
day. That is how numerous the blessings I have received from your hand are. May each breath
of mine be an expression of my boundless gratitude. In Jesus' name, I pray. AMEN.

October 1

SENT

Read: Acts 13:1–3

Then after fasting and praying they laid their hands
on Paul and Barnabas and sent them off.
ACTS 13:3

WE ARE CALLED toward God, only to be sent back into the world. The Spirit prompts us to gather for worship, prayer, and fasting so that we can discern where we are called to go and what we are called to do in this life. Church is not the destination of faith. Being sent into the world in the Lord's service is the purpose of our belief. We come in to go out. We turn to God to be returned to the world. Worship, prayer, fasting, and other spiritual practices inform us of the mind of God and point us in the right direction. God's call on our lives always sends us out into the world.

Where are you being sent?

Lord, I falter in my faith disciplines. My prayer life is inconsistent. I attend worship when it fits into my schedule. I can't remember the last time I attempted a fast. If I can't maintain simple faith practices that can bring my will in line with your will, how will I know which way to go? Help me to cultivate a disciplined life that seeks to wait on you so that you can send me on your way. In Jesus' name, I pray. AMEN.

October 2

SUCCESS

Read: Acts 14:1–7

And when an attempt was made by both Gentiles and Jews, with their rul-
ers, to mistreat them and to stone them, the apostles learned of it and
fled to Lystra and Derbe, cities of Lycaonia, and to the surround-
ing country; and there they continued proclaiming the good news.
ACTS 14:5–7

IT IS DIFFICULT to know if you are successful without some quantifiable means of measurement. How many units were sold? How many customers were gained? By how much has the profit margin increased? If Paul and Barnabas had tried to measure success by counting, they would have perceived themselves to be failures, for they were kicked out of nearly every community in which they preached. And yet, in retrospect, we know Paul to be the most important and influential evangelist in church history.

God uses different metrics when gauging success. Did you do what I asked? Did you go where I told you to go? Did you say what I laid on your heart to say? Paul didn't count converts, he merely spoke the words God asked him to share with others . . . the rest is history!

Are you successful?

Lord, I am a counter. I judge success and failure by what I can see and by what I can measure. I do not have the eternal view you have. I do not understand that seeds planted today may reap a remarkable harvest in a future I will not be around to take credit for. How limited my understanding, how shallow my insight, how small my vision! Success is obedience to you . . . All else is worthless. Allow me the courage to live in such obedience. In Jesus' name, I pray. AMEN.

October 3

DISCERNMENT

Read: Acts 15:1–35

Therefore I have reached the decision that we should not trou-
ble those Gentiles who are turning to God.
ACTS 15:19

JAMES, THE BROTHER of Jesus, was the leading authority in the church in Jerusalem. He presided over a council that was gathered to decide the expectations that the new Gentile converts were to live by. James's word would be the final word—a word that would reshape the life and mission of Jesus' followers forever.

Before James could render faithful judgment, however, he had to engage in careful and deliberate discernment. Silence was kept as testimony was given. Vigorous debate was encouraged. Scripture was consulted. Prayer was central. When trying to determine the mind of God, communal discernment is essential.

How do you make decisions?

Lord, I often make my decisions based on what feels right to me. What does my gut tell me? I might toss in a prayer for good measure after a decision is made. No wonder I have made so many poor choices in the past. I need to learn to listen—to you and to others around me, so that I learn what I need to know. In your name, I pray. AMEN.

October 4

SEPARATION

Read: Acts 15:36–41

> *The disagreement became so sharp that they parted company; Barnabas took*
> *Mark with him and sailed to Cyprus. But Paul chose Silas and set out . . .*
> *ACTS 15:39–40*

OUR FAILURE DOES not thwart God's success. When we stumble, God can still use our falling to further God's mission. Paul and Barnabas, two men of faith commissioned together by the apostles in Jerusalem, got in an argument and that argument escalated into a separation. This was a moment of failure for both Paul and Barnabas, their fellowship could not withstand their fight. They severed their relationship and went their separate ways. However, the breakup was still used by God in redeeming ways. Because of this separation, the ministry expanded. Paul and Silas went on to Macedonia, and Barnabas and Mark went to Cyprus. Somehow the separation served to further spread the mission. Our brokenness can be the catalyst for God's ever-expanding blessing. Our failures can be a prelude to God's success.

How can God use your failure for good?

Lord, I so often view failure as a dead end—I hesitate to believe that there can be positive byproducts of thwarted mission or ambition. And yet, you seem to be able to use all our experiences to further your message. You love us through thick and thin. Success or failure, unity or separation, cross or crown . . . there is not a situation in which you cannot bring about salvation. Glory, glory be to you! In Jesus' name, I pray. AMEN.

October 5

FITTING IN

Read: Acts 16:1–5

Paul wanted Timothy to accompany him; and he took him and
had him circumcised because of the Jews who were in those
places, for they all knew that his father was a Greek.
ACTS 16:3

THIS SEEMS TO be a rather inconsistent choice, when viewed in relationship to the agreement that Gentiles did not need to become circumcised to join the faith. Paul, who championed inclusion of Gentiles without circumcision, had Timothy undergo that very procedure. Why? Had the mission changed? No. To win Jews to the faith, you must become like a Jew. That was Paul's personal conviction about faith leaders. To win people to Christ, you need to become like them. While there are certainly exceptions, as well as lengths to which a person of faith should not go to connect with others, the general rule is sound. In fact, God demonstrated a similar willingness in Jesus Christ. To win us, God took on our corruptible human form and dwelled with us in all our sin and brokenness. Fitting in can be an important step toward sharing faith.

What lengths would you go to, to share your faith with others?

Lord, I cannot imagine undergoing a painful surgery in order to more effectively share my faith with others. My faith is as private as my genitalia. Why? Please help me to answer this question. Help me to know why I remain silent about you. Help me to change. In Jesus' name, I pray. AMEN.

October 6

AN OPENING

Read: Acts 16:6–15

Having been forbidden by the Holy Spirit to speak the word in Asia
. . . we immediately tried to cross over to Macedonia, being convinced
that God had called us to proclaim the good news to them.
ACTS 16:6 & 10

THE HOLY SPIRIT opens some doors while closing others. Paul had wanted to take the message of Jesus Christ to Asia, but he was prevented from doing so—a door closed. As one avenue was shutting down, however, a vision revealed that another avenue was opening up. Paul was supposed to bring the message and ministry of Jesus Christ to Greece—which he did with tremendous effect!

It is cliché to say *"Whenever God closes a door, he opens a window,"* but perhaps it is cliché because it is true. The door to Asia is shut so a window to Greece could be opened. A door to one job closes just as a window opens to your dream job. A seemingly ill-timed *"no"* can open the way to a perfectly timed *"yes."* For Paul that was more than a T-shirt slogan. For Paul, the opening and closing of doors was the Spirit's work, and it needed to be respected and followed.

What doors or windows are opening and closing in your life?

Lord, thank you for the many times that you have closed doors that might have led to my destruction . . . and thank you for opening windows and doors that have led to my salvation. In Jesus' name, I pray. AMEN.

October 7

FREEDOM

Read: Acts 16:16–40

> *Suddenly there was an earthquake, so violent that the founda-*
> *tions of the prison were shaken; and immediately all the doors*
> *were opened and everyone's chains were unfastened.*
> *ACTS 16:39*

GOD'S SPIRIT IS a Spirit of freedom. Christianity's mission breaks bonds. Freedom stands at the heart of our faith. In this brief passage of scripture, there are at least four occasions in which freedom is offered to particular individuals. A slave girl was released from the possession of both a demon and the oppressive demands of her owners. An earthquake broke open the gates of the jail in which Paul and Silas had been imprisoned. Paul and Silas's announcement freed the jailer from the shackles of death. And finally, Paul and Silas were publicly and apologetically released from their jail cell. Even Paul and Silas's singing and praying within the prison testifies to the Spirit's refusal to be caged. God creates us to be free, and God finds ways to release us when we are bound.

What binds you?

Lord, I know you have created me to be free—but free from what? Free for what? Whatever the answers are, one thing is sure . . .We are more than free to offer you our thanks. So, thank you, Lord. Thank you. In your name, I pray. AMEN.

October 8

IDOLS

Read: Acts 17:16–34

*Then Paul stood in front of the Areopagus and said, "Athenians, I see how extremely
religious you are in every way. For as I went through the city and looked carefully
at the objects of your worship, I found among them an altar with the inscription 'To
an unknown god.' What therefore you worship as unknown, this I proclaim to you."*
ACTS 17:22–23

THE GREEK PLAZA or mall was filled with the shrines and altars of gods that the
Athenian people worshiped. The many idols on display spoke of a deep need and a
deep spiritual hunger in Athens. Paul understood that while the spiritual pursuits
of the people of Athens were flailing about, the desire for objects of faith were real.
In an attempt to spiritually nourish the people, Paul tried to direct them away from
images *"formed by the art and imagination of mortals"* and toward the living and expansive God who was able to supply their every need.

If you walk through any of our malls or plazas today you will see the many
images and idols we worship in the displays at countless outlets and retailers. At
first glance, our consumptive appetites might seem sacrilegious, but are really signs
of misplaced spiritual desire. We feel a deep emptiness within us, and we are ravenous to fill it. The truth is, only the living and expansive God of the Bible is able to
soothe our spiritual ache.

What do you worship?

*Lord, because I do not know you as well as I should, I feed my deep spiritual hunger with
idols and images that leave me feeling even more empty. I need you to fill my life. I don't want
you to be the "unknown God" to me. I want to know you and be known by you. I want you to
come in and complete my life. In Jesus' name, I pray. AMEN.*

October 9

I HAVE PEOPLE

Read: Acts 18:1–11

Do not be afraid, but speak and do not be silent; . . . for
there are many in this city who are my people.
ACTS 18:9 & 10

ONE OF THE most common admonitions in the Bible is *"Do not be afraid," "Do not fear,"*
"Do not worry." While we know fear to be a potent enemy to the vitality of our lives,
the Bible is not always clear *why* we should not be afraid. In this story, however,
Paul's vision is clear. You don't need to be afraid because God has people around
you who will take care of you. Just as God is working in your life, God is working
in the lives around you, and God will use those people to sustain you in your life
and ministry. God has people in the city, God has people in all countries, God has
people in every boardroom, classroom, emergency room, and courtroom in the
world. Therefore you should not fear, for protectors hover about you even when
you are unaware of them.

What people has God placed around you?

Lord, I tend to believe in what I can see and measure and control. And yet, you are at
work behind the scenes in my life and in the lives of countless others. Perhaps I should trust
more and fear less, knowing that protectors are gathered around me just beyond my sight. In
Jesus' name, I pray. AMEN.

October 10

NO SUBSTITUTE

Read: Acts 19:1–7

"Into what then were you baptized?"They answered,"Into John's baptism."
ACTS 19:3

PAUL ENCOUNTERED MEN of faith in Ephesus who knew only of the teachings and baptism of John. They did not know Jesus. They were not followers of the Way. They had not received the gift of the Holy Spirit. While John the Baptist was a powerful and important prophet and teacher, he himself testified that he was no substitute for Jesus.

We often substitute other teachers, other leaders, and other messages for Jesus. We follow the latest guru or the popular motivational speaker or perhaps our own internal sense of direction. But when we substitute anyone or anything for Jesus, we miss out on the empowering blessing of his Spirit in our lives. There is no substitute for Jesus.

Are you settling for a substitute when you have been invited to learn from Jesus?

Lord, I get distracted, but when I focus on what is most important, I am reminded that there is no substitute for you in my life.Your guidance, your direction, and your counsel lead to life. All other paths are but shadows that dim the light you draw us to. In your name, I pray. AMEN.

October 11

THE LORD'S WILL BE DONE

Read: Acts 21:1–14

> *Since he would not be persuaded, we remained silent*
> *except to say, "The Lord's will be done."*
> *ACTS 21:14*

IN THE END, they agreed to disagree and to put their trust in the Lord. Paul's disciples wanted to steer their leader away from trouble, and Paul wanted to face trouble head on. Those who loved Paul wanted to preserve his life, while Paul wanted to extend God's mission. By traveling to Jerusalem, Paul might have become a martyr, and yet, avoiding Jerusalem might have compromised his ministry. Paul and his followers disagreed about the course of action to be taken. Paul wasn't budging, and those who loved him held firm to their position.

There is little doubt that Paul was a stubborn fellow; when he made up his mind no one was going to change it—even if he was wrong. Paul's followers possessed a similarly stubborn love for their teacher and friend. In the end, the disagreement was dropped and all involved decided to entrust all things to God. They believed that their wills were ultimately subject to the sovereign will of God. They trusted that God was able to use their efforts—those well planned and those ill advised—to further the kingdom. The evidence is in the conclusion of the story itself—Paul became a martyr, the message continued to spread, and the ministry flourished.

Where in your life do you need to surrender and say, *"God's will be done?"*

Lord, I like to make plans, and I am often stubbornly wedded to my own will. And yet, I know how many mistakes and missteps I have made and taken in my life. How remarkable it is that I still doggedly insist on my own way! Thankfully, you are able to use my clumsy efforts to further your will. You have been clear from the beginning, your will is going to be done on earth as it is in heaven—whether I embrace that reality or not! In Jesus' name, I pray. AMEN.

October 12

FAITH WITNESS

Read: Acts 22:3–16

While I was on my way and approaching Damascus, about noon a great
light from heaven suddenly shone about me. I fell to the ground and heard
a voice saying to me, "Saul, Saul, why are you persecuting me?"
ACTS 22:6–7

HOW WILD A claim, and how provocative a witness! Paul, the great persecutor of
the church, was stopped in his tracks on his way to Damascus by Jesus, and from
that day forward the orientation of his life changed. Three times in the book of
Acts, Paul recounted his conversion experience. There was a great light. There was
a voice. Jesus appeared and commissioned Paul. It must have sounded preposter-
ous to the critical minds of the day. That sort of thing just doesn't happen. At the
same time, the evidence of conversion was undeniable. Whatever happened on the
road to Damascus, Paul was an entirely different person as a result of the experience. Whether or not it sounded crazy to those who would listen, Paul regularly
witnessed to his encounter with Jesus—and Paul's witness continues to inspire our
faith even today.

Do you remember a time when someone shared their faith with you?

Lord, I keep silent about you and about my faith in you. Give courage to my voice. Grant
me some of the courage you offered Paul. In Jesus' name, I pray. AMEN.

October 13

THE MISSION

Read: Acts 23:12–22

Now the son of Paul's sister heard about the ambush; so he went
and gained entrance to the barracks and told Paul.
ACTS 23:16

ACCORDING TO THE story of Acts, it was God's desire to use Paul to bring the good news to the Gentiles, and Paul knew that the seat of power for the Gentiles was Rome. Rome was the mission. To preach before Caesar was the goal. To take the good news to the heart of the empire was the plan. Political posturing, evil plotting, and even court proceedings cannot get in the way of God's plan. When God's will needs to be accomplished, the most unlikely of characters can get swept up in the drama even if unwittingly so.

When you gain clarity about God's mission and purpose for your life, you begin to see that no power in heaven or on earth will be able to stand in the way of God's aims. God's will cannot be thwarted—even people who have no interest in God are employed to carry out divine initiatives!

What mission God is calling you to today?

Lord, life becomes more clear when I am trying to align my life with your will. This doesn't mean that life gets easier, it just means that clarity often comes with call. Though impressive obstacles may seem to be arrayed against your will, you provide a way forward. Even enemies prove to be aids. You win. That is the story. You win. In Jesus' name, I pray. AMEN.

October 14

TROUBLEMAKERS

Read: Acts 24:1–8, 14–16

We have . . . found this man a pestilent fellow, an agitator among all
the Jews throughout the world. . . . I admit . . . that according to the
Way, which they call a sect, I worship the God of our ancestors.
ACTS 24:5 & 14

PAUL WAS ACCUSED by his own people of being a troublemaker. Paul was disrupting the established order of a Jewish community. In his defense before Felix, Paul outlined the values and authorities by which he lived. He said, *"I am a Jew who follows the way of Jesus.""I believe in the authority of scripture.""I believe in the resurrection of all people." "I strive for honesty in all that I do."*

It is more than plausible to believe that both Paul and his accusers were correct. Paul was making trouble for the religious authorities because he was living out his faith in uncompromising ways. Paul was committed to telling the truth in a world that liked to lie. As scripture commanded, Paul cared for people who those with position and power often chose to overlook. Paul yielded to God's authority instead of claiming authority for himself. Such a person as that is bound to make life uneasy for those who enjoy the comfortable and well-worn patterns of a corrupting social order.

Are you a holy troublemaker?

Lord, I too often play it safe. I give in to the culture in which I live. I swim with the current instead of against it. I don't cause trouble because I believe good people are nice and polite and don't rock the boat. However, I know that injustice and hatred swirl about me, and I am often caught up in it unwittingly—and sometimes intentionally. Paul reminds me that to be a Christian is to be willing to risk being a holy troublemaker. Christianity is in tension with the evil vices of our world . . . and I suspect that tension should be more evident in my own life.Why is it not? Correct my way, Lord, so that I can trouble the ways of this world. In Jesus' name, I pray. AMEN.

October 15

AN EMPIRE UNDER GOD

Read: Acts 25:1–12

Festus, after he had conferred with his council, replied, "You [Paul]
have appealed to the emperor; to the emperor you will go"
ACTS 25:12

WHEN WE THINK of the Roman Empire and early Christianity, we may think of brutal oppression that pitted lions and fearsome gladiators against frail people of faith. There is no doubt that Roman persecution of the church was a fact of life for the first Christian people—a reality that might make this text all the more remarkable. It was Roman authority that preserved Paul's life against the death plots of the Jews, and it was the Roman justice system that completed Paul's mission by sending him to Rome. How amazing to think that Paul's ministry was carried to Rome by the Roman authorities themselves!

Clearly God is able to use the powers and principalities of this world—either wittingly or unwittingly—to accomplish God's aims. The same empire that brutally tried to crush the little Jewish sect that followed Jesus was the very force behind the spread of Christianity throughout the world. Even empires find themselves ultimately under God's authority.

Where is God at work in the ruling powers of the world?

Lord, we tend to think governments are corrupt, uncaring, and incompetent. But you,
Lord, remind us that you can use the messiness of this world to further your desires for us.
Perhaps that means that you can even use the messiness of my life for the good of those around
me. Imagine that! In Jesus' name, I pray. AMEN.

October 16

THINKING BIG

Read: Acts 26:1, 24-32

Agrippa said to Paul, "Are you so quickly persuading me to become a Christian?" Paul
replied, "Whether quickly or not, I pray to God that not only you but also all who
are listening to me today might become such as I am—except for these chains."
ACTS 26:28–29

KING AGRIPPA DID not convert to Paul's faith. In fact, most people who heard Paul remained unmoved and unchanged. If you look critically at Paul's career, you might assume that most of the time Paul's efforts met with failure. And yet Paul sought and received a private audience with King Agrippa and his wife, Bernice, and the Roman governor Felix. Not bad for someone written off as insane! During this audience with the ruling authorities, Paul tried to convert Agrippa, Bernice, Felix, and everyone else who was within earshot.

Paul's goals were inspired by the Lord he worshiped, and those goals were big. Huge! God encourages us not to play small but to dream on a gigantic scale. Creating a nation of people from a shriveled old couple from Ur, freeing a nation of slaves from Egypt, encouraging the world to fall in line behind Jesus—we are encouraged to think big because our God acts big.

What big thought is the Lord encouraging in your life?

Lord, so often I feel as if my efforts in this world are of no consequence. But the Bible
testifies that you use little people like me to accomplish remarkable—unimaginable—work.
Perhaps I should demand more from myself, and expect more from you. In Jesus' name, I pray.
AMEN.

October 17

Retirement

Read: Acts 28:11–16, 30–31

He lived there two whole years at his own expense and welcomed all
who came to him, proclaiming the kingdom of God and teaching about
the Lord Jesus Christ with all boldness and without hindrance.
Acts 28:30–31

Church history tells us that Paul died a martyr's death in Rome, but his biblical history only says that he continued to teach and preach unimpeded. Whatever the case, Paul's ministry continued. Having reached his goal of arriving in Rome, Paul did not retire quietly into the background but continued to blaze a path forward.

In our culture, if we are blessed with health and longevity, we believe retirement should be our reward. We can sit back on our investments and accumulated good works and allow others to pick up the mantle of leadership and stride forward. We believe we have done our part, now it is someone else's turn to step forward. God does not put people out to pasture. As people of faith, we are called to strive—right up to our very last breath—for the kingdom of God. We can't afford the luxury of retirement—there is too much important work to be done. Thank God!

Do you plan to retire?

Lord, I don't want to die old and useless. I want to live my days purposefully and with my boots on. I want to be working for you until my dying day. Retirement is not for me any more than it is for you. In Jesus' name, I pray. AMEN.

October 18

ASHAMED

Read: Romans 1:1–17

For I am not ashamed of the gospel; it is the power of God for salva-
tion to everyone who has faith, to the Jew first and also to the Greek.
ROMANS 1:16

HAVE YOU EVER been embarrassed to be with someone? The way they were dressed or the way they acted or the things they said made you feel uncomfortable. You may have even tried to pretend you were not really with them. The claims early Christians made, the way they chose to live, and the people they hung out with made plenty of people uncomfortable. Those early Christians pooled their resources and divested themselves of their hard-earned property. They were a motley bunch of poor, troubled, and morally questionable people. Their central faith practice was gathering together to share a meal that they referred to as their leader's "body and blood." It was a seemingly crazy way to live, but Paul and others found deep and fulfilling life in and through it all, and Paul was not ashamed to share his experiences with others . . . even if it got him in trouble from time to time.

We live in an age when many folks—even ourselves at times—are a bit ashamed of our faith or the church, and of Jesus himself. Clergy sex abuse, philandering televangelists, messages of bigotry wrapped in scripture, and the fact that average Christians just don't seem to practice what they preach can make anyone feel a bit awkward about being even loosely associated with Christianity. Hypocrisy, bigotry, homophobia, anti-intellectualism are just a sampling of the charges levied against those who claim to follow Jesus. For those who have dared to orient their life toward Jesus, however, there is this undeniable sense that it is the most daring, true, and rewarding way to live. If only we were not ashamed to admit it!

Are you a bit ashamed to be a Christian?

Lord, I am a quiet Christian most of the time. I try to convince myself that Christian actions speak louder than words . . . but without words, how are new Christians to be made and sustained? The truth is that I am embarrassed. The idea of announcing that I am a Christian makes me feel uncomfortable. I don't want people to think less of me . . . and I believe my association with you might do just that. And yet, your words and my relationship with you are life-giving! Why should I not be willing to shout that truth from rooftops and street corners like Paul? I know I should be less ashamed of my faith . . . I'm just not sure how to break that cycle. Help me, I pray . . . in your name. AMEN.

October 19

Hope in Suffering

Read: Romans 5:1–11

Suffering produces endurance, and endurance produces character, and
character produces hope, and hope does not disappoint us.
ROMANS 5:3–5A

IN OUR CULTURE, suffering, struggle, and trial are experiences to be avoided at all costs. We have succumbed to the belief that if it is uncomfortable for us, it must be bad for us. However, our God can use even the deep and heart wrenching challenges in our lives to produce something of lasting value in us: endurance, character, and hope.

Do you remember a time when you suffered?

Lord God, I long for everything to go well in life, but that is rarely the case. I find I am often beset by hardship, disappointment, and anxiety. I pray that you will indeed use my present affliction to strengthen my faith, my resolve, and my hope in you. In Jesus' name, I pray. AMEN.

October 20

FREE GIFT

Read: Romans 6:15–23

For the wages of sin is death, but the free gift of God
is eternal life in Christ Jesus our Lord.
ROMANS 6:23

FREE GIFTS TEND to come with strings attached. You get a free gift for opening a checking account at the local bank. You get a free gift when you enter the stadium on opening day. You get a few extra knives for free when you make that late night infomercial purchase. But we know these offers are not free. Everything costs something. Bank fees and ticket prices and the cost of the first dozen knives are the actual price of the gift.

When we read Paul's announcement of the free gift of grace and eternal life, we assume there must be a transaction to be made. What's the catch? Do we have to be good enough to earn the gift or believe the right theology to deserve the gift or make the correct profession of faith in order to receive the gift? If you have to do something for a gift, then it is not free. Eternal life is either free or it is earned somehow. Paul insisted that the price of eternity had already been paid by Jesus; therefore all we can do is accept the gift and live the rest of our lives with gratitude for all we have received.

Do you believe in free gifts?

Lord, gifts can make me feel a bit uncomfortable, particularly if I don't feel I deserve them. I would feel much better if you allowed me to earn my way forward in life. Even if I failed to please you, at least I would be in charge of my destiny. Your grace has a way of highlighting my limitations. If I can't earn your love, what good am I? However, I realize that might just be the point of your free gift to us. It reminds us that we are not in control, we are not in charge, and we are not the independent creatures we strive to be. We must rely on you. I may not always be comfortable with that reality, but I am grateful for your grace all the same. In Jesus' name, I pray. AMEN.

October 21

STILL SINFUL

Read: Romans 7:14–25

I do not understand my own actions. For I do not do what I
want, but I do the very thing I hate. . . . For I do not do the
good I want, but the evil I do not want is what I do.
ROMANS 7:15 & 19

IF YOU READ only these two sentences from Paul, you might assume that he was an evil tyrant. He seems to know what is right and good, but he finds himself doing what is wrong and bad. These statements appear to stand in such stark contrast to the faithful apostle who did so much to inspire our own faith. Did Paul not have an encounter with the risen Lord? Was Paul not a changed man leaving behind his violent past? Was he not the very one to bring the peaceable and loving message of Jesus to the Mediterranean world?

There can be no question that Paul is one of the great heroes of our Christian faith. However, he was always aware that he was in need of God's grace. He knew that his proclivity toward sin was always at hand. One careless judgment, one callous remark, one hostile impulse would reveal that he was still the fallen creature who had once persecuted followers of Jesus. It may be a great gift to always remember the sins of our past, for that allows us to be aware of our sins of the present and our continual need for forgiveness and grace. Paul knew that he was in constant need of Jesus' healing presence in his life—without it he would be entirely mired in sin and selfishness. If that was true for someone as remarkably faithful as Paul, perhaps it is true for us too.

Do you know what is like to want to do good, but find yourself doing what you know to be bad?

Lord, I am so very grateful for the witness of Paul. I am grateful that this hero of our faith never lost touch with his sinful past and his awareness of his present failings. Somehow, Paul's willingness to reveal his weakness gives me hope. If Paul felt as broken and sinful as I often feel and yet still went on to make a lasting and positive impact on the world, then perhaps there is hope for me too. In Jesus' name, I pray. AMEN.

October 22

No Condemnation?

Read: Romans 8:1–11

There is therefore now no condemnation for those who are in Christ Jesus. For the law of the Spirit of life in Christ Jesus has set you free from the law of sin and of death.
Romans 8:1–2

THERE ARE A lot of claims about Jesus. There are countless popular slogans bandied about that pertain to him. Some beliefs about Jesus are so simplistic that the entire line of thinking can be captured on a bumper sticker. Debates rage about salvation, judgment, and sin and how Jesus is involved in it all. However, if there is one profound claim that seems perhaps most important, it is that in Jesus we find freedom. Jesus calls us into a new life that is free from past mistakes, painful histories, and poor choices. Jesus frees us from deathly patterns of thinking, acting, and believing so that we can fully embrace and enjoy the life we have been given. Jesus is not in the condemnation business, he is in the liberating business. Jesus is less interested in laws than he is in life!

Are you free?

Lord, when I think of all I have been told about you over the years—all that I have been encouraged to believe and struggled to believe—I hope and pray that my freedom can be found in you. There are so many times when I feel bound—bound by my past, bound by my present commitments, and bound by a future that seems so uncertain. This is quite alarming to me. I long for a life that is free and joyous and meaningful. Please break into my life and break the bonds that tie me down in enslaving ways. In Jesus' name, I pray. AMEN.

October 23

ABBA! FATHER!

Read: Romans 8:12–17

When we cry, "Abba! Father!" it is that very Spirit bearing wit-
ness with our spirit that we are children of God . . .
ROMANS *8:15B–16*

HOW DO WE know that there is a God? How do we know that what the Bible tells
us about Jesus is true? How firm is the foundation of our faith, really? The truthful
answer, of course, is that there is no real way to know. There are times, however,
when it feels as if deep down in the core of our being we are petitioning God, crying out for our Lord, or offering a word of thanksgiving. It might even surprise us
when unexpectedly we feel the spirit within us craving something—something
deep and true and foundational. That is our spirit reaching out to the Spirit of God
. . . It is the creature longing for connection with the Creator. It is the cry of our
human soul for our truest home. That inner desire is probably the closest thing we
have to proof that our belief in God is well founded . . . It is our spirit bearing witness to the Almighty.

Do you sense God in your spirit?

Lord God, I am not sure I can fully explain what I feel . . . but within me there is a long-
ing, a cry, a welling up of my spirit that craves connection with you. It almost feels physical
in nature. I think it is my spirit calling out for you . . . or perhaps, my spirit responding to
your call. Whatever it is, I thank you for the sense of you that I have in my life. In Jesus' name,
I pray. AMEN.

October 24

Present Sufferings

Read: Romans 8:18–25

I consider that the sufferings of this present time are not worth comparing with the glory that is about to be revealed to us.
Romans 8:18

THERE ARE TIMES in our lives when we feel as if we are aching and groaning under the weight of so many expectations, anxieties, and demands. Life feels like a strain, and not the joy we want it to be. Even in moments of true suffering, however, our trials are not nearly as arduous as those that Paul and the earliest Christian had to endure. Life for them was harsh, and life as a Christian was downright dangerous.

In the midst of it all, Paul had a vision of the future that gave him immense hope. He believed in a liberated creation in which the entire world and all who are in it are redeemed, made whole, healthy, and joyful. Through his faith in Jesus Christ, Paul sensed that the world was on the brink of a new and glorious age, guided by the very Spirit and presence of God. To Paul's mind, all suffering in the world paled in comparison to the glory that he sensed just on the horizon.

How do you endure suffering?

Lord God, there are times when grief, disappointment, and despair get the best of me. There are moments when I am tempted to lose heart and hope. I want to believe that the pain of life will be overcome by your plan for the world. But sometimes I doubt. I wish I had Paul's faith in the future. Please build my confidence in you, and in what you are doing in the world, so that even in the face of suffering I can look forward to that which is to come. In Jesus' name, I pray. AMEN.

October 25

Spirit Interceding

Read: Romans 8:26–27

Likewise the Spirit helps us in our weakness; for we do not know how to pray
as we ought, but that very Spirit intercedes with sighs too deep for words.
Romans 8:26

OUR SPIRIT AND God's Spirit are connected. That means God's will, God's endurance, God's patience, and God's love dwell within us. God's Spirit even knows what we need and where we ache before we speak of it. This reality should not be simply a comfort but also an encouragement. Having something of God's Spirit within us means we have capacity and resources for living that go well beyond our wildest imaginations. We possess an infinite reservoir of generosity, love, courage, compassion, and wisdom with which to navigate our way through life. Therefore, we should be particularly attentive to the promptings of our spirit within us . . . It is God's Spirit directing us.

What does it mean for you to be endowed with God's Spirit?

Lord, I have a sense of your leading at times. I might call it a hunch or a gut feeling or just some deep sense of where I am supposed to go and what I am supposed to do at a particular moment. There are also moments when I feel broken or distraught or prepared to quit the fight, but somehow a resolve bubbles up within me that carries me forward and encourages me on my way. I may think of this as my own inner strength, but perhaps it is your Spirit within me urging me on. I thank you for that gift. In Jesus' name, I pray. AMEN.

October 26

ALL THINGS WORK TOGETHER

Read: Romans 8:28–30

We know that all things work together for good for those who
love God, who are called according to his purpose.
ROMANS 8:28

WHAT AN AMAZING statement! All things work together in life to produce what is considered "good." We are quite familiar with people of faith—and people of no faith—saying, *"I know everything works out for the best,"* or, *"I know everything happens for a reason."* These statements reflect the ways we try to comfort ourselves when we are facing disappointment, failure, or loss. They are loosely based on Paul's belief articulated in his letter to the Romans that the good, the bad, and the ugly of life can work together to bring about something positive. What people often forget, however, is the caveat that Paul tacks on to this statement. Things tend to work out well *"for those who love God, [and] who are called according to his purpose."*

God does have a way of taking a dark situation and using it to bring new light and life into our lives. How many times have we experienced disappointment and failure, only to find that in that low moment was the beginning of a new and extraordinary chapter in our lives? However, the promise that good things can come out of bad circumstances is a promise made to people who love God and try to align their lives to God's will. This is not a promise made to everyone. And it is certainly not a promise that everything that happens to us is for the best. The promise is simply that those who orient their love and life toward God will find that darkness can turn into light, disappointment can be transformed into delight, and death can be overcome by life.

Do you love and serve God—or do you simply hope for things to work out for the best?

Lord, I have often echoed the secular belief that life is oriented toward good results no matter what misfortune befalls me. But, in truth, I know that my life should be oriented toward you so that whatever I experience in my living can be infused and interpreted through your presence, love, and guidance. Help me to maintain that focus. In Jesus' name, I pray. AMEN.

October 27

INSEPARABLE

Read: Romans 8:31–39

Who will separate us from the love of Christ?
ROMANS 8:35

PAUL ELOQUENTLY ASSERTED that there is no external power on earth that can severe us from God's love as revealed to us through Jesus Christ. Paul believed that nothing in life or death, not the powers and principalities of the world or physical distance or depth can drive a wedge between ourselves and the God who has loved us since before we were born.

The one point of separation that Paul does not mention in his litany of obstacles is *ourselves*. It may be true that no external force can get in the way of God's love for us, but God has allowed us the freedom to ignore or refuse that divine love. We can get in the way. We can separate ourselves from God. We can drive a wedge into that relationship. God's love abounds, but we always have the ability to deflect it.

Do you get in the way of God's love for you?

Lord, you have given me the power and freedom to reject or accept your love. I assume that is because love that is coerced is not real. That means the most significant barrier to our relationship is my unwillingness to receive you and your love into my life. I don't want to refuse . . . but perhaps I just don't know how to accept what you offer. Help me to receive your love so that I can live in it and share it with others. In Jesus' name, I pray. AMEN.

October 28

CONFESS AND BELIEVE

Read: Romans 10:5–21

Because if you confess with your lips that Jesus is Lord and believe in
your heart that God raised him from the dead, you will be saved.
ROMANS 10:9

MANY OF US grew up believing that these were the magic words of the Christian faith. Confess Jesus as Lord and believe God raised him from the dead, and all will be well—for eternity. Upon that simple statement hung eternal consequences. It answers the questions, *"Who is your Lord?"* and, *"What do you believe?"* As a first-century Jew, Paul knew that there were actual lords and kings and even an emperor in Rome who demanded devotion. Also, Paul's concept of salvation was not just otherworldly but had concrete application in this world. How is one saved from anxiety? How is one saved from despair? How is one saved from hurtful sins and bad choices?

For Paul, the answer was following Jesus and trusting in God. Those might be the keys to heaven, but they can also unlock a profound sense of joy and peace on earth. Follow Jesus and trust God. That was Paul's solution. Orient your life in the most meaningful and hopeful direction, and your life will come together in ways that are both rich and rewarding. Christian faith is not about saying magic words in just the right way—it is about turning your life in the right direction and trusting that God will make sure life and death, and life after death, work out just as they should.

Whom do you follow and trust?

Lord, I want to know the magic words that will make life come together for me in ways that I have yet to experience. I want to live with a deep sense of peace in my heart, free from the nagging little worries of this life, and the great uncertainties of the death and life that is to come. I do not know the way. I do not know what to believe. And the more I think about it all, the more unraveled I become. Why don't I just leave the worrying to you and focus on the life you have given me? I pray this in the name of Jesus, my Lord and Savior. AMEN.

October 29

LIVING CHRISTIAN

Read: Romans 12:9–21

Let love be genuine; hate what is evil, hold fast to what is good; love one another with mutual affection; outdo one another in showing honor.
ROMANS 12:9–10

WHAT DOES LIVING like a Christian look like? Is there a to-do list? Is there a three-step, or seven-step, or twelve-step program for following Jesus? The answer to these questions can be both "yes" and "no." There are so many different ways to follow Jesus, it is difficult to prescribe a specific path. In fact, if you look at Jesus as he is represented in the Gospels, you can see Jesus offering different advice to different people about how to live more faithfully.

In the twelfth chapter of Paul's letter to the Romans, Paul offered his own list of Christian pursuits that are fairly clear and quite inspiring. Let your love be genuine. Extend hospitality to strangers. Live in harmony with one another. Care for the poor. Take care of your enemies as if they were your friends. This is a list of steps that could benefit anyone wishing to live their life as Jesus urged us to. Are they the right steps or the only steps to faithful Christian living? In the end, following Jesus isn't just about taking certain well-defined steps—it is about walking in a new direction that takes us away from ourselves and our selfish longings and toward people and a world in need of love, grace, mercy, and forgiveness.

How do you live as a Christian?

Lord, I want a few simple steps to salvation. I want a formula to follow. I want a clearly defined path toward you. I fear, of course, there is no perfectly defined way forward. I just pray that my desire to walk toward you and with you is enough for you to enter into my life and guide my steps. In your name, I pray. AMEN.

October 30

Respect for Authority

Read: Romans 13:1–7

> *Pay to all what is due them—taxes to whom taxes are due, revenue to whom*
> *revenue is due, respect to whom respect is due, honor to whom honor is due.*
> *Romans 13:7*

PAUL BELIEVED—OR HE at least communicated to the Christians who lived in Rome—that there was *"no authority except from God."* Throughout this passage Paul encouraged the Christians in Rome to respect those who governed them, for the rulers of the world have been given their authority by God. This teaching is deeply disturbing to those of us who understand that power can, and has, been abused. Should we believe that Adolf Hitler or Joseph Stalin or Mao Tse-Tung were authorities endorsed and placed in their position by God? Given our knowledge of history, we are more likely to be wary of governmental leaders than to freely give ourselves over to their leading.

What prompted and sustained Paul's belief in the divine nature of authority? It is possible that there was greater civility and character among the Roman leaders of Paul's time. Paul might have been unaware of abuses of power in hidden corners of the world. Or perhaps Paul was just being overly cautious and mindful of the unique demands placed upon Christians who had to live out their faith in the very heart of the empire that seemed to rule the world. Whatever we make of Paul's understanding of authority, perhaps we should not be too quick to condemn it as overly naïve. Respect and obedience to authority might not be a bad first instinct for those of us who so readily choose to be our own masters. In fact, being subject to the rulers of our world might not be bad practice for learning how to be obedient to the ultimate ruler of the world—God. If we can obey human authority, perhaps we will develop a greater competency to respect and obey divine authority.

To whom do you give respect, and whom do you choose to disobey?

Lord, I worry about the abuse of power. History had shown us that power corrupts, and we feel the need to be always vigilant for signs of overstepping by those who are given charge of us. In fact, we feel not only free but also empowered to belittle and bemoan those who rule over us. Why is that, Lord? As a Christian, should my response to those in public office be provocative or prayerful? Should I treat them as if they are my servants or yours? Help me to know how to offer respect and honor, even when I am reluctant to do so. In Jesus' name, I pray. AMEN.

October 31

Faithful Remnant

Read: 1 Corinthians 7:1–16

For the unbelieving husband is made holy through his wife, and
the unbelieving wife is made holy through her husband.
1 Corinthians 7:14

THE BIBLE CONTAINS a theme that suggests that the faithfulness of the few winds up sanctifying the many. God told Abraham that through him—because of his faithfulness—all the nations of the world would be blessed. The Hebrews—a remnant people to be sure—were supposed to pray for and serve as a blessing to communities of which they were a part. In Paul's letter to the Christians in Corinth, he asserts that a believing spouse may make their entire family holy. A faithful remnant of people can serve as an avenue through which people who do not recognize or observe God's commands are saved. If you are a person of faith—even if your faith is less than sure—your efforts please God enough to cover not only your own sins but also the errors of others.

What does it mean to be a faithful remnant?

Lord, in a culture that appears to have little interest in you, I understand what it means to be a "remnant." While I am reluctant to call myself "faithful," I am intrigued by the possibility that living my faith might turn out to be a saving grace for others. When I read the bible I am drawn to consider the possibility that a small group of people devoted to you can help to redeem the world. What a great honor and even greater responsibility! Help me to live as a faithful remnant in a hostile world. In Jesus' name, I pray. AMEN.

November 1

GIFTED FOR THE COMMON GOOD

Read: 1 Corinthians 12:4–11

To each is given the manifestation of the Spirit for the common good.
1 CORINTHIANS 12:7

YOU ARE GIFTED. You have talent. You have a special ability that when uncovered can shed a little bit of light in some darkened corner of the world. Some people are gifted athletes. Others are gifted students. There are people who are just naturally gifted communicators, carpenters, or competitors. When you are gifted at something, it means that you have been given a talent that allows you to accomplish certain tasks easily and proficiently. However, we tend to assume that gifts we have received have been conferred upon us for our own good. Like receiving a birthday or Christmas present, we assume the gift is *for us*. But God does not give gifts for our own benefit; God gives gifts with a much wider receivership in mind. We are gifted for the common good of the world. We are given gifts intended for the benefit of all creation. We have been blessed to be a blessing.

What gift do you possess that God intends for you to share with others?

Lord, when I find I have a talent, I begin to think of ways to utilize that talent for my own gain. Yet again, my thinking is so small and your ways are so expansive! The gifts you have offered me are not mine alone, but rather are intended to be shared for the good of all around me. In Jesus' name, I pray. AMEN.

November 2

LOVE AND WORK

Read: 1 Corinthians 13

Love is patient; love is kind; love is not envious or boastful or arrogant
or rude. It does not insist on its own way; it is not irritable or resent-
ful; it does not rejoice in wrongdoing, but rejoices in the truth. It bears
all things, believes all things, hopes all things, endures all things.
1 CORINTHIANS 13:4-7

PAUL'S "HYMN OF Love" is likely the most frequently read passage of scripture in Christian weddings. Countless adoring couples have gazed into each other's eyes as this beautiful love poem has been read to them and for them. Enraptured in the moment, and confident that their love will last, most brides and grooms never fully hear the demands of love, believing that affection comes easily to those who are truly soul mates.

However, if love is indeed patient and kind, never insisting on its own way, then that means love is work. And it takes work not to be irritable or resentful of your partner when they don't seem to be pulling their weight. It takes work to believe and hope that you can make it as a couple, when other couples begin splitting up. It takes work to endure the demands of life with someone who does not always see things the way you see them. Love isn't simply a pretty collection of words spoken on a wedding day—love is a lifetime work that is worth all the effort needed to nurture and sustain it.

Do you expect love to be easy?

Lord, I want love to be easy…and perhaps you do too. I have no doubt that it is a chore
to love me, and I am so grateful that you do. Help me to be similarly committed to the work of
love that my relationships require. In Jesus' name, I pray. AMEN.

November 3

OF FIRST IMPORTANCE

Read: 1 Corinthians 15:1–11

> *For I handed on to you as of first importance what I in turn received: that Christ*
> *died for our sins in accordance with the scriptures, and that he was buried,*
> *and that he was raised on the third day in accordance with the scriptures.*
> 1 CORINTHIANS 15:3–4

OF ALL THE teachings about faith and Jesus that Paul tried communicate to the churches he was in relationship with, the most critically important had to do with the resurrection of Jesus Christ. Jesus lives! Life is eternal! Everything has changed! That was the heart and soul of Paul's message to the early Christians. Service to the poor, healing of the sick, working for social justice and equity all flowed from a belief that we don't need to cling too tightly to this life. When we embrace the truth that life is eternal, we find we can loosen our grip on our possessions, on our desires, and on our compulsive need to always be safe. Resurrection can allow us the courage to move from a position of self-interest to a place of genuine interest in the needs and well-being of others. Paul believed that death did not have ultimate claim on us, which meant that Jesus could. We were created for life not death, hope not fear, love not hate, and joy not sorrow. This truth was of first importance to Paul, and he hoped it would be of first importance for us as well.

What is of first importance to you?

Lord, it is an incredible belief that is supposed to ground our faith. You live. Resurrection is real. Death does not win. While I know such a belief should change me and change the world . . . I am slow to be moved . . . and perhaps even slower to fully believe. I want to believe. I want to live without fear. I want to trust that life is eternal and that my relationship with you will endure forever. Help me to believe, help me to really live, and help me to claim that which is of first importance. In your name, I pray. AMEN.

November 4

COURAGE AND STRENGTH

Read: 1 Corinthians 16

Keep alert, stand firm in your faith, be courageous, be
strong. Let all that you do be done in love.
1 CORINTHIANS 16:13–14

GROWING UP, KIDS used to fight each other on the playground, behind the school, or in the bathroom to prove their strength and worth. Bloody lips, black eyes, and defeated foes were badges of courage. As we age, physical demonstrations of strength give way to the battle to move up the corporate ladder and to continually acquire more wealth, prestige, and power. But even as we rack up impressive accomplishments, we are still not showing the strength the Lord wishes us to have.

Biblical courage and strength are always connected to love, for loving is often the most difficult and humbling act a human being can engage in. Love is worth fighting for and working at. It takes courage to love your spouse when others seem more alluring. It takes firmness of spirit to love the child who disappoints you time and time again. It takes strength to respond in love to that employee who is not as gifted or as bright as the rest. To God, a person of great strength and courage is a person who possesses great love.

Is your love strong and courageous?

Lord, it is easy to get angry and frustrated when the people around me do not live up to my expectations. It is difficult to love myself when I feel as though I am falling short. On my best day and on my darkest day, help me to have the courage and strength to respond to those around me with love. In your name, I pray. AMEN.

November 5

FREEDOM IN SPIRIT

Read: 2 Corinthians 3:12–18

Now the Lord is the Spirit, and where the Spirit of the Lord is, there is freedom.
2 CORINTHIANS 3:17

WHEN THE APOSTLE Paul was talking about freedom, he was not talking about the ability to do as we please. He wasn't extolling the virtues of a free society or the blessing of self-determination. Paul was talking about being freed from sin, oppressive religious laws, and death. Paul's view of freedom wasn't merely about being freed *from* something but rather being freed *for* someone. Jesus Christ—our Lord—offers us freedom from the bondages of sin and death so that we can live and love and give ourselves to others for the good of all. The Spirit of Jesus has nothing to do with the freedom to do as we wish. Being free in the Spirit means being free from our sinful and selfish desires so that we can offer ourselves to the world in the same transformative ways Jesus did. To be free in Christ means to be called to others. We are freed from sin so that we are freed up for service.

What does freedom mean to you?

Lord, freedom has become a bumper sticker slogan in our culture. Freedom has become an idol that we worship in our society. We believe freedom is our right, and a right that permits us to do as we please as long as we don't injure others too badly. But the freedom you offer us is not a freedom from obligation but a freedom for service. There is indeed a cost to freedom . . . It requires me to conform to the ways of the one who offers it to me—Jesus Christ, our Lord . . . in whose name, I pray. AMEN.

November 6

Clay Jars

Read: 2 Corinthians 4:1–15

But we have this treasure in clay jars, so that it may be made clear that
this extraordinary power belongs to God and does not come from us.
2 Corinthians 4:7

By all accounts Paul was not much to look at. His body had been broken by years of torture and abuse. He had been beaten, whipped, shipwrecked, nearly drowned, and even bitten by a deadly viper. His body bore the scars of affliction for living, preaching, and professing what he believed. There are also indications that his preaching wasn't all that engaging. His words could fill people with rage or put them to sleep. But to some, Paul's presence and his words reflected something of the power and presence of God. In fact, Paul believed that the more cracked and humble our lives, the more God could be seen through them. Fancy and shiny lives have a way of distracting our attention from the One who created them. However, rustic clay jars do not draw our attention away from that which fills them. Likewise, the imperfections of our lives may be the cracks through which the Spirit of God can be witnessed by others.

What imperfection in you can demonstrate God's power to the world?

Lord, we feel as if our imperfections, flaws, and painful histories are dark stains on our appearance. We strive to hide our faults and failures so that those around us will not take notice of our weaknesses. What if our weaknesses are those very spaces in our lives through which you can be seen? What if you are more fully revealed in clay jars that do not demand more attention than their contents? What if less-than-remarkable parts of our lives demonstrate your presence better than those few well-polished aspects we desire to present to others? That would be a miracle . . . and that sounds just like you. In Jesus' name, I pray. AMEN.

November 7

MOMENTARY AFFLICTION

Read: 2 Corinthians 4:16—5:10

For this slight momentary affliction is preparing us for
an eternal weight of glory beyond measure.
2 CORINTHIANS 4:17

LIFE IS HARD. Love can lead to heartbreak. Failures often seem to mount up with greater frequency than successes. There is joy and beauty in life to be sure, but life begins with an infant's uncomfortable scream and can end with the whimper that may accompany a person's final breath. As Paul said in his first letter to the Christians in Corinth, *"If for this life only we have hoped in Christ, we are of all people most to be pitied."* Life in this world can seem cruel and unkind and unfortunate. But we must always view this life through the promise of an eternal life that exists beyond all we can see. Our life in this world is but an instant. So, live it well, love others, and take your lumps along the way, trusting that a glory awaits us that will quiet every cry, wipe away every tear, and convert all sorrows into joy.

What affliction do you need to remind yourself is only temporary?

Lord, help me to cleave to the reality that life in this world is preciously short, while eternity with you lasts forever. Help me to live this life well—even when the living is not easy—knowing that with you there will be wonderful and renewing eternal rest. In your name, I pray. AMEN.

November 8

BECOMING NEW

Read: 2 Corinthians 5:11–21

So if anyone is in Christ, there is a new creation: everything
old has passed away; see, everything has become new!
2 CORINTHIANS 5:17

THERE IS SOMETHING about following Jesus, inviting Jesus into our lives, and living by Jesus' example that remakes us in important ways. When commit ourselves to living in relationship to Jesus, we become new. Our self-centered, self-absorbed, and sinful lives are converted into lives that focus on the needs and concerns of others. We are transformed from self-interested creatures into people whose primary interest has something to do with the interests of God. This is not to say that we become perfect people—by no means! But, with Jesus, our orientation and the course on which we find ourselves in life has us pointed in the right direction. Following Jesus is just better than following our own selfish instincts and desires. That new beginning we long for can be had when we get into Christ more than we are into ourselves.

Do you long to be made new?

Lord, I want to be made new. I hear so many people who believe they are good people who focus on making good decisions. I just do not have that kind of confidence in my own righteousness. I know I am flawed and sinful and on a path that is less than ideal. I am so very tired of following my own whims and fancies. I want something more, something profoundly new, something only you can provide. I want to be a new creation, your creation. In Jesus' name, I pray. AMEN.

November 9

GOOD GUILT

Read: 2 Corinthians 7:2–16

For godly grief produces a repentance that leads to salva-
tion and brings no regret, but worldly grief produces death.
2 CORINTHIANS 7:10

THERE HAS BEEN a tremendous shift in mainstream Christianity away from sin and guilt. We dismiss any concept or conviction that might make people feel uncomfortable—especially ourselves. Hellfire and brimstone preaching is a relic of the past. Sin and damnation are out. We don't dare do or say anything that would induce people to feel guilty. We believe faith should be about love, freedom, and the ability to lead a happy life. When people attend church or gather with Christian friends, they should leave that gathering feeling better about themselves and better about life in general than when they arrived. Christianity is about "good news," so it stands to reason that we should have a good time practicing it!

However, Paul believed that there was a kind of *good guilt*—what he referred to as *"godly grief."* This was guilt applied to someone's life not to simply make them feel bad but to produce repentance. Sometimes we cannot merely be *affirmed* into the right direction, rather we need to be confronted with the painful truth that we are not living our lives as we should. We need a course correction. We need a spiritual traffic cop. We need someone who is unafraid to speak hard words to our lives. Guilt can be good. Guilt is an indication we have acted in ways that are beneath our created purpose. Guilt can spin us around and get us back on track. Guilt may not be fashionable these days, but that doesn't mean it isn't good for us.

When was the last time you felt really guilty?

Lord, we would like our faith to affirm us and assure us that we are doing our best. That means we would prefer a faith that lies to us. But that is not the faith of Paul, it is not the faith of Jesus—it is not faith in you. You speak truth to our lives. You don't tell us what we want to hear but what we need to know. You can use guilt for our own good. Help us to accept that teaching when we feel guilt welling up within us. In Jesus' name, I pray. AMEN.

November 10

RÉSUMÉ

Read: 2 Corinthians 11:16–33

Are they ministers of Christ? . . . I am a better one: with far greater labors,
far more imprisonments, with countless floggings, and often near death.
2 CORINTHIANS 11:23

WHEN WE THINK of accomplishments that commend us to others—those things that lend credibility to our person—we tend to think of all the impressive work we have done. When we build a résumé or fill out an application or apply to a school of some kind, we list out all our accomplishments, achievements, and successes. Paul's résumé was quite different from ours. Paul reveled in his weaknesses and his failures. The obstacles he encountered and the failures he endured were for him a measure of the fortitude and persistence of his faith. Paul had been beaten but not broken, he had been flogged but not forestalled, and he had been shipwrecked but not shaken. Even after every kind of harm had befallen him, Paul stood firm in his faith. Success in worldly terms was not nearly as important to Paul as the strength and resolve a person demonstrated when the world turned against them. Christian résumés should be filled with the trials and testing that befall us when we try to live out our faith in a world that was, and still is, hostile to Jesus. For Christians, worldly success and praise are not nearly as commendable as resilience in the face of hardship and hostility.

What moments of resilience would you include on your Christian résumé?

Lord, I don't like failure, and I am even less enamored with the idea of facing people who are hostile toward me. I try to avoid conflict. I view success as managing through life in ways that bypass opposition. And yet, when I think of the grand mission you call us to, a call that draws us to the side of people our world often discounts and maligns, when I consider that you call us to do what is right rather than what is popular, and speak truth even when truth is the last thing so many people want to hear, it shouldn't be surprising that Christian success can look a bit different than what I might envision for myself. Lord, help me to build a résumé of love and faith and action that isn't afraid of confrontation, conflict, and failure. For this I pray, in your name. AMEN.

November 11

THORNS

Read: 2 Corinthians 12:1–10

Three times I appealed to the Lord about this, that it would leave me, but he said
to me, "My grace is sufficient for you, for power is made perfect in weakness."
2 CORINTHIANS 12:8–9A

PAUL HAD SOME mysterious ailment that plagued him to the point where he prayed
that the Lord would take it away from him. Paul referred to the ailment as a thorn
in his flesh. Many scholars have speculated on the nature of the thorn, but we will
never know for sure what it was that afflicted Paul. All we know is that Paul asked
for this ailment to be removed from his life, and the Lord said *"no."* In fact, Paul
believed that the Lord wanted this weakness to be present in Paul's life to remind
him that it was God's power, not his own, that his life and ministry depended upon.

There are so many imperfections in us that we would like to change. We don't
like the way we look or the way our voice sounds or how our face reddens at the
slightest embarrassment. Our hands shake or our body is marred or misshapen
or an illness plagues us in uncomfortable ways. We lament these weaknesses, but
Paul encourages us to claim them as gifts given for our own well-being. For if we
are not reminded of our frailty, we might assume we can rely on our strength to
get us through life. That is not what God wants for those in God's service. When
we are weak, that is when God's power can shine through our lives. Our weakness
demonstrates God's strength.

What thorn do you wish was taken out of your life?

Lord, I am weak in so many ways, and I loathe being reminded of it. I want to appear
strong, confident, and self-assured. However, if I find assurance in my own abilities, then I
begin to depend upon them more than I depend on you. That I do not want. Therefore, I thank
you for the thorns in my life. They remind me that I need you, and that you can work through
me . . . even, and perhaps especially, in moments of weakness. In your name, I pray. AMEN.

— 359 —

November 12

LAW ABIDING

Read: Galatians 5:1–15

For the whole law is summed up in a single command-
ment, "You shall love your neighbor as yourself."
GALATIANS 5:14

MANY PEOPLE THINK of the Bible as a book of rules, and, in truth, there are plenty of commands and laws that our faith ancestors wanted us to keep. In fact, one of the great blessings that God offered the world through the Hebrew people was a set of laws that were intended to help give order to what can often feel like a rather chaotic existence. The apostle Paul was a Jew. He had lived much of his life trying to uphold all the laws of the Jewish people. Paul knew the law inside and out. But as he began to follow Jesus, he began to cleave to and preach about one of Jesus' most important teachings. All the laws in the Bible can be reduced to a single command: love. Love God and love your neighbor. Treat people the way you want to be treated, and you will fulfill every command God gave to Moses and the Israelite people on Mount Sinai. Love fulfills the law—always! When we love both our God and those around us, we discover that we are in fact being law abiders.

Do you need rules because you are reluctant to love?

Lord, I have a choice to make. I can try to follow and fulfill every rule in the Bible, or I can ignore them as if they do not pertain to me, or I can try to act out of a love for all people and trust that love will fulfill every rule you have set for me. Love is hard . . . If it were easy everyone would be doing it. But following all the commands and rules in the Bible may be even more complicated. Help me to choose the simple but demanding path toward pleasing you: love. In your name, I pray. AMEN.

November 13

FLESH AND SPIRIT

Read: Galatians 5:16–26

Now the works of the flesh are obvious: fornication, impurity, licentiousness, idolatry,
sorcery, enmities, strife, jealousy, anger, quarrels, dissensions, factions, envy, drunken-
ness, carousing, and things like these. . . . By contrast, the fruit of the Spirit is love,
joy, peace, patience, kindness, generosity, faithfulness, gentleness, and self-control.
GALATIANS 5:19–21A, 22–23

WHEN THE CHOICE is as black and white as the type on this page, who would choose the works of the flesh? We don't dream of being people who live in dissension and careless self-indulgence. We don't want to be people like that. When we read the list of the fruits of the Spirit, the spirit within us really does groan and ache to live in such ways. If we could just choose between these two lists and stick with that choice once and for all, all would be well!

But that is not what life is like. You want to stay faithful to your spouse, but then someone attractive comes into view. You don't want to have another argument with your child, but then they make the same darn mistake yet again. You don't want to be jealous and envious, but then you see the life someone else is living and you can't help feeling a bit covetous. On paper we would not choose the desires of the flesh, but we do not live on paper—we live in a world full of temptation and sin. So, how do we live by the Spirit and not be entirely dominated by the flesh? Keep the words of the Spirit before us at all times, pray to always live by them, and trust that God's Spirit within us is stronger than our desire to gratify our flesh.

How would you choose to live?

Lord, I would not want to be known as a jealous or envious person. I don't want to be
a drunk or divisive or difficult person. I don't want to live out of control. I long to be known

as generous, kind, and thoughtful. But the things I want and the things I do are so often in conflict with one another. It is as if I am two entirely different people—the person I am and the person I inwardly long to be. Help me to become one person in you, the loving and faithful person I dare to believe you created me to be. In your name, I pray. AMEN.

November 14

It Takes Time

Read: Ephesians 1:3–14

With all wisdom and insight he has made known to us the mystery of his will,
according to his good pleasure that he set forth in Christ, as a plan for the full-
ness of time, to gather up all things in him, things in heaven and on earth.
EPHESIANS 1:8D–10

"WHY IS IT taking so long?" That is a fair question. The Bible claims that God's intent is to bring order and harmony and righteousness to the world . . . but there seems to be scant evidence of that plan gaining much ground in our age. What is the holdup? Why can't Jesus return in an instant and make all wrongs right once and for all?

According to this passage of scripture, God does not want to lose anyone or anything as the plan for the salvation of the world unfolds. Salvation—the union between God and all that God has made—is not for a select subgroup of religious people, it is for *everyone*. Jesus will not return, and God will not draw this age to a close, until *"all things"* are gathered up in God's will, reflecting God's way. This is a colossal task. It will take something Paul refers to as the *"fullness of time."* If God is eternal and everlasting, then the wait for all creation to conform to God's desires might take a very, very long time. The plan is in motion, but the timer is in God's hands.

Do you get impatient with God?

Lord, I sometimes wonder—perhaps oftentimes wonder—why the promises of unity and peace and love in the Bible do not seem to be taking root in the world on the scale the Bible suggests they will. Why is your grand design taking so long to unfold? Is my impatience with the "fullness of time" a result of being a finite being with limited time to understand and par-ticipate in your expansive work? I just don't know. Help me to be at peace with my ignorance of your plans, and encourage me to do my part, trusting that the final result is in your hands. In your name, I pray. AMEN.

November 15

MORE THAN WE CAN IMAGINE

Read: Ephesians 3:14–21

Now to him who by the power at work within us is able to accomplish abundantly far more than all we can ask or imagine, to him be glory in the church and in Christ Jesus to all generations, forever and ever. Amen.

EPHESIANS 3:20–21

WE CAN IMAGINE so much for ourselves. We have the ability to dream big, and perhaps even begin to pursue those dreams in the hope of making some of them a reality. We have visions for the way we would like our lives to look and feel. Whether a casual daydream or a profound sense of personal mission, we can envision a whole universe of possibilities for ourselves . . . We just have some serious doubts about our ability to accomplish all that we desire to do with our lives.

Paul lets us know that as big as we feel we can dream for ourselves and our world, God's vision for our lives is even more expansive. God has an eternal and infinite imagination that far surpasses our own. In fact, our most outlandish ask of God—our most fervent prayer and desire—is not nearly as grand as what God is prepared to do in our lives. God's dreams for you are so much bigger than your dreams for yourself. Perhaps, then, we should leave some of the dreaming to God while we get to work on following God's commands.

What is your most expansive dream for yourself right now?

Lord God, you are eternal, your imagination is infinite, and your life is everlasting. How could I possibly out-think, out-dream, or out-imagine you? It is not possible. You are able to accomplish in my life and in the world more than I could ever imagine. I am small, you are expansive . . . Thank you for allowing me to participate in what you have planned for creation. In Jesus' name, I pray. AMEN.

November 16

GROWING UP

Read: Ephesians 4:1–16

We must grow up in every way into him who is the head, into Christ . . .
EPHESIANS 4:15B

DO YOU REMEMBER, as a child, what you wanted to be when you grew up? A police officer? A firefighter? A doctor? A veterinarian? In the Christian faith we can choose to pursue a career in any field we desire, but whatever our chosen profession is, we are also supposed to be finding ways to live, behave, and resemble Jesus. The goal of our lives, according to the apostle Paul, is to serve as reflections of Jesus in the world. When we finally grow up in faith, we should somehow take on the characteristics of Christ. You can *do* whatever vocational work you want to in this life, but when it comes to who you are called to *be,* the answer is clear: you are to be like Jesus.

Have you ever thought of trying to live like Jesus?

Lord, I can't even begin to envision trying to live my life as you lived yours. I suspect that is because I have always been told you were, and are, perfect. I look at my own life and my own choices in living . . . and perfection is simply not a word that describes who I am. Living like you seems an impossibility. Perhaps simply trying to live by your words and your example is a start. I am willing to try, if you are willing to help me grow up. In your name, I pray. AMEN.

November 17

Relationships at Sunset

Read: Ephesians 4:25—5:2

Do not let the sun go down on your anger.
Ephesians 4:26b

PAUL GIVES PLENTY of relational advice in this passage of scripture, and there is at least one note of instruction that is worth living each and every day of our lives. Don't go to sleep angry. Anger has a way of festering when the world goes dark, and we are left tossing and turning through the night, getting ever more worked up about contentious relationships and difficult encounters. What a blessing it would be to marriages if couples would commit to staying awake and working through the issues that plague them rather than going to bed on edge with one another. How much more soundly we would sleep if we made up with those with whom we are at odds! As the sun sets, we might want to remember Paul's admonition and make tracks to people who have angered us and who we have angered. Make amends, make reparations—make love—before you choose to end the day angry.

What do you do when you are angry?

Lord God, sometimes I think it would be better to end the day not giving up any ground in the arguments and disagreements I find myself embroiled in. Somehow I believe going to bed angry is preferable to making amends and sacrificing my positions. However, when the sun sets and my rage is still hot . . . I find I am lost already. Help me to swallow my pride—or better yet, allow my heart to enlarge so that empathy and not anger is the way I end my days. In your name, I pray. AMEN.

SUBJUGATION

Read: Ephesians 5:21–33

Be subject to one another out of reverence for Christ.
EPHESIANS 5:21

THIS MAY BE one of the most disagreeable texts in the New Testament. In this passage, Paul encourages women to be subject to their husbands. In fact, Paul seems to indicate that the man is the head of the household just as Jesus Christ is the head of the church. However, as often happens when we are alarmed by a biblical passage, we miss out on the overarching message of a text.

Paul's hope for families, and his hope for the church, was for people of faith to be subject to *one another*. Paul viewed service to others as a vital passageway toward peaceable and healthy relationships. Only when you treat others as if they were better than yourself can you truly value a person as Jesus values them. Service—or willing subjugation to others—fulfills all the relational dreams the Lord has for us. When you gladly serve others—whether a spouse, a child, a friend, a church member, or a stranger—you enter into relationships just as God intended. Respect, care, and support become the hallmarks of your interactions with those around you.

Can you subject yourself to others so that your relationships can be more careful and thoughtful?

Lord, I don't like the idea of surrendering my authority to anyone for any reason. I prefer to engage in relationships in ways that allow me to press my rights. I want respect. I want people to treat me the way they would like to be treated. I believe I deserve to be well cared for. Those are my desires . . . and they are so often unfulfilled. Perhaps I spend more time thinking about what I want than I do about providing others what they may need. Can it be any surprise to me that so many of my relationships are not as well developed as they could be? Maybe if I was more focused on serving rather than being served, I would find the relational peace I truly desire. In your name, I hope and pray. AMEN.

November 19

HUMBLED

Read: Philippians 2:1-11

Do nothing from selfish ambition or conceit, but in humil-
ity regard others as better than yourselves. Let each of you look
not to your own interests, but to the interests of others.
PHILIPPIANS 2:3—4

PAUL ENCOURAGED THE Philippian Christians to humble themselves and to place the interests of others before their own desires, because that was what Jesus did for us. Paul's interpretation of Jesus' actions were that Jesus "*emptied himself, taking the form of a slave, being born in human likeness. And being found in human form, he humbled himself and became obedient to the point of death—even death on a cross.*" Jesus was King among kings, Lord of lords, and the very Son of God—and yet Jesus was willing to embrace the life of a humble servant for our benefit. Jesus became a "man of the people" to save people just like us. If Jesus was willing to cast away his rightful position and royal claim in life in order to interact with and suffer for people like us, what should we be willing to do in order to be a saving presence in other people's lives?

Can you humble yourself for the sake of others?

Lord, you do not stand aloof from my life. You do not keep the world at a safe distance. You plunge right in, even if it means drowning along with us. Encourage in me a willingness to dive to whatever depths I need to in order to reach the people you want me to serve. You are not only my Lord and Savior, you are also the example I wish to model my life after. In Jesus' name, I pray. AMEN.

November 20

What Matters Most

Read: Philippians 3:1b–10

More than that, I regard everything as loss because of the sur-
passing value of knowing Christ Jesus my Lord.
Philippians 3:8

IT IS A revelation that hopefully grips every Christian at one time or another in his or her life of faith: nothing is more important than our relationship with Jesus. This realization can come from the trials of life and the deep longing for something better. Or, having accomplished your dreams and achieved the goals you have set for yourself, you come to recognize that you still have a gnawing emptiness in your soul.

Paul had been a zealous, faithful, and successful Jew, meeting every expectation of the law. He had also been a frequent prisoner and a constant target of persecution for sharing his newfound faith in Jesus. Paul knew success and failure, he experienced acceptance and rejection, and at different times he had lived a life of ease and a life of hardship. Through his experiences Paul's belief was confirmed: life lived with Jesus and living life according to the example of Jesus were what mattered most. No pursuit was more fulfilling than being in daily relationship with the Lord. For Paul, nothing else mattered.

What matters most to you?

Dear Lord, in moments of hardship and in moments when all appears well in my life, I am aware of a sense that my life is not complete. Oddly, the experiences of both challenge and accomplishment make me aware that something is missing within me . . . something that seems as if it should be absolutely central to my existence. You. You are what I am missing. Your guidance, your presence, and your life intertwined with mine is what I crave. Help me to focus on our relationship so that I can keep in touch with what matters most: you, and your call on my life. In your name, I pray. AMEN.

November 21

Not from Around Here

Read: Philippians 3:12—4:1

But our citizenship is in heaven, and it is from there that
we are expecting a Savior, the Lord Jesus Christ.
PHILIPPIANS 3:20

WHERE ARE YOU from? How do you answer that question? Do you think of the place of your birth or your childhood home? Do you identify yourself with a particular town or state or country? Paul was a Jew, he was also a Roman citizen from the city of Tarsus. Paul could have claimed to belong to quite a number of places. But Paul recognized that his true citizenship was in heaven—his truest home was in the presence of God. Paul never renounced his Jewishness or his rights as a Roman subject, but he was clear where his primary allegiance was.

There are times when we feel far from home. We may struggle to identify ourselves with institutions and governmental authorities that do not seem to exemplify the best of what we believe. We might not even feel particularly at home in our own skin. We make our way through life with a spiritual restlessness that makes it difficult to settle into any one place or job or relationship. This soul-angst may be our internal recognition that we are not from around here. Our home is with God. Our citizenship is in heaven.

Where *are* you from?

Dear Lord, I am uncomfortable with flag waving, and I am not always filled with civic pride. There are plenty of times when the town I live in and the country I pledge allegiance to and the institutions I have chosen to associate with do not seem to reflect who I truly feel I am. There are plenty of times when my church affiliation makes me uncomfortable. What is this restlessness of place within me? Is it my soul's ache for my true home—my residence with you? In Jesus' name, I wonder and pray. AMEN.

WORRY FREE

Read: Philippians 4:2–7

Do not worry about anything, but in everything by prayer and supplica-
tion with thanksgiving let your requests be made known to God.
PHILIPPIANS 4:6

IT IS ONE of the most common refrains of the Bible: do not worry. Living worry free appears to be an identifying characteristic of those who claim to follow Christ. Of course, it is often easier said than done. But Paul indicates that if we simply share our worries, our concern, and our anxieties with God in prayer, somehow we will find ourselves free of them. Confessing our concerns to God has a way of releasing us from the bondage of anxiety. Paul goes on to say that if you speak your concerns to God with a grateful heart, *"the peace of God, which surpasses all understanding"* will settle upon you and allow you to remain calm. It doesn't say that the source of your worry will disappear, but somehow your anxiousness will be replaced with a sense of peace from God. Confessing concerns has a way creating calm.

What worry will you share with God today?

Lord, I do feel like I share my concerns with you, but there are times I am silent. My wor-
ries so consume me that I waste time fretting instead of spending time praying. Frankly, I am
not entirely sure what it means to pray thankfully in the midst of my anxiety. Do you want me
to be grateful in the midst of my concerns, and if so, how do I do that? I have so much to learn
. . . I need you to teach. In your name, I pray. AMEN.

November 23

THROUGH HIM

Read: Philippians 4:8–14

I can do all things through him who strengthens me.
PHILIPPIANS 4:13

THERE IS SOMETHING about life in Jesus—living our lives in accordance with Jesus' commands—that gives us strength. When Jesus is our guide, his example, his faith, and his ability to endure can encourage us on our way. That is the power of witness. One life lived courageously can inspire another life to do the same. However, Jesus wasn't and isn't merely a *witness*, he is a *presence*. Paul knew Jesus as a resurrected Lord. This meant Jesus was available for relationship and ready to offer support. For Paul, there was no need that Jesus could not supply, and there was no pit so deep and dark that was beyond Jesus' grasp. Paul's strength was impressive—he was a blazing and passionate human being. But Paul knew his strength was not his own. On his own, Paul would have been nothing more than a limited, scared, and failed person. With Jesus . . . Well . . . all things were suddenly possible!

Can Jesus strengthen you?

Lord, I can't imagine feeling strong on my own—when I attempt to give off that impression to others, I worry it looks as false as it feels. I want your life to fill my life. I want your example to be my example. I want your will to be my way. There is so little I can do on my own . . . I long to be able to do all things through you! In your name, I pray. AMEN.

November 24

PROPER ATTIRE

Read: Colossians 3:1–17

Above all, clothe yourselves with love, which binds every-
thing together in perfect harmony.
COLOSSIANS 3:14

WE SPEND A fair amount of time deciding what we will wear in the morning. We think about our schedules—what meetings and appointments we have—and we choose attire that seems appropriate for our interactions. We dress differently if we have an interview than if we plan on spending the day working in the yard. Clothing is so important to us that we might even get mildly annoyed if we can't find what we were planning to wear.

The Christians in Colossae were told that they were supposed to dress in love. Love was supposed to be their daily attire, and love is a choice that is perfect for every occasion. Love does not clash with any clothing choice—it even goes with plaid! Love never goes out of style. And when you decide to clothe yourselves in love, everyone is able to see it. Perhaps you become a trendsetter—your style encouraging others to start dressing in love too!

How do you choose what to wear in the morning?

Lord, I spend more time deciding on shoes and slacks than I do about what demeanor I will wear throughout the day. In fact, I spend far more time thinking about how I look than how I will choose to act. Why is that? I know that is not a priority that reflects the faith I claim to believe and practice. Help me to consider my attitude as much as my attire. Help me to wear my "Sunday best" at all times—not my most fashionable clothes, but the best of my faith: love and compassion. In Jesus' name, I pray. AMEN.

November 25

Do It for Jesus

Read: Colossians 3:18—4:1

Whatever your task, put yourselves into it, as done
for the Lord and not for your masters.
COLOSSIANS 3:23

SLAVERY WAS SIMPLY a part of life in the first century. In fact, people often offered them-selves and their families as slaves, because the life of a slave could be easier than a life of starvation as a serf. This is not to say that slavery wasn't harsh at times, but it wasn't necessarily the oppressive institution we imagine. For the New Testament writers, all people had masters—earthly or heavenly. In the end, Jesus was believed to be Lord and Master of all. Therefore, obeying earthly masters and doing daily tasks as if they were being done for Jesus allowed people to understand their service to others as sacred work. Work done well, with a cheerful spirit, was a way of glorifying God.

We often grumble when it feels as if tasks are stacked too heavily upon us. At times we bemoan both our work and our bosses. We accomplish the tasks before us, but we do so grudgingly. As a result, we don't put forth our best efforts, and our work and our relationships with those with whom we labor suffer. What if we treated all the work before us as tasks to be done for Jesus himself? When we are called to serve a family member or put in extra time in the office or volunteer in ways that are more taxing than we anticipated, we can imagine ourselves doing it all for Jesus himself. How might that change the spirit with which we work?

What service or work do you engaging in grudgingly?

Lord, there are times when I feel embittered by the work that is left for me to do. When I am forced to serve in ways that are not pleasing to me, I perform in ways that negatively affect my work and my relationships. Help me to think more often of the service you rendered to me and to the world. You gave your life for us . . . Perhaps I can more cheerfully offer my services to others. In your name, I pray. AMEN.

November 26

OPEN DOOR

Read: Colossians 4:2–6

At the same time pray for us as well that God will open to us a door for the word . . .
COLOSSIANS 4:3A

OPPORTUNITY. OF ALL the things we could pray for and desire, opportunity might be the most intriguing. Paul prayed for open doors, not specific outcomes. He wanted the opportunity to do his work in the world, and he didn't really care where his work took him. He was primed to be a part of God's adventure in the world; open doors and opportunities were his heart's desire.

We often pray for specific outcomes for the issues and situations that concern us. We want our lives and our relationships to unfold in somewhat predictable and pleasing ways. We long for a sense of certainty and control in our lives. But where is the adventure in that? Perhaps we should begin to request opportunities and open doors that will lead us more deeply into the mystery of our faith. Maybe we should be more open to the adventures of faith and the opportunities for service that God can afford us. An open door, and the resolve to walk through it, can be an exciting and enlivening opportunity to grow in faith. It can be the adventure of a lifetime!

Where is a door opening in your life?

Lord, open doors for me that you want me to walk through. Usher me into adventures of faith that will give shape to my life. Light a path before me that you want me to follow. I am ready to seize the opportunities you set before me. In Jesus' name, I pray. AMEN.

November 27

AUDIENCE

Read: 1 Thessalonians 2:1–8

Even so we speak, not to please mortals, but to please God who tests our hearts.
1 THESSALONIANS 2:4B & C

WHO IS YOUR audience? Whom do you try to please? From whom do you desire applause and recognition? We may not think about it much, but we are all performers. We perform routine tasks, we receive performance reviews from our employers, and we long to perform well academically or athletically or financially. As a result, we can have an overwhelming need to meet countless expectations—regardless of the appropriateness of those expectations. There is also the issue of so craving applause and approval that we seek it out whatever the cost. Either way, we can easily fall into lives and ways of living that are unmanageable and unfulfilling.

Paul understood his audience. He knew for whom he performed. It wasn't the civil authorities that so often sought to run him out of town. It was not even the fledgling bands of new Christians he helped to form and found around the Mediterranean world. He did not seek the admiration of his peers or other religious teachers. Paul's audience was Jesus alone. His singular desire was to please God. God's applause was the only affirmation he sought.

So . . . who is your audience?

Dear Lord, I feel worn out from trying to please and impress a thousand different audiences. It is overwhelming. Why do I set myself up with expectations I can never meet? Help me to be clear about whom I need to please—you and you alone. In your name, I pray. AMEN.

November 28

INTIMACY

Read: 1 Thessalonians 2:1–16

So deeply do we care for you that we are determined to share with you not only the
gospel of God but also our own selves, because you have become very dear to us.
1 Thessalonians 2:8

THERE IS A spoken but unwritten rule that religious leaders should not befriend members of their congregations. It can blur roles and create a relational hierarchy in the church. This is often true in the secular world as well. Bosses aren't supposed to fraternize with their employees. Coaches and teachers don't befriend the students who are in their care. Doctors, bankers, politicians, and countless other professionally trained people are taught to maintain a professional distance between themselves and the people they serve. Don't get too close—that would be inappropriate!

How odd this all would seem to the apostle Paul. The goal of all relationships is love and intimacy. Not sexual intimacy—though that is appropriate in certain relationships, of course—but a deep sharing of ourselves with others. People of all ranks and classes and professional standing are called to open themselves to others. As Christians—leaders and laity alike—we are called to friendship and intimacy without setting up artificial boundaries for protection. We don't need as much protection as we think; what we need is what Paul strived for—intimacy, love, and a mutual sharing of life with others.

Whom do you need to be more open with?

Lord, I claim that I keep a professional distance from others for their safety. If I stand
apart from the people I am called to serve, then I won't get caught up in the emotional chal-
lenges that complicate relationships. "It is better for them," I tell myself. But the truth is, Lord,
the boundaries I erect around me are for my protection. If I stand apart from the people I serve,
then I don't have to risk having people know me for who I really am. But Lord, you call us to
risk intimacy for the sake of relationship and love and compassion . . . the very things that
make life worth living. Help me to take that risk today. In your name, I pray. AMEN.

November 29

The Quiet Life

Read: 1 Thessalonians 4:1–12

Aspire to live quietly, to mind your own affairs, and to
work with your hands, as we directed you . . .
1 Thessalonians 4:11

Live out loud! Express yourself! Make a statement! Be bold! There is significant cultural encouragement for people to make themselves known and not shrink from view. You can see it in the way we dress, the color of our hair, and the art and piercings we may have applied to our bodies—we are encouraged to live loud and expressively.

Paul had a different idea for Christian living. Live quietly. Keep out of other people's business. Work simply. I suspect that when we live large as a way of expressing ourselves and our individuality, that is when our personality begins to push other people to the side, and the space that could be reserved for God in our own lives gets cluttered with our own self-image. In a culture that says, *"Live big and loud,"* Paul might say, *"Live smaller and quieter"* as a way of being respectful to others and open to God.

How can you live more quietly?

Lord, I know that when issues of justice are at stake, we, as people of faith, must speak up and speak loudly so that your will can be made known to the world. But most of the time, Lord, we would benefit from a more quiet way of life. Help me to claim a way of living that isn't so large and loud that it serves as a barrier to my relationship with you and with those around me. Help me to embrace quietness and simplicity as a way of living more faithfully and fully. In your name, I pray. AMEN.

November 30

BEING DIFFERENT

Read: 1 Thessalonians 4:13–18

But we do not want you to be uniformed, brothers and sisters, about
those who have died, so that you may not grieve as others do who have
no hope. For since we believe that Jesus died and rose again, even so,
through Jesus, God will bring with him those who have died.
1 THESSALONIANS 4:13–14

THE CHRISTIANS IN Thessalonica had a problem. They had been taught—and believed—that Jesus would return to the world and usher everyone into an age of peace and unity and faithfulness. However, as they awaited Christ's return, members of their community had begun to die. This was certainly the natural course of life in the world, but those first Christians believed that Jesus had changed the world, and that life as humanity had known it up until that point had changed. Everything had been made new . . . or so they hoped. Jesus had come to save people, not to let them die! So, why were they losing loved ones? What was going on?

In this passage, Paul attempted to calm the Thessalonians fear by assuring them of God's eternal care for all people living and dead. However, Paul's statement covers more ground than that. Christians do not grieve, they do not worry, and they do not fear as others do. Jesus had been victorious over the forces of evil and death; therefore, there was nothing on earth or in heaven that people should be concerned about. Christians are to be different. Our concerns are not to be for ourselves and our own personal welfare. Our primary concern is to be focused on others. We are saved in life and in death; the only thing we need to concern ourselves with is the care of others here and now.

How does being a Christian make you different?

Lord, new life in you means giving up my old life of worry and fear. There is no need for it any-
more. You have shown us that we move from life to life . . . Therefore, the only thing we should concern
ourselves with is sharing that abundant life and love with others. In your name, I pray. AMEN.

December 1

GO WITH IT

Read: 1 Thessalonians 5:12–28

Rejoice always, pray without ceasing, give thanks in all circumstances; for
this is the will of God in Christ Jesus for you. Do not quench the Spirit.
1 THESSALONIANS 5:16–19

LIFE IS HARD. Being a Christian in the first century, with the Romans and everyone else looking down at you as if you were part of some bizarre religious sect, must have been very difficult. There are some Christians who believe that somehow life should get easier because of faith, but the apostle Paul knew that fidelity to Jesus had a way of placing even heavier burdens on people. Christians didn't cut corners. Christians didn't fight back when challenged. Christians shared what they had and what they earned with people who were in need. Walking the path of Jesus could be a very hard road indeed.

Paul believed that a little hardship is well worth the deepening relationship between ourselves and the Lord. The key is not getting hung up on that hardship. Be joyful in all situations. Pray through all the challenges you face. Be grateful for every experience that comes your way. That is God's will for you—not that everything will always work out well, but that you welcome and embrace every moment of every day. That is living with the Spirit! Life comes at you, and you go with it . . . with gratitude and good cheer.

Does hardship stop you in your tracks?

Lord, I would like my life to be peaceful and happy and blessed. I would prefer to avoid the hardships of life. However, when I think about it, it is in times of hardship that I find myself clinging most closely to you. If I long with my whole being to be more closely knit to you, I should probably welcome moments of challenge as opportunities for you and me to work more closely together. The next time a challenge comes my way, help me to rejoice, to pray, and to give thanks for a new opportunity to deepen our relationship. In your name, I pray. AMEN.

December 2

GET TO WORK

Read: 2 Thessalonians 3:6–15

We did not eat anyone's bread without paying for it; but with toil and labor
we worked night and day, so that we might not burden any of you.
2 THESSALONIANS 3:8

THE APOSTLE PAUL did not tolerate idleness in himself or others. He believed in the value of work and in the ability of people to provide for themselves. This is an interesting twist, because Paul also believed in a person's need to be totally dependent on God. So, Paul's work ethic must have been grounded in a belief that God helps those who help themselves. Whatever you make of such a belief, Paul's emphasis on labor, and the value he put on work, can be instructive. Work is essential. Work adds value to one's life and one's community. Work is a holy act that is required of all people. Work is not something you retire from, but something you should engage in as if it were an act of faith. Productivity, for Paul, was a powerful witness of the need for all people to participate in the building and strengthening of community. Paul could have chosen to be a preacher who was provided for by the people he served, but he believed that there was great value in labor and didn't want to divorce himself from the treasures of toil. Paul encourages us to do the same.

Do you think of your work as a sacred task?

Lord, I often grouse about the work before me. I often can't wait to be done with my work so that I can get on with my living. That means I perceive a divide between my work life and the activities I more fully enjoy. But what if work is holy? What if work is good for me? What if you desire productive people who not only witness to your presence in the world but also work to support and sustain the world you love? Lord, I don't want to spend my life waiting to retire from an activity you might be calling me to. Help me to value the work set before me as if it is a central part of the holy vocation to which you have called me. Allow me to work as if every task I engage in can somehow witness to your glory. In Jesus' name, I pray. AMEN.

December 3

Prayer for Our Leaders

Read: 1 Timothy 2:1–7

*First of all, then, I urge that supplications, prayers, intercessions, and thanks-
givings be made for everyone, for kings and all who are in high positions, so
that we may lead a quiet and peaceable life in all godliness and dignity.*
1 Timothy 2:1–2

We often malign our political leaders. We believe our leaders to be corrupt, out
of touch with the needs of real people, and willing to say and do whatever will win
them approval for the next election. We are cynical about our leaders, because we
know how often political power is abused. Frankly, there are plenty of times when
we just flat out disagree with a perspective or a stance that one of our leaders has
or takes. We have few qualms about blaming our president or Congress for inaction
and division, or claiming that our courts are either intensely biased or engaging in
reckless political activism. We freely voice our disagreement and our dissention
and assume that our freedom to speak up and out is our most foundational, God-
given right.

But Christians are supposed to use our freedom and our speech to offer peti-
tions and prayers on behalf of those who have power and position over us. Like
them or not, we are supposed to pray for those members of our society who hold
office. And our prayers aren't just for political will to turn in our direction—our
prayers are supposed to be for the benefit and blessing of those who have charge
over us. We can disagree with our leaders, but we must never fail to pray for them
and for their well-being.

Do you criticize politicians more than you pray for them?

*Lord, I am not particularly careful with my critique and criticism of the people who hold
positions of leadership. I can view them to be problematic and downright pathetic at times. But*

who am I to judge? How would my life and my choices hold up under intense public scrutiny? Not well, I suspect. So, Lord, I pray now for those who hold office and try to serve the public good. Bless them, be gracious to them, and help them to tend faithfully to those they lead. In Jesus' name, I pray. AMEN.

December 4

Taking Care

Read: 1 Timothy 5:1–8

And whoever does not provide for relatives, and especially for family members, has denied the faith and is worse than an unbeliever.
1 Timothy 5:8

WE ARE SUPPOSED to take care of each other. That is a central message in this letter to a young pastor named Timothy. Treat old men as if they are our fathers, tend to older women as if they are our mothers. Young men and women are to be regarded as siblings. Therefore, all people are to be treated as if they are family members—because they are! And our responsibility is to provide for family members in need. To shirk our duty to tend to people in need is to forsake the faith we claim to believe in and live by. Moral support, financial support, and relational support are the central work of pastors and people who claim to be followers of Jesus. Our faith is only as real as our care.

Do you treat the people around you as carefully as your family?

Lord, you are our Creator, you are our eternal parent, you are the originator of our human family. Thank you for reminding us in scripture that we are all connected. We are related—to you and to one another. Therefore, we are supposed to offer familial support and care to everyone we meet. That is an expansive request, Lord—one we need your daily assistance to meet. Help us to embrace and support all our family members—help them to become as dear to us as they are to you. In Jesus' name, I pray. AMEN.

December 5

FINDING CONTENTMENT IN A DISCONTENTED WORLD

Read: 1 Timothy 6:6–10

> *There is great gain in godliness combined with contentment.*
> *1 TIMOTHY 6:6*

WE LIVE IN a restless age. We aren't satisfied by what we have, and we are ever striving for more. More money. More accomplishments. More prestige. Even though we may have a good life, we dream of an even better life, which we believe we can attain if we only work hard enough. We spend countless hours and days in pursuit of a life of paradise and perfection that always seems to elude our grasp. In the end, if we are not careful, the dream, the vision, the allure of the perfect life can and will kill us. We will die grasping for a dream instead of taking hold of life.

Contentment with what we have—contentment with what we have been given—is a way to quiet the restless longings within us. This is not an endorsement of laziness or sloth, but a word of encouragement that helps us to gain perspective on what is and is not possible in our lives. The restless desires of our hearts will kill us, while cultivating a sense of godly contentment can lead to life . . . and, frankly, a far greater appreciation for life.

Where in your life are you feeling restless?

Lord, I do not want to live lazily, but I also do not want to waste my life in vain pursuits. I want to be content with what you have given me . . . and simply appreciate it and give you thanks. In Jesus' name, I pray. AMEN.

December 6

Faith Ancestry

Read: 2 Timothy 1:3–7

I am reminded of your sincere faith, a faith that lived first in your grand-mother Lois and your mother Eunice and now, I am sure, lives in you.
2 Timothy 1:5

HOW IS FAITH born in a person? What relationships play a role in directing people toward God? How is Jesus Christ made known to people? Sometimes—perhaps oftentimes—faith is transmitted through family members. Mom or Dad or Grandpa or Grandma was a person of faith, and their faith was passed on to future generations. This doesn't mean that if a parent or grandparent is a person of faith, the rest of the family will automatically follow. There will be family members who do not catch the Spirit no matter how effectively we try to douse them with it. However, a faithful family member is a much more effective conveyor of the gospel than a church or the local pastor or a total stranger. The regular spiritual diet of family prayers at bedtime and mealtime, the commitment to worshiping as a family, and the encouragement of faith discussions within the household can set the conditions for faith to be transmitted from one generation to the next. A faithful grandmother, a prayerful aunt, or a devoted sibling can be the agent through which the Holy Spirit can claim the lives of an entire family.

How are you transmitting the faith to the next generation?

Lord, I want my children and grandchildren to be in relationship with you. I want them to have a faith they can lean on when times are hard, and I want them to know that they should find time to thank you when all is well. I want them to know you and serve you and love you. In fact, I worry that somehow they might miss out on a life of faith because I have failed to properly instill it in them. Lord, help me to live out my faith in plain sight of all my family—without being holier than thou—and then I will entrust the rest to you. In Jesus' name, I pray. AMEN.

December 7

HELPFUL SCRIPTURE

Read: 2 Timothy 3:10—4:8

All scripture is inspired by God and is useful for teaching, for reproof,
for correction, and for training in righteousness, so that everyone who
belongs to God may be proficient, equipped for every good work.
2 TIMOTHY 3:16–17

MANY PEOPLE ARE scared of the Bible. It seems like an ancient and confusing book that has very little to do with our contemporary lives. The few times we have decided to open the book—perhaps deciding on a whim to finally read it from cover to cover starting with Genesis—we have been alarmed by its content. The story seems so violent, God seems so vengeful, and humanity seems embroiled in more sin than we could ever be free from. There are reasons why our Bibles are on a shelf collecting dust somewhere or lost in some long-forgotten location. We don't understand the Bible, we don't trust the teaching inside, and we feel intimidated by other Christians who claim that the Bible is an easy to use manual for living.

For all our doubts, however, there is a sense within us that the Bible might just hold the answers to the gnawing questions within us. Printed on those delicate pages just might be some direction we desperately need. In a world held captive by uncertainty, violence, and a desire to do our own thing and find our own way, the Bible might be able to take our intense focus off ourselves and refocus us on God. Maybe it is time to locate our Bibles, dust them off, take them to a study group in a church, open them with greater regularity, and discover the faith that has given direction and hope and purpose to countless people over thousands of years.

Where is your Bible right now?

Lord, I want faith to be easy and for the books I read to be accessible. The Bible is neither of those things. If it is full of words you have inspired, why have you made it so difficult to comprehend? Is it because you want me to wrestle with the mystery in its pages? Do you want me to be pressed into relationship with other people who can make the biblical stories intelligible to me? Is it because you want all my attention to be focused on your word and not drawn in a thousand other distractions? I realize that may be the case. So, Lord, let me find my Bible, dust it off, and begin to engage it as if it were part of the conversation you want to have with me. In Jesus' name, I pray. AMEN.

December 8

A Good Equation

Read: Titus 3:1–11

I desire that you insist on these things, so that those who have
come to believe in God may be careful to devote themselves to good
works; these things are excellent and profitable to everyone.
Titus 3:8

THE EQUATION TURNS out to be fairly simple. God is good, God saves us, therefore, we go on to do the good work of God. For countless generations there have been questions about what it takes to receive eternal life. The question has turned into heated arguments at times. Are we saved by good works, or are we saved by the grace of God? During the Protestant Reformation, the answer that was offered was that human beings cannot do anything to deserve God's grace and love—we can only receive it. In fact, Martin Luther encouraged his followers to *"sin boldly,"* and some have taken that to mean that you can do any sinful act you want as long as you pray for forgiveness. That kind of thinking has left many a person of faith wondering about the integrity of a belief system that so diminishes good works. If we are saved by grace, how do good works fit into the equation? The Bible is wonderfully balanced on this point. Thanks to the goodness of God, we are all extended grace and forgiveness, but once we have accepted the grace and forgiveness of God, we should respond to those gifts by living in ways that reflect God's goodness. God is good. By the grace of God we are saved. Our response should be to do work in the world that reflects God's goodness. Fairly simple.

What good works do you do?

Lord, perhaps the equation of our faith isn't as easy to accept as it might be, because we struggle to understand how you could choose to love us and save us before we have even done anything to deserve your graceful attention. We live in a world where work is done for a reward. But that is not the equation of faith. You love us in the hope that we will share your love with others. You are good, and your desire is for us to be like you. Help me to do good works today in response to the grace you have already afforded me. In Jesus' name, I pray. AMEN.

December 9

BEING UP FRONT

Read: Philemon

> *I am appealing to you for my child, Onesimus, whose father I have become*
> *during my imprisonment. . . . I am sending him, that is, my own heart,*
> *back to you. I wanted to keep him with me, so that he might be of ser-*
> *vice to me in your place during my imprisonment for the gospel; but I*
> *preferred to do nothing without your consent, in order that your*
> *good deed might be voluntary and not something forced.*
> PHILEMON 10,12–14

ONESIMUS, A SLAVE of Philemon, somehow found his way to Paul and wound up serving Paul during one of Paul's imprisonments. From this letter we can gather that Philemon was a convert of Paul's, and thus in Paul's debt. For some reason Paul wound up sending Onesimus back to his master with this letter requesting that Philemon free Onesimus from slavery. This is an odd request, because Paul openly advocated that slaves dutifully and contentedly serve their masters as if they were serving Jesus Christ himself. But Paul went to great lengths to advocate freedom for Onesimus. What is most impressive is that Paul clearly insisted on being up front about his desire for Onesimus to be free. I suspect Paul could have kept Onesimus in his care without telling Philemon. Or, Paul could have unapologetically kept Onesimus as compensation for all Paul had done for Philemon. Paul, however, chose to be above board in regard to his request. He returned the slave, made his request, and trusted that Philemon would respond faithfully. For Paul, there were no shortcuts, no cutting corners, and no deceptive dealings when living out faith. To be righteous means to be up front about all our human dealings. Secrets, dark dealings and whispered words behind someone's back are not the marks of a Christian. All things are to be done in the light. Even when presented with challenging circumstances, we should be able to conduct ourselves and our business in plain sight of the world.

Are you upfront, direct, and transparent in your dealings with others?

Lord, I confess that I often make choices that I would not want others to witness. I can make determinations without involving everyone I should in the decision-making process. It is easier to keep my own council than to allow all my dealings to be done in ways that invite scrutiny. Help me to be more up front in my interactions with others. Help me to take the right road instead of the path of least resistance. Help me to live my life in the light for all to see. In Jesus' name, I pray. AMEN.

WHO IS JESUS?

Read: Hebrews 1:1–4

> *He is the reflection of God's glory and the exact imprint of God's*
> *very being, and he sustains all things by his powerful word.*
> *HEBREWS 1:3*

THE LETTER TO the Hebrews tries to explain Jesus' identity. Jesus' ministry up until his crucifixion was not particularly unique. There had been other charismatic prophets that had called Israel to faithfulness over the generations. There had been healers and miracle workers who spellbound the Hebrew people. A Jewish religious teacher dying in Jerusalem was just a standard part of the résumé for a Hebrew prophet. This is not to say that Jesus' ministry was insignificant—but most scholars agree that his true significance was recognized only after his resurrection. Resurrection made Jesus unique, and after that remarkable event, Gospel writers started piecing together the stories of Jesus' life in the hope of discovering his true identity. Was Jesus a Messiah? Was he the Son of God? Was Jesus the one the Hebrew people had been waiting for to redeem their common life and reestablish their special position in the world?

The writer of the letter of the Hebrews is fairly explicit. When a person looked at Jesus they saw God. Jesus was God's reflection in the world. God had been imprinted in human form, and that representation was Jesus. Who is Jesus? Jesus is what God looks like in human form.

What do you imagine God to look like?

Lord, I am told in scripture that to see you is to see God. I long for such a vision. I strain to see you at work in the world and in the words of scripture. You can be a bit difficult to make out. Please reveal yourself to me . . . I want to know what you look like so that your reflection of God can be the image I model my life upon. In your name, I pray. AMEN.

December 11

LIVING WORD

Read: Hebrews 4:1–13

Indeed, the word of God is living and active, sharper than any two-
edged sword, piercing until it divides soul from spirit, joints from mar-
row; it is able to judge the thoughts and intentions of the heart.
HEBREWS 4:12

THE GOSPEL OF John tells us that the *"Word became flesh and lived among us."* The Word is Jesus. This is a way of saying that Jesus is the embodiment of all that God has said from the beginning of time, starting with God describing creation as *"good."* It has been a long-held Christian belief that if Jesus is the Word, then we can have an actual encounter with Jesus through the Word—that is, through scripture. As the writer of the letter to the Hebrews attests, there is a living quality to scripture. When reading God's word in the Bible, one can feel as if the words themselves are at work in one's life. Who has not been struck by how a particular verse of scripture—even when it is taken a bit out of context—can illuminate our lives? There are moments when it can feel as if God is speaking directly to us through a biblical text. As Christians, we dare to believe that voice is the voice of Jesus, the living Word, and our resurrected Lord.

Do you remember reading a particular passage of scripture and feeling as if it was meant just for you?

Lord, speak to me. Allow me to hear your voice. Encounter me as I feebly try to encounter
you. I need your word—I need you today. In your name, I pray. AMEN.

December 12

Sympathetic Priest

Read: Hebrews 4:14—5:10

For we do not have a high priest who is unable to sympathize with our weaknesses,
but we have one who in every respect has been tested as we are, yet without sin.
Hebrews 4:15

In Jesus' day, the Hebrew people were looking for a Messiah who would be a conquering hero, not a suffering servant. However, for those of us who believe, having a high priest who knows our pain, understands the challenges of our lives, and can empathize with the burdens we carry is indeed a saving grace. Jesus is a Savior, because he understands our plight. Jesus knows brokenness. Jesus is familiar with temptation. Jesus can sympathize with those of us who live in fear and are afraid of death. Because our high priest and judge understands our lives, we should have no hesitation in approaching his throne. Grace resides in the presence of Jesus, because Jesus knows what it is like to have to live in a sinful and broken world. If Jesus did not understand us, then that would be cause for great fear and trepidation. But Jesus knows what it is like to be disappointed by followers and friends. Jesus knows what it is like to be wrongly accused and unfairly convicted. Jesus knows what it is like to have God remain silent in a moment of great trial. Jesus lived and died in our world, and he chose to return to us out of love . . . love for God and love for us. Trusting in such faithfulness, how can we not approach his throne of grace with some degree of boldness? Jesus is a sympathetic priest who is ready to forgive us before we are even aware of our need for pardon!

Has a sympathetic priest or pastor or person of faith ever been gracious to you beyond your expectations?

Lord, knowing the thoughts that run through my mind and the actions of my life, I don't think I could bear standing in your presence. I do not possess boldness when it comes to our relationship. I feel hesitant, not believing myself worthy of relationship with you. And yet, scripture urges me to trust in your grace. You who called Judas a friend and forgave Peter his denial and returned to the disciples who deserted you will likely be just as gracious and forgiving of me. In your name, I hope and pray. AMEN.

December 13

OBEDIENT SON

Read: Hebrews 5

> *[As] a Son, he learned obedience . . . ; and having been made perfect,*
> *Jesus became the source of eternal salvation for all who obey him.*
> HEBREWS 5:8–9

OBEDIENCE IS NOT a hallmark of American culture. As Americans, we prize freedom above all else. *"Give me freedom or give me death"* is so often the cry of the American soul. So, like disobedient teenagers, we spurn the rules and laws of our God and set our minds on doing things our own way. And we suffer for it. Too often our marriages, our careers, and our relationships with our children are compromised by our belief that we know best.

We do not know best. God, the Creator of the heavens and the earth, knows best. God set rules in place so that we would experience joy and blessing in this life and live forever in the next. The good news is that Jesus Christ has entered our broken lives and broken world with perplexingly divine wisdom. Love your enemies. Turn the other cheek. Give to those in need. Observe the Sabbath. Love and serve God. Follow me.

These rules do not always make sense to us. We are tempted to ignore them. There comes a time, however, when we have to own up to our failed efforts and finally decide to trust that doing things God's way will lead to salvation.

Where in your life do you need to start being obedient to God?

Lord, I disobey you at every turn—intentionally and unintentionally. Help me to trust that your word, your rule, and your leading can guide me to salvation. Help me, like Jesus, to be more obedient, even when that is about the last thing I desire. Lead me to your salvation, now and forever. In Jesus' name, I pray. AMEN.

December 14

BELIEF AND FAITH

Read: Hebrews 11:1–7

Now faith is the assurance of things hoped for, the conviction of things not seen.
HEBREWS 11:1

THERE IS A difference between belief and faith. Belief is theoretical, whereas faith is practical—it is the difference between "in theory," and "in practice." Belief has to do with the activity of our minds and faith has to do with the actions of our lives. The difference between belief and faith can be explain through observing a high wire act. A performer steps onto a platform with a bicycle, preparing to ride across the wire to the opposite platform. *Belief* is thinking that the performer will succeed in the act . . . *faith* is choosing to get on the shoulders of the performer and joining in the ride.

Faith is not about right *thinking*, it is about right *acting*. It is taking the belief that one has and putting that belief into some sort of concrete practice. The great stories of the Bible are not stories of people merely believing in God, they are stories of people taking leaps of faith and moving with God. The writer of the letter to the Hebrews lists numerous people who didn't merely believe but who acted on their belief . . . and the hope of their faith became reality.

Are you a believer, or do you put your faith into action?

Lord, I am not always sure my convictions are all that strong . . . Just believing sometimes feels like a stretch. How can I act on my beliefs if my believing is a bit anemic? However, perhaps the practice of acting on some of the things I want to believe might actually produce in me a faith that can grow. I am as confused as ever . . . Please take me on your shoulders and strengthen my faith in ways that I am unable to produce in myself. In your name, I pray. AMEN.

December 15

CLOUD OF WITNESSES

Read: Hebrews 12:1–13

Therefore, since we are surrounded by so great a cloud of witnesses, let us also lay aside every weight and the sin that clings so closely, and let us run with persever-ance the race that is set before us, looking to Jesus the pioneer and perfecter of our faith, who for the sake of the joy that was set before him endured the cross, disre-garding its shame, and has taken his seat at the right hand of the throne of God.
HEBREWS 12:1–2

WE HAVE A fan club . . . or perhaps more aptly, we have a cheering section. Through resurrection and the history of our faith, we have innumerable examples of people living out their convictions and their love of God in the world. The Bible is filled with stories of people who served as examples of faithful living. Abraham, Moses, Ruth, David, Mary . . . The list is impressive—and it is headed up by Jesus. It can be daunting to think about trying to live our lives as the luminaries of our faith did so many years ago. We too often feel like failed sinners, not faithful saints. To read the great and heroic stories of the Bible can make us feel as if we are living in the shadows of lives that somehow darken our own by comparison. But the cloud that the writer of this letter refers to is not one that casts a shadow over who we are, but it is a sea of cheering faith siblings who encourage us on our own way. The names in the Bible, the list of saints, and Jesus himself are all part of a divine cheering section that can embolden us to run well the race that is set before us. What an amazing image—to think that Abraham and Sarah, Moses and Ruth, Mary and Jesus, Peter and Paul are among a crowd of faithful people who cheer us on our way! How can we fail to run well and live well when we have that kind of support!

Can you imagine Jesus cheering you on as you make your way through life?

Lord, most of the time I feel like my life of faith is a solitary exercise. Like working out at the gym, there may be others around, but the effort put forth is my own, and no one is taking particular notice of what I am doing. You challenge me to think of my life of faith as a very public affair—a race that is eagerly watched by countless people who have traveled many of the same paths I now take. I had not considered that before. You have people cheering me on. Thank you for that encouragement. Help me to claim the truth of it. Allow that encouragement to strengthen my stride. In Jesus' name, I pray. AMEN.

December 16

AWESOME!

Read: Hebrews 12:18–24

*You have not come to something that can be touched, a blazing fire, and dark-
ness, and gloom, and a tempest, and the sound of a trumpet, and a voice whose
words made the hearers beg that not another word be spoken to them.*
HEBREWS 12:18–19

HOW CAN WE possibly describe the presence of God? What would it be like to encounter Jesus? Is there a way to sum up the experience of entering eternal life?
Such descriptions have been attempted. Moses' encounter with God left him aglow
with God's Spirit and presence. Paul was struck blind and entirely stripped of his
old sinful identity by Jesus. We have heard stories of what a new heaven and a new
earth might look like if we found ourselves there—and the majesty of such a place
is awe inspiring. However we try to describe connection with that which is divine,
we believe the experience to be awesome. It is as if a blazing fire and an utter darkness are entangled with one another, it is like a blaring trumpet and the sound of
sheer silence in concert with one another—it is as if the very last word has been
spoken, and that word was so good that we longed never to hear another voice
speak as long as we live. It is all things together in one. Completion. In the presence
of God all people and all things are made whole . . . even us. How awesome is that?

Can you imagine yourself complete?

*Lord, how I long for wholeness—for my soul and my entire self to feel fully united in
my person and at one with you. There are moments when I feel as if one word from you could
set everything right within me. My deepest desire is to hear you speak so that all the noise
inside me and all the clamoring of my life might be stilled and silenced. For this I pray, in
your name. AMEN.*

December 17

Entertaining Angels

Read: Hebrews 13:1–19

Do not neglect to show hospitality to strangers, for by doing
that some have entertained angels without knowing it.
Hebrews 13:2

We teach our children to fear strangers. Don't talk to or entertain unfamiliar people. If we don't know someone, we feel it is best to steer clear of an encounter. In fact, if someone we don't know smiles at us as we pass them on the street, we might be tempted to wonder what is wrong with them. Even eye contact with strangers is not considered a prudent way to navigate through life. Can it be any surprise that angels so seldom appear in our world when strangers are not welcome in our lives?

Some may scoff at the notion of angels in disguise, as if it is nothing less than another fanciful religious notion. But whatever you might make of the implied connection between strangers and angels, the message is clear that strangers can serve as a blessing to us. When showing hospitality to someone, we often think we are the ones offering the gift. But somehow, when we extend ourselves to others, particularly those for whom we have little or no expectations—strangers perhaps—we find the encounter to be enlivening, hopeful, and spirited. The time we give is returned to us in joy experienced. And somehow, what we feel we have given is outweighed by what we sense we have gained. What a shame to be unaware of an experience like that!

When was the last time you extended yourself to someone you didn't know?

Lord, what must we miss because of that which we fear! How many angels have I passed on the street with my head down and my eyes averted? Have I taught my own children to behave in ways that prevent divine encounters? Give me courage to welcome strangers as if they are angels sent by you. In Jesus' name, I pray. AMEN.

December 18

SPEED LIMITS

Read: James 1:19–27

> *You must understand this, my beloved: let everyone be*
> *quick to listen, slow to speak, slow to anger.*
> *JAMES 1:19*

MANY OF US like to talk, and we believe it is our right to get angry when we choose. The impulse to speak and the speed with which we can become enraged are shockingly quick. We tend to speak before we think, and we get enraged before we consider how our anger will exacerbate a particular situation, which is unfortunate, because, as the writer of James says, our *"anger does not produce God's righteousness."*

One possible antidote to anger that can damage relationships and further aggravate difficult situations is to slow down. Don't be in a hurry to speak, and don't rush to judgment. Ask questions. Listen to the responses given. Try to truly understand the person or situation that is producing an emotional charge in you. When we accelerate our ability to listen and understand, we find that our impulse to respond in anger is greatly reduced.

Are you in a rush to be heard, and are you quick to anger?

Lord, help me to slow down and listen. I need to listen to you. I need to listen to those around me. Instead of forming a response in my mind while someone else is speaking, I should listen deeply and slowly as you advise. Perhaps when I am quick to listen, without worrying whether I get the first or last word, a sense of peace will overcome my impulse to anger. For this I pray, in Jesus' name. AMEN.

December 19

Faith Demonstration

Read: James 2:14–26

But someone will say, "You have faith and I have works." Show me your faith
apart from your works, and I by my works will show you my faith.
JAMES 2:18

FAITH SHOULD SHOW. That is the point the writer of James makes in this passage of scripture. A faith that does not practice what it preaches is hypocritical. That is so often the knock on Christians: we proclaim one belief and then act contrary to what we say we believe—and the world mocks us for such inconsistence. The reason for this inconsistency is, of course, sin. As Paul said, we know the good we should be doing, but somehow the bad that we do not want to do continues to infiltrate our choices in life.

No matter how often or how far we fall short of fulfilling the call of our faith, we must strive to allow that which we believe to shape how we behave. For while it is true that *"faith without works is dead,"* when works accompany faith, our Christian witness can truly come alive!

Do you live what you say you believe?

Lord, I know I am a hypocrite, I know I am a sinner, and I know I fall short of your glory
in ways great and small each and every day. But I refuse to quit, because I believe you can
take my sinful life and help me to produce acts of faith that demonstrate your presence in me.
If you can produce a good work in me, then there must be hope for the entire world. In Jesus'
name, I pray. AMEN.

December 20

TOMORROW'S PLAN

Read: James 4:13–17

> *Come now, you who say, "Today or tomorrow we will go to such and such*
> *a town and spend a year there, doing business and making money." Yet you*
> *do not even know what tomorrow will bring. What is your life? For you*
> *are a mist that appears for a little while and then vanishes. Instead you*
> *ought to say, "If the Lord wishes, we will live and do this or that."*
> JAMES 4:13–15

LIFE IS SHORT. We often forget that reality as we plan for the future and get caught up in our own sense of self-importance. We may not like to think of it at first, but we are as impermanent as a mist that appears at dawn only to be burned off by the midmorning sun. One of the ways we deal with our fleeting presence in this world is to further invest ourselves in it. We make plans. We set goals. We strive to make an imprint on the world in which we live. But as our last breath nears, we come to the hard realization that nothing we do is permanent, and we would have been better off simply following the commands of God and trying to live our lives according to the desires of the one who is eternal. Rather than planning for tomorrow, we should strive to serve God today.

Why do you make so many plans?

Lord, if is your will that I should live beyond this moment, I offer that life to you. I don't want to feverishly try to leave my imprint on this world. What I really want—what I so deeply desire—is for your imprint to be evident in my life . . . however long I have to live. I will embrace today, and if it is your will . . . tomorrow I will do the same. In Jesus' name, I pray. AMEN.

December 21

BUILDING PROJECT

Read: 1 Peter 2:1–10

Like living stones, let yourselves be built into a spiritual house, to be a holy priest-
hood, to offer spiritual sacrifices acceptable to God through Jesus Christ.
1 PETER 2:5

AS KIDS, WHEN someone would share an accomplishment that was underwhelm-
ing to those listening, we would snidely respond, *"So, what do you want, a medal or*
a monument?" That was a rather painless and even playful way of putting a boasting
peer back in their place. Youthful boasting and retorts about medals and monuments hints at our very real human desire for legacy. We want to do something
significant with our lives. We want to leave an impression on the world. We want
to be remembered.

The first letter of Peter encourages us to believe that, as people of faith,
we are indeed being built into a unique form of monument. The building project is not for our own glorification, however. We are living stones that are set
into place to form an edifice that brings glory to God. Our lives have abundant
significance when we allow ourselves to be used for that which God desires to
construct. Our lives, when set in place with the saints from every generation,
serve as a memorial—a testament to what God is able to do in the world. If God
can take our frail and sinful nature and build us into something lasting and eternal, then there is no limit to the good work God can do in our lives and in our
world. If there are medals and monuments to be offered in this life, they should
be offered to God!

Think of all the monuments you have seen in your lifetime . . . How many
were dedicated to God?

Lord, you do not need anything. You are complete. You are not impressed with the churches, temples, and holy shrines dedicated to you. What you value, according to scripture, are lives that are dedicated to you and ready for your use in this world. I am ready to be used according to your will. Take me. Set me in a place of service. I submit to your building plan. I pray that I am suitable for your designs. In Jesus' name, I pray. AMEN.

December 22

DOING RIGHT

Read: 1 Peter 2:11–17

For it is God's will that by doing right you should silence the ignorance of the foolish.
1 Peter 2:15

A PERSON OF faith can't go too far wrong in the world by doing what is right. That is the conviction of the writer of this passage of scripture. When we try to do the right thing—especially when it is costly to us—it can serve as a powerful and moving witness in the world. This is not to say that there aren't plenty of *"damned if you do, damned if you don't"* scenarios at play in the world. There is no hard and fast promise that doing the right thing will work out well for us. However, while there are opportunities to suffer for doing what is right, more often than not, making faithful choices and living by them can be a prudent path forward in life. By doing right you can live well. Difficult situations and difficult people can be overcome and transformed for the better when people dare to live out the best of their faith. It is very difficult to fault someone for being faithful.

Do you do what is right?

Lord, I am reluctant to claim to know what is right. I am aware that much harm has been done in your world by people who believe they know your will and claim to know what is best. In truth, I am only one act of hubris away from joining the self-righteous. However, while I am never entirely certain about right behavior, I feel fairly clear about behavior that is wrong. I don't want to be hurtful, I don't want to be divisive, and I don't want to be destructive. With all my heart I want to be a healing, unifying, and encouraging member of your family. Help me to choose well . . . so that I might do well. In Jesus' name, I pray. AMEN.

December 23

Nothing Fancy

Read: 2 Peter 1:16–21

For we did not follow cleverly devised myths when we made known to you the power and coming of our Lord Jesus Christ, but we had been eyewitnesses of his majesty.
2 Peter 1:16

What do we say about our faith? How do we share what we believe? How would we invite others into this value system that has nurtured, shaped, and sustained our lives? There is a sense that a person needs to be part theologian to speak about their faith. As a result, few of us feel qualified to talk about our relationship with God in ways that could be compelling to others.

The first Christian witnesses were nothing fancy. It is true that the apostle Paul spent much of his time trying to prove Jesus was the Messiah by using his vast knowledge of Hebrew scripture, but most Christian witnesses were not cleverly devised theological treatises. Early Christians just spoke plainly about their experience of the God they had come to know through Jesus Christ. They simply shared their experiences, without worrying too much about how systematic their beliefs were. The way you witness to your faith is to share with others your experience of God. You don't need fancy theological proofs—your willingness to speak of your relationship with Jesus is often proof enough.

What keeps you from speaking your faith?

Lord, I am more than tempted to leave faith talk to the pastor on Sunday morning. It is just easier that way. I convince myself that I would make a mess of a faith conversation anyway, so I remain silent. But my silence has a way of disquieting me, as well. Do I not have a story to tell? Have you done so much for me, only for me to refuse to talk about you? That's not right, and I do not want that to be my way any longer. Open a door for me this week to talk about our relationship with someone who needs to know about you. Sweep aside my fears of theological correctness, and help me to speak from the heart about how I feel your presence in my life. In Jesus' name, I pray. AMEN.

December 24

BEING PATIENT

Read: 2 Peter 3:8–15

With the Lord one day is like a thousand years, and a thousand years are like one day.
2 PETER 3:8

PATIENCE. SOME OF us seem to have it, others don't. Long lines, traffic, and being left on hold can drive some of us absolutely crazy, while others seem perfectly content to wait. Anticipation can get the best of many of us, while others always seem completely sanguine and peaceful. The patient ones among us seem to understand something that alludes the rest of us—they seem to comprehend the divine nature of waiting, and they can see the value of taking time. The rest of us can only pray for such insight.

God is patient. God doesn't rush. God's time is different from our time. God understands that it takes time to form a life. It takes time for transformation to take place. It takes time for the Word to sink into our souls so that it can bloom and grow in our actions and living. God is patient with us, wanting all of us to come to repentance. Perhaps that is an indication that we should be patient with others . . . and even ourselves.

Are you patient?

Lord, I am not patient by nature. I want what I want, when I want it. In fact, I get bent out of shape when I have to wait. I see only inconvenience when my time is taken up by standing in line. Help me to understand the holy nature of waiting. Help me to learn to wait as you wait: with patience, trust, and the hope that all things will eventually mature and grow and improve. In Jesus' name, I pray. AMEN.

December 25

Truth

Read: 1 John 1:5–10

If we say that we have no sin, we deceive ourselves, and the truth is not in us.

1 John 1:8

THERE ARE CHRISTIANS who want to believe they are good people. They would prefer not to hear about our bondage to sin. They feel that talk about sin brings people down and turns our faith into an oppressive and depressing belief system. They would prefer that we hold up our good works as evidence of our intrinsic value and spiritual wellness.

There is no question that we are empowered by the Holy Spirit to do good works in accordance with our faith. We do have within us a divine spark that prompts us to seek God and attempt to model our lives after Jesus. But sin is always close at hand, and behavior that serves to separate us from the will and ways of God is a constant temptation. There are an infinite number of thoughts and actions in our lives that we would prefer to keep secret, because exposing them to others would reveal the depth of our imperfection. This inherent sinfulness, which is as much a part of us as our uncharitable thoughts and deeds, is not a cause for depression, it is rather a call to confession and forgiveness. When we recognize and embrace the fact that we are sinful creatures, that is when we can finally confess our faults and receive the forgiveness for which we deeply long. That is the truth.

Why do you struggle to understand yourself as a sinner?

Lord, if I am to be completely honest, while I don't like being tagged a sinner, I know that is exactly what I am. If my secret thoughts and actions were somehow brought out into the light for all to see, I would be revealed for the fraud that I am. I like to think of myself as good, but that is not the truth. I am a sinner, and I am grateful that you are a Savior! In your name, I pray. AMEN.

December 26

LOVE AND GOD

Read: 1 John 4:7–21

God is love, and those who abide in love abide in God, and God abides in them.
1 JOHN 4:16B

GOD IS LOVE. We have heard that said, and perhaps we have said it ourselves. God's character, as revealed to us through the life and ministry and resurrection of Jesus, is ultimately loving. But that statement may be an even more profound description of what God is actually like. God is like love. Invisible, but fully present. Disembodied, but keenly felt. Inexplicable, but so very real. The experience of love might be the most dynamic proof we have of God. There is no reason for love to exist in the world. Darwin didn't cite love as part of the evolutionary progression of life in the world. Science cannot measure love any more than scientists can locate God. We all believe in love. Love is real. If God is love, then it stands to reason that God is just as real. Why is that so difficult to believe?

How are God and love alike?

Lord, love may be the very best descriptor of who you are and how you exist in the world. Your presence is like the presence of love in the world. Where do you exist? Can we pinpoint your location in the created order? I suspect you are present in every loving act that graces this world. In Jesus' name, I pray. AMEN.

December 27

FACE TO FACE

Read: 2 John & 3 John

I have much to write to you, but I would rather not write with pen and ink;
instead I hope to see you soon, and we will talk together face to face.
3 JOHN 13–14

THESE TWO SHORT letters end with nearly the identical wording and sentiment: there is much more to say, but what needs to be said is best done face to face. While this is not the thrust of the message of these two letters, it still seems to be a very important message to embrace.

We live in a world where people can communicate with one another in near anonymity. Technology allows us to have conversations in countless ways without ever having to stand directly in front of another person. We have been told that we can create virtual relationships and communities. That may be true, but the Holy Spirit of God is best communicated when people physically come together. The Internet, email, text messaging, and other social media can be easily abused and misinterpreted. As people of faith, we might be well served to keep our technologically facilitated communications brief, trusting that relationships and communities are at their best when people choose to speak face to face and stand hand in hand.

How do you choose to communicate with others?

Lord, it is so much easier to communicate with people while standing at a distance. Distance and anonymity allow us to share words that we would not dare to speak if we had to stand face to face with certain people. It is so easy to send off a heated email or a hurtful text or a hateful tweet. In fact, it is too easy. You do not call us to easy interactions but rather to deep sharing that can only happen when we are in close proximity to others. Help me to possess the restraint and the resolve to limit my communication to that which can be done face to face. In Jesus' name, I pray. AMEN.

December 28

HAVE MERCY

Read: Jude

*And have mercy on some who are wavering; save others by snatch-
ing them out of the fire; and have mercy on still others with
fear, hating even the tunic defiled by their bodies.*
JUDE 22–23

JUDE APPEARS TO be an angry little letter that breathes threats and condemnation for people who teach unrighteousness and live ungodly lives. For many of us these charges unsettle us, because even as people of faith, we recognize that we often fail to teach what is right, and we make choices in our living that are less than holy. Oftentimes we do this without even realizing it. We are uncertain of our own righteousness, and we are rather skeptical of others who proclaim their own correctness.

But there is a gracious note in this letter that should not be overlooked. Even the unrighteous are offered mercy. We can hate sinful acts, but we must be gracious to all people no matter their choices in life. God desires to save all of us, not just a select few. Jude lets us know that there will be judgment, but there is also mercy. And according to the letter of James, mercy always triumphs over judgment—praise God!

Are you a merciful person?

Lord, talk of your wrath and judgment are terrifying. Who could stand in your presence? Who would not wither under your critique? Who could endure your examination? We dare to believe that person to be none other than Jesus. And Jesus has proclaimed that judgment is stayed by mercy. I pray with my whole heart for that to be true. The whole world is in need of your grace . . . so please have mercy on us all. In Jesus' name, I hope and pray. AMEN.

December 29

STILL SPEAKING

Read: Revelation 1:9–20

I was in the spirit on the Lord's day, and I heard behind me a loud voice like a trumpet
saying, "Write in a book what you see and send it to the seven churches, to Ephesus,
to Smyrna, to Pergamum, to Thyatira, to Sardis, to Philadelphia, and to Laodicea."
REVELATION 1:10–11

HAVING BEEN EXILED on the sun baked island of Patmos, John continued to observe
the Sabbath and to pray to his Lord Jesus Christ. One day when he was *"in the spirit,"*
he heard a voice and saw a vision, and he began to write a powerful, creative, and
disturbing witness to his faith. We don't know if John was the only Christ follower
on that Greek isle at the time, but he was not alone—Jesus was somehow wonderfully and vividly present to him. The product of that encounter is a book that
continues to challenge and hearten Christians around the globe.

Whatever one makes of the descriptive and cataclysmic nature of John's writing, the book itself is witness to our belief that Jesus is still speaking. Through the
Spirit, Jesus continues to teach us and reveal God's desires for us. Our faith is not
a memorial to the acts of God done in the distant *past*, our faith is a testament to
the ability of our Lord to communicate and lead us in the *present*. That is a powerful
revelation in and of itself: God is still speaking, desiring us to listen and respond.

Is God still speaking in your life?

Lord, if you can speak to an exiled person of faith living in a cave on the hills of Patmos,
I long to believe you can speak also to me. I do not need to see you as some blinding and
soul-arresting light . . . I would be more than content with hearing a still small voice from
you. However you choose to reveal yourself, know that I deeply desire that encounter. In your
name, I pray. AMEN.

December 30

OPENING THE DOOR

Read: Revelation 3:14–22

Listen! I am standing at the door, knocking; if you hear my voice and open
the door, I will come in to you and eat with you, and you with me.
REVELATION 3:20

THERE ARE A seemingly infinite number of claims made about what someone needs to do to enter into a relationship with Jesus—you have to say specific words or believe a particular doctrine or behave a certain way. However, this passage in the book of Revelation indicates that it is Jesus who takes primary responsibility for the relationship. Jesus comes to the door. Jesus knocks. Jesus calls to us through the door. Jesus enters through the doorway. Jesus shares a meal with us. In this passage of scripture, Jesus does most of the work to initiate the relationship. All we need to do is open the door—open ourselves up to Jesus, and he will enter in. Maybe as Christians we need fewer rules and more openings for Jesus to work through.

Have you opened a door in your life to Jesus?

Lord, I admit that I close a lot of my life off to you. Only when I am in need and at the end of my options do I turn to you. Which means that most of the time you are standing out-side my life waiting to enter, like a visitor to a house who rings a doorbell that goes unheard and unheeded by the family inside. Lord, for all the times I have kept you out of my life, I apologize. Enter in today. Enter into my life every day. I want you to always feel welcome. In Jesus' name, I pray. AMEN.

December 31

THE END?

Read: Revelation 21:1–8

And I heard a loud voice from the throne saying, "See, the home of God is among mor-
tals. He will dwell with them as their God; they will be his peoples, and God himself
will be with them; he will wipe every tear from their eyes. Death will be no more;
mourning and crying and pain will be no more, for the first things have passed away."
REVELATION 21:3–4

JOHN'S VISION FOR the end of all human affliction and strife echoes the vision Ezekiel received during Israel's exile to Babylon in 597 BC. God will create an entirely new heaven and earth—there will be a new world, and a new Jerusalem at the center of it all. For all the groaning and aching of creation throughout the ages, a day will dawn when our world and our lives will be made whole and God will choose to dwell in our midst.

The description of this heavenly Jerusalem that resides at the center of God's established kingdom is beyond imagining. John does his best to capture what heaven on earth might look like, but his efforts still have a way of confounding our ability to envision it for ourselves. What is clear is that at the end of all things, life is gloriously renewed. The end turns out to be a new beginning. Death itself is swallowed up by irrepressible life. Through John's efforts, we learn that there is no ending eternity.

At the end of this year, how do you envision beginning anew?

Lord, you promise to make all things new. You challenge us to believe that there is no
final chapter to our lives and to your world. Every end is just a new beginning, a clean slate,
another opportunity to live well, right wrongs, and live in love. Oh, how I long for just such
an ending! In Jesus' name, I pray. AMEN.